THE ROYAL LINE OF FRANCE

LOUIS XI.

[*Frontispiece*

THE
ROYAL LINE OF FRANCE
THE STORY OF THE KINGS AND QUEENS
OF FRANCE

BY E. THORNTON COOK

Essay Index Reprint Series

BOOKS FOR LIBRARIES PRESS, INC.

FREEPORT, NEW YORK

First published 1934
Reprinted 1967

LIBRARY OF CONGRESS CATALOG CARD NUMBER:
67-26789

PRINTED IN THE UNITED STATES OF AMERICA

CONTENTS

v

CONTENTS

NOTE.—The lives of Louis XVII, Louis XVIII, Charles X, and the consorts of the two last-mentioned Kings are touched upon in chapters XIII and XIV.

LIST OF ILLUSTRATIONS

ix

   * By permission, from photographs supplied by Établissements Lévy et Neurdein Réunis, Paris.

   † By permission from *Les Rois Français*, at the Victoria and Albert Museum.

PREFACE

THIS is the story of the Kings and Queens of France shown against the romantic background of French history. The tale begins with Louis XI, for during his reign monarchical France rose out of the ruins of the feudal territorial houses and became a unified nation; under the earlier Kings she had been little more than a geographical expression.

Of the sovereigns who go to the making of this story, Charles VIII and Henri II met death by accident—the latter being mortally wounded in a tournament. Henri III and Henri IV were struck down by assassins, and Louis XVI went to the guillotine; Charles X abdicated, and Louis-Philippe was deposed.

In five cases the crown descended from father to son; once it passed direct to a fourth generation. When Henri of Navarre ascended the throne in the sixteenth century, the nearest common ancestor was St. Louis (1226). The longest reign lasted seventy-two years, the shortest, seventeen months.

Five of the seventeen Kings married twice, and one three times. François I and Henri IV were rivals in gallantry. Of the former it was said: " les Dames, plus que les ans, lui causèrent la mort " ; the latter acknowledged over fifty mistresses—and there were others " of small importance."

Of the Kings' consorts, two were Scottish Princesses and one was English born.

Marguerite de Valois, Jeanne, and Claude were Daughters of France ; the last-named is unique in that she was discarded by the King and beatified by the Church.

Marie Leczinska was Polish. Margaret (returned after having spent ten years at the French court), Éléonore, who was forced upon France by the point of the sword, Elizabeth, Marie-Antoinette, Anne, and Marie-Thérèse were all called Austrian, though the two last at least were actually Spanish. Charlotte of Savoy, Anne de Bretagne (who married two Kings), and Louise de Vaudemont came from adjoining principalities. The daughters of the Medici were Italian; Catherine saw five sovereigns on the throne, and was one of the trio of Queens who gave ten children to France. Three of her sons wore the crown in succession, and a daughter became the wife of Henri IV, although she was not permitted to share any other title than that of Navarre.

One other woman, a King's wife for thirty years, was never acknowledged as Queen.

The kingdoms of Sardinia and Naples sent France her last three Queens, all of whom died in exile. The sisters Marie-Joséphine and Marie-Thérèse (consorts of Louis XVIII and Charles X) never reigned in France, and Marie-Amélie de Bourbon, niece of Marie-Antoinette, lived through six revolutions before finding a last refuge in England.

E. T. C.

ACKNOWLEDGMENTS

THIS book would never have been written if it had not been for the help generously volunteered by Miss Henrietta Tayler, who has been untiring in her reading of innumerable old French Chronicles and in correcting proofs. To her are due the thanks of all who find interest in *The Royal Line of France*, as well as the gratitude of the author.

Thanks must be given also to Mrs. Arnold Bennett, Mrs. Edward H. Angle, and to Basil S. Long, Esq., Deputy Keeper of the Department of Paintings in the Victoria and Albert Museum, for the infinite trouble they took in helping to secure the interesting series of portraits which illustrate this volume. Nor does it seem possible to let a sixth of my books appear through the famous firm of John Murray without an expression of my deep appreciation for all the courtesy and kindness that has been shown to me at Albemarle Street, from the day when my first manuscript was welcomed by the late Sir John Murray.

As usual, I acknowledge my indebtedness to the authors of the long list of books mentioned in the Bibliography.

E. T. C.

" If you want romance, why not look for it in history ?   There one finds the human heart displaying its most vivid passions. . . ."

Guizot.

HOUSE OF VALOIS

CHAPTER ONE

LOUIS XI (1461–1483)

I

Louis (XI) (as Dauphin of France) and Margaret of Scotland.

"Fie de la vie de ce monde !"

II

Louis (XI) and Charlotte of Savoy.

"Qui scit dissimulare, scit regnare !"

Louis XI

Born at Bourges	. .	1423
Married (1)	. . .	1436
Married (2)	. . .	1457
Ascended	. . .	1461
Died at Plessis-lès-Tours	.	1483

Contemporary Sovereigns

ENGLAND : Henry VI, Edward IV, Edward V, Richard III.
SCOTLAND : James III.
SPAIN : United under Ferdinand and Isabella, 1469.

Popes

Pius II, Paul II, Sixtus IV.

Descent

(House of Valois)

PHILIPPE VI
|
JEAN II
|
CHARLES V
|
CHARLES VI
|
CHARLES VII
|
LOUIS XI

Consorts

(1)

JAMES I OF SCOTLAND *m.* JANE BEAUFORT (niece of Henry IV of England).
|
MARGARET OF SCOTLAND

Born	. . .	1424
Married at Tours	.	1436
Died at Châlons-sur-Marne		1445

No issue.

(2)

AMÉDÉE VIII OF SAVOY (anti-Pope Felix V)
|
LOUIS II, DUKE OF SAVOY, *m.* ANNE OF CYPRUS
|
CHARLOTTE OF SAVOY

Born	. . .	1445
Married	. . .	1457
Died	. . .	1483

Issue : three children who died young ; also Anne (de Beaujeu), later Regent of France, 1461–1522 ; Jeanne (married Louis XII), 1464–1505 ; Charles (Charles VIII), 1470–1498.

MARGARET OF SCOTLAND.

CHARLOTTE OF SAVOY.

3]

CHAPTER ONE

LOUIS XI (1461–1483)

I

SINCE Hugh Capet was crowned at Rheims (987), so founding the royal line that was to endure for nearly nine centuries, no French King had sought a bride from either England or Scotland till the time of Charles VII.

For five hundred years the courts of Russia, Holland, Spain, Denmark, Hungary, and the greater duchies had provided Queens for France; no one seemed aware that in the little island in the North Sea there were princesses sufficiently civilised to wear a consort's crown. Then Charles VII found himself in dire straits, for the English, while they held half his territory, jeered at him as " le petit roi de Bourges," and crowned the child Henry VI in Notre-Dame, King of France as well as of England.

In desperate need of an ally, Charles looked towards Scotland and asked the hand of Princess Margaret for his eldest son (nearly a century was to elapse before an English princess was selected for the honour of a French marriage).

The Treaty was signed at Chinon (Oct. 30, 1428), but since bride and bridegroom were only four and five years old the affair could go no farther for the moment.

A Scot (John Earl of Buchan) was Constable of France, and Scottish troops were fighting alongside the almost exhausted French forces, but Charles stipulated that an additional 6,000 stalwarts should

accompany Princess Margaret when she came to her
marriage, and offered the fair province of Saintonge
in proof of his eternal friendship—provided that the
Scots could wrest it from the English.

Five months after the signing of the marriage
treaty a country girl arrived at the Castle of Chinon
and demanded to see the King. He listened to her
incredible story, as did *Parlement*,[1] and the Maid's
unshakeable faith gave fresh hope to the stricken
country. She would raise the siege of Orléans and
bring the King to his coronation at Rheims :

" No one in the world, neither Kings, nor dukes,
nor the daughter of the King of Scotland, can recover
the Kingdom of France ; in me alone is help ! " said
Jeanne d'Arc.

She was examined, and her interlocutors found no
harm in her, " but only good, humility, virginity,
devotion, honesty, and simplicity." So the girl was
nominated Chef de Guerre and sent out her ultimatum
to the English :

" Je suis cy venu de par Dieu le Roy de Ciel pour
vous bouter hors de toute la France."

Within four months England had been forced to
relax her grasp and Rheims resounded to the cry of
" Vive le Roi ! "

When the Dauphin was thirteen years old Charles
VII sent to fetch " our most redoubtable and mightie
Ladie Margaret from her Kingdom of Scotland."
Envoys were secured after much difficulty, for the
journey was both dangerous and expensive, but the
Comte de Vendôme, Regnault Girard, and one Pymor,
were ultimately coerced into making a start, when
Charles, in good faith and on the word of a king, under-
took to pay a ransom if the trio was captured by the
dangerous English, whose fraud all men knew.

[1] *Parlement.* Not a representative body, but a close corporation
of lawyers. It was the judicial court and claimed the right of registering, or refusing to register, the royal decrees.

Few expected to see the unwilling ambassadors return, and many tears were shed as they embarked. Four days later the Scilly Isles were sighted, and just as everyone began to hope that the journey might be accomplished a " marvellously great storm " compelled the fleet to seek shelter under lee of the Irish coast. Then contrary winds drove the battered galleys out of their course and Pymor's vessel disappeared into the mists apparently bent on reaching the fabled New World, but Girard kept his head, and promised St. Ringan a silver ship should the party reach Scotland alive. The storm abated almost instantly, the galleys ran past the Mull of Cantyre, effected a reunion with Pymor, who had been given up as lost, and all landed after a memorable journey of fifty-six days.

Before the storm-beaten ambassadors had had time to repair the ravages of the voyage a warning reached them that the perfidious English were at work ; a brother of the Scottish Queen was even now in Scotland endeavouring to prevent the marriage of Princess Margaret and the Dauphin !

An appeal to those inclined to the French match brought in a band of knights and squires and the envoy rode towards Edinburgh with sixty horsemen behind him, much relieved that he was able to present as dignified an appearance as any Englishman.

King James I came from Edinburgh to meet his guests and put up at the Convent of the Franciscans at Linlithgow, " according to the wont of Scottish Kings, who, in these times, lived as much as they could in convents and priories, not only in consideration of the Holy Character of such places, but because living there cost them nothing. . . ."

To the immense relief of the Comte de Vendôme, King James set aside the specious arguments advanced by the rival ambassadors and held to the Treaty of Chinon, although he insisted that every point of the contract should be re-examined : their majesties were playing for time, each being anxious to delay the departure of their beloved daughter. Between them they raised so many queries that the ambassadors felt compelled to refer to their own sovereigns, so once more unwilling messengers were despatched to brave the seas between Scotland and France. Departing on Shrove Tuesday, they returned in late September.

Charles VII was willing to approve of all the arrangements made, but suggested that since France was now in comparative peace he had no need of the 6,000 Scottish archers for whose services he had stipulated —and could not afford to pay them.

By the time the lesser figure of 2,000 had been reached and Scots and Frenchmen had agreed as to the provisions each was to supply for the benefit of Margaret and her retinue, fresh reasons had been found for delay.

King James wished the Dauphine to have so fine a galley that its like could not be built in either France or Scotland, but only in Spain, but that country was at war and could spare no gilded vessel for the transport of a bride. Only after long argument would James yield the point; and now Queen Jane stepped into the breach, insisting that her daughter should take with her a large number of Scottish attendants, though the French argued that with Scots all about her the Lady Margaret would never learn French, nor the manners of a Frenchwoman. As the Dauphine was to be placed under the care of the Queen of France, who would treat her as if she were her " carnal daughter," she would have no need of Scots. Compromise was reached, but now it was July " when winter was in sight and no marriage could be made between right-minded people," so Margaret's departure was delayed till March.

March came and the round of farewell ceremonies began, culminating in a State banquet at Perth, where Margaret was so lectured on the honour shown to

Scotland by the King of France in selecting her as a
bride for his son that she was reduced to tears, and
James had to distract public attention by directing
Regnault Girard to kiss Queen Jane, whereupon
the Queen of Scots " kindly kissed him too."

An exchange of gifts followed. Margaret was
bidden to carry a Scottish sword to her bridegroom,
and James received with great joy " a very strange
animal." It was a mule.

Embarkation began, and on March 27 the King
saw his daughter aboard, after which he went away
" weeping tears of sorrow."

The convoy sailed, was beaten back, sailed again,
and reached the coast of France, where a sudden
storm made an immediate landing imperative.
Margaret was hurried ashore, " but was not shown to
the people that day because it was late and the town
not decorated."

Each city through which the Princess passed on her
journey towards the court vied with the next in
pageantry, but the palm was awarded to Poitiers,
where triumphal arches had been erected, from one
of which a child in angel's garb let down a crown upon
Margaret's head, " this being very genteelie and
craftilie performed."

The Dauphin and Margaret met for the first time
at Tours on the morning of their marriage. Years
later Louis XI was to say that he had been married
against his will and regretted it ; now the children
played their parts with unprotesting decorum, accepted the blessing delivered by the Archbishop of
Rheims, shared the wedding feast, and, one hopes,
found pleasure in the organised festivities.

Tours had decided upon a display of Morris dancing
as a suitable bridal entertainment, and the town had
paid out fifteen sols to one Richard Gaugain for four
old bedsheets from which the costumes for the dancers
were made, also fifteen sols to the tailor who sewed
the said dresses, and another forty sols to the painter-

glazier who had hastily painted the same dresses and provided beards for four of the dancers. Yet a further expense was occasioned by " Robert the Devil," who demanded a *douceur* for organising the affair, and something extra for a pair of hose which he had burst when dancing.

If the Dauphin never learnt to love the charming child who was his bride, she won the good-will of her father-in-law and also of the Queen under whose ægis she was to see the proxy betrothal of Henry VI of England to Margaret of Anjou,[1] but for the most part court life in the fifteenth century was a dull affair, for the Queen lived chiefly among women, while the King, the Dauphin, and their knights warred in various parts of France.

Shut away from the world, knowing nothing of great events, the little Princess turned to the writing of poetry, seeking an outlet for her pent-up youth.

There is a pretty story of how she had once dropped a swift kiss on the lips of Alain Chartier, poet and singer, as he lay sleeping, explaining to her horrified ladies that : " I do not kiss the man, but only the mouth which has uttered such golden words ! " But a too exact modern writer has produced figures to prove that Chartier died some years before Margaret reached France !

Be that as it may, other impulsive actions did the Princess harm, and the culminating scandal occurred one evening when Jamet de Tillay and Regnault de Dresnay, two evil-minded members of the royal household, discovered the Dauphine lying on a couch, surrounded by her ladies it is true, but also in the company of two gentlemen of the court, one of whom had ventured to rest an elbow on the couch as all talked in the firelight.

Presently it was whispered that Margaret's conduct was that of a wanton, and Jamet de Tillay saw to it

[1] See *Her Majesty : The Romance of the Queens of England.*

that the absent Dauphin heard all the court gossip.
Now, when Louis came to Amboise he ignored the
Dauphine still more completely, devoting himself to
his falcons and his dogs and going about shabby, even
dirty, wearing a hat (which he vowed he would burn
if he believed it knew his thoughts) around the crown
of which were pinned tiny images of different saints,
to each of whom in turn Louis would vow offerings,
provided that his prayers were answered.

To distract Margaret from her excessive writing of
poetry (which was considered dangerous to health)
Charles took his daughter-in-law with him on a pilgrimage in a hot August. She caught a chill and
presently the court physician was explaining that
" a rheum had been bred in her brain . . . and perhaps from her said brain a corrupt humour had fallen
on her lungs." Others, more sentimental, saw the
Scottish Princess dying of a broken heart by reason
of the calumnies that had been circulated.

" I have never done my lord a wrong ! " she vowed,
and when those around tried to distract her thoughts
by talking of happier times when she should be Queen,
Margaret turned away impatiently :

" Fie de la vie de ce monde—ne m'en parlez plus ! "

After the death of this Princess her father-in-law
instituted an enquiry into the cruel statements that
were being circulated concerning her. Much, and
varying, evidence was taken, but no verdict was pronounced.

Never till the day of Mary Stuart was France to
seek another Scottish bride for a King's son.

LOUIS (XI) AND CHARLOTTE OF SAVOY

"Qui scit dissimulare, scit regnare!"

LOUIS was still merely Dauphin of France when at the age of twenty-nine he plighted himself to six-year-old Charlotte of Savoy and her dowry of 600,000 écus. Since he had antagonised his father and was suspected of treason he was living in Brabant under the protection of the Duc de Burgogne.

Charlotte had an interesting ancestry, her grandfather, Amédée VIII, being the anti-Pope Felix V who was elected by the Council of Basle on the deposition of Pope Eugenius IV. Having held the high office for some five years, Felix V retired (officially for the peace of the Church), became Amédée once more, married Marie de Bourgogne, daughter of Philip " le Hardi," and begat Louis, the father of Charlotte.

Any husband should be able to train any wife secured at the tender age of six, and there are no records of complaints by Charlotte, either before or after the more formal ceremony which took place a few years later, although Louis stinted her in clothes and other necessities. She gave him his first child when she was fourteen—it died in infancy, as did the second—but in the year of her husband's accession Charlotte was more successful, and her daughter Anne lived to make a name for herself in the history of France.

Together, Louis XI and the powerful Duke who had been his financial stay for sixteen years, rode to Rheims for the crowning, but Charlotte was sent to Amboise, where, in due course, she produced three more children, Jeanne, for whom Louis found a use when she was four days old by betrothing her to unwilling Louis d'Orléans (later Louis XII), the Dauphin Charles, and one more small son who so entered into his father's heart that on the child's death he made an impulsive vow of conjugal fidelity, " qu'il n'observa pas longtemps ! " observes Philippe de Comines with admirable terseness.

Perhaps as a reward for the exemplary manner in which the Queen fulfilled her wifely duties Louis allowed her to accompany him upon one of his triumphal progresses through France, and Charlotte was amazed to find herself welcomed with music and flowers by a President of *Parlement* who had had four beautiful baths prepared for her, all *richement adornez.* Unfortunately the Queen thought the weather somewhat dangerous for bathing, so, being unwilling to hurt the President's feelings, sent her sister and four maids-of-honour rather than risk a bath herself.

Paris was more fortunate in her efforts, and Charlotte accepted a sweetmeat model of a stag ornamented with the royal arms of Savoy. It was the only treasure this consort of a King is known to have possessed.

Louis XI had little time to spare even for a wife as amiable and chaste as Charlotte. His oppressions had stirred the great vassals of the crown and driven them to form the League of Public Weal to bring their sovereign to reason. No sooner was this dissolved than Edward IV of England landed at his port of Calais and succeeded in marching into the heart of Picardy before Louis could check the ruthless advance.

The two Kings met on a bridge to sign peace terms, a grated barrier between them, and near-by two strong box-like edifices in case it became necessary for them to take cover.

Upon succeeding to the crown Louis XI had found his country merely a collection of scattered provinces and himself scarcely more powerful than his stronger vassals, but he was true to his favourite motto, " Qui scit dissimulare, scit regnare," and beneath his rule France became a nation.

An apoplectic seizure warned the King that he must hasten if he would hand France on to his son as the heritage of his dreams. He started on a pilgrimage with 6,000 fighting men behind him, after having sent Charlotte into Savoy. He had no further use for a wife and had never deemed her worthy of bringing up her children ; even Jeanne, less important than the others because deformed, had been taken from her, and so meek was Charlotte that once when one of the child's guardians lay ill of a malignant fever, and the other suggested that the Princess should be fetched away, "lest evil befall her," the Queen was shocked :

" I have written to the King of the matter that he may give orders as he wishes, for I would not dare to send and fetch my said daughter without first telling him." The most she could venture was to urge that letters should be sent to the King, " and that quickly so that my lord may be pleased and write to me what occurs."[1]

A second stroke followed the first. Louis retreated to his gloomy gibbet-encircled castle of Plessis to seek what distraction he could. Throughout France processions marched from shrine to shrine and saintly men were fetched from distant lands to pray for this King who dreaded Death. Once he had gone so meanly clad that people marvelled and cried that his whole outfit, horse included, was not worth twenty francs. Now he poured out money on remedies " terrible and marvellous." Courtiers whispered of a bath of infant's blood, and the doctors went in fear of their lives till one Jacques Coctier boldly faced the dying King and turned his superstitions to account :

" Sire, I know full well that some morning you will order me to be put to death, but I warn you—you will not survive me eight days ! "

[1] Bib. Nat. MSS., F. 2907.

Within eight months that doctor had amassed a fortune of ninety thousand crowns.

" If God had given me but a few more years I would have set the whole state in order," sighed Louis XI, remembering that the English still held Calais, and summoned the shrinking, half-educated son who was to succeed him.

" Let the land rest, for it is lean and poor," he told the heir, " and avoid quarrels, especially with England and Bretagne."

Pain overwhelmed the King, and he had himself re-anointed with the Holy Oil sacred to Coronations. So great was his fear of treason that four hundred archers kept watch night and day around the moated castle wherein he lay, and sharp-shooters waited in the turrets ready to account for unwary mortals should they venture to approach. In constant fear of poison, Louis would eat barely enough to keep life in his wasted frame and had become " une anatomie cheminante." Few were allowed entry save the King's eldest daughter, Anne, and her husband, Pierre de Bourbon, Seigneur de Beaujeu.

To Anne, not to half-forgotten Charlotte, fell the honour of the Regency[1] when Louis, turning his face to the wall, sent the Chancellor with his seals, his hounds, and his hawks to the boy who was to succeed him.

So died the man of whom Francis Bacon wrote as one of the greatest monarchs in Europe, placing him with Ferdinand of Castille and Henry VII of England as " the three Magi." But a contemporary, seeing him as man, not sovereign, wrote bitter lines beneath his portrait :

> " Louis renversa tout pour suivre son caprice !
> Mauvais fils, mauvais père, infidèle mary,
> Frère injuste, ingrate maistre et dangereux amy. . . ."

Of the great fiefs only Bretagne remained unannexed.

[1] " She is least of a fool of all women, for wise one there is none ! " said the King, and made his will in favour of his elder daughter.

Charlotte died three months after Louis. In her will (which is the only document relating to this Queen which has been preserved) she distributed her few possessions among favourite *religieuses* and servants, making no mention of Anne, Jeanne, or Charles, her three surviving children.

CHAPTER TWO

CHARLES VIII (1483–1498)

CHARLES VIII WITH MARGARET OF AUSTRIA, ANNE DE BEAUJEU, AND
ANNE DE BRETAGNE.

" La gentille Demoiselle et la Maîtresse femme."

LOUIS XI
m. CHARLOTTE OF SAVOY

	CHARLES VIII				ANNE OF FRANCE		
Born at Amboise	.	.	1470	Born at Amboise	.	.	1461
Married (1)	.	.	1483	Married the Sire de Beaujeu			1474
Succeeded	.	.	1483	Became Regent	.	.	1483
Married (2)	.	.	1491	Died	.	.	1522
Died	.	.	1498	Issue : one child (Suzanne).			

CONSORTS OF CHARLES

(1)

Maximilian II, K. of the Romans,
m. Marie, d. of Charles the Bold.

MARGARET OF AUSTRIA

Born in the Netherlands	.	1479
Marriage ceremony at Amboise	. . .	1483
Returned to the Flemings		1493

(2)

Francis II, Duc de Bretagne,
m. Marguerite de Foix.

ANNE DE BRETAGNE

Born at Nantes	.	.	1476
Married (1) (proxy)	.	.	1490
Married (2), Rennes	.	.	1491
Crowned at St. Denis		.	1492
Widowed (April)	.	.	1498

Married (3), Nantes	.	.	1499
Re-crowned	.	.	1503–4
Died at Blois	.	.	1514

Issue—

By Charles VIII : three sons and a daughter, who died in infancy.

By Louis XII : two still-born sons, and Princesses Claude and Renée, who survived their mother.

CONTEMPORARY SOVEREIGNS

ENGLAND : Richard III, Henry VII.

SCOTLAND : James III and IV.

SPAIN : Ferdinand and Isabella.

POPES

Sixtus IV, Innocent VIII, Alexander VI.

[British Museum.

ANNE DE BRETAGNE.

CHARLES VIII.

17]

CHAPTER TWO

CHARLES VIII (1483-1498)

ON the death of Louis XI his son was declared King
as Charles VIII, and Margaret of Austria, to whom
the young Prince had been affianced a few months
before, assumed the title of Queen of France. As the
royal pair were only thirteen and four years old
respectively, life continued its ordinary routine.

Under the will of the late King, Charles's elder
sister, Anne, was named " gouvernante du royaume
et tutrice de son frère,"[1] so Madame de Beaujeu now
gathered the reins of government into her capable
hands and made herself unique in the annals of France.

By the Salic law [2] no daughter could succeed to her
father's throne, even though he lacked male heirs.
Indeed, the restriction extended to inheritance
through a woman, with the curious result that though
foreign princesses had been, and were to be, Regents,
when their sons succeeded as minors, no daughter of
France could normally hold this position of authority.
Even in Anne's case, despite her father's will, there
were murmurings. "Why," asked the indignant
nobles, " should Louis, a tyrant in life, be permitted
to continue his tyranny after death and impose this
monstrous rule on France ? "

But Anne was a " Maîtresse femme " and feared no

[1] " C'était la première fois qu'on voyait une fille de France Régente "
(Dreux de Radier).
[2] The Salic law was promulgated by the *Parlement* de Paris in 1316 in
order that Philippe V, the uncle of the deceased King, and not that
King's five-year-old daughter, might come to the crown, this being
the first occasion since the death of Hugh Capet, three centuries before,
that son had not succeeded father.

one. She escorted her young brother to an assembly of the Estates held at Tours, and saw to it that he announced his intention of being guided by her counsel, after which she exerted tact, strategy, and personality till the duly impressed Assembly forgot its disapproval. But a Council of Twelve was appointed to assist her, and one of the twelve was Louis d'Orléans, heir-presumptive to the throne and brother-in-law to Charles and Anne by virtue of his forced marriage to their young sister Jeanne.

Had Louis been twenty-one instead of twenty, he could have claimed the coveted office held by Anne. As it was he lost no chance of thwarting, and even insulting her, till she was driven to lead an army against him, taking Charles with her so that d'Orléans could be charged with *lèse-majesté* in fighting against his sovereign. There were those who whispered that in the beginning Anne had " loved Louis with love, so that if Monsieur had been willing to take her he might have had better luck."

No King, however youthful, could long remain a child in the fifteenth century, and while Madame de Beaujeu ruled France she saw to it that her brother and the Queen-designate were being prepared to face the future.

In Anne's own babyhood she had been used as a pawn in the royal game for the aggrandisement of France, having been pledged when two months old to Nicolas Marquis de Pont-à-Mousson, grandson and heir of King René of Anjou, who claimed the crown of Naples. When the Marquis repudiated his contract (dying soon afterwards), Louis XI had turned upon René, demanding sovereign damages for his daughter, and terrorised his frail neighbour into the ultimate bequeathment of his territories. So the jilting of a French princess had secured Maine, Anjou, and Provence to the French Crown.

Now Anne looked across the frontier and saw Bretagne an independent duchy under Duke François, whose elder daughter was his heir, since the Salic law had never run in Bretagne.

It was obvious that if Charles VIII could marry Anne de Bretagne, France would gain this last out-standing fief; but unfortunately the child was al-ready affianced, and Charles too was bound. A few months before his father's death he had been be-trothed in the market-place so that all men might see, and there had followed a stately ceremony near Amboise.

"... In a robe of cloth-of-gold Monsieur le Dauphin came to the place prepared for the wedding —near the bridge and surrounded by barriers—and within the barriers all those invited, and archers to prevent the crowd pressing in as the King came.

"The Dauphine was then brought in her litter, and carried within, and they were betrothed by the notary nephew to the Grand Seneschal, who asked Monsieur le Dauphin in a voice so loud that everyone heard him, whether he would take Margaret of Austria in marriage, and he replied '*Yes*.' Then Madame la Dauphine was asked, and she replied the same, which done they took hands, and Monsieur le Dauphin kissed Madame la Dauphine twice, and then they both returned to the Castle, and all the streets of Amboise were hung with draperies. . . ."

Since then Charles VIII had been kept too busy to think of his wife, though the more precocious Margaret was very sure of her position as Queen of France.

The years of Anne's Regency continued, and every twelve months saw France stronger. Men spoke with respect of this "Maîtresse femme" who quelled insurrections, defended frontiers, and effected eco-nomies. Yes, she had ruled well for France. And now Charles was a man and a warrior, but he had never claimed his wife, and Margaret, for all her eight years as titular queen, had never been crowned.

The battle of St. Aubin-le-Cormier (July 1488) was

a notable victory for Charles, and Anne was quick to
seize an opportunity by inserting a clause in the
Treaty of Peace which secured to the conqueror a
right of veto in connection with any marriages the
Duc de Bretagne might arrange for his daughters.
Then Duc François died, leaving Anne, the elder child,
to take up her inheritance. Since the duchy was
almost bankrupt, ravaged by plague, and still smarting
under the defeats inflicted by Charles, her guardians
decided that safety could only be found in marriage.

The little Duchess had been plighted to that
pathetic boy King Edward V of England, but his death
in the Tower of London had left her unattached.
Now a strong party urged that she should wed a
Breton noble and advanced the claims of the Seigneur
d'Albret, a widower of forty-five, renowned alike for
his fierce temper and harsh voice, to whom she had
been tentatively betrothed when ten years old.
Others considered that Maximilian, King of the
Romans, would be a more suitable match, although
he had a son who was as old as the suggested
bride.

Anne had seen the Seigneur d'Albret and retained
a vivid recollection of his spotty face, so decided that
the unknown was preferable to the known evil, inclined towards Maximilian, and lodged a statement
with the Ecclesiastical Court to the effect that her
betrothal had taken place under duress.

On account of the provisions of the Treaty of St.
Aubin the new bridal ceremony was a secret affair,
but, to make it binding upon both parties, Anne was
put to bed, and while her nobles, their ladies, and the
city fathers surrounded the State couch, Maximilian's
proxy, the Marshal von Polhain, bared his leg up to
the knee and placed it beside her. Anne was now
entitled to sign herself " Queen of the Romans."

Immediately Charles VIII discovered what had
occurred, he came marching into Bretagne once more,
and " La Grande Madame," Anne de Beaujeu, feeling

that this was an affair requiring woman's guile, came
with him.

Alain d'Albret took his revenge by yielding up
Nantes to the enemy, but Anne de Bretagne was not
to be intimidated. If a child in years still, she was
a daughter of her age, and now, having sold her jewels
and plate to replenish the treasury and buy food for
her soldiery, she marched with the army—and soon
found herself besieged in Rennes. Maximilian sent
mercenaries, but they failed to effect a rescue, and
the war continued ; a war in which knights from the
opposing ranks would sometimes sally forth to break
a lance together while the child Duchess watched them
from the castle walls. She was lonelier now, for the
little sister who had been her close companion from
babyhood had died from privation.

The time for parley arrived. Anne received a
deputation and listened to Charles's offer. If she
would relinquish her war-stricken duchy, he would
supply her with a pension and a husband, provided
she selected one of an approved trio. Duchess
Anne ignored the financial offer and replied that she
was already married, adding with a touch of youthful
temper that even if her present husband refused to
have anything to do with her, she would marry none
but a king, or the son of a king.

Nothing dismayed, Charles bought off the mercenaries, proclaimed an amnesty, repeated his offer of a
pension, and added the promise of a safe-conduct
which would enable the intrepid little Duchess to
join Maximilian.

Now Anne's counsellors had an inspiration. Why
should not their Duchess marry King Charles VIII
and so ensure permanent peace between Bretagne and
France ? (Had the older Anne insinuated the suggestion ?)

The matter was argued for three long days, and
when the Duchess still remained obdurate they
called in her Confessor to point out that such a union

was clearly decreed by God, who required that she should sacrifice herself for the good of her people.

Now Charles, having made confession at the little church of Notre-Dame outside the gates of Rennes, arrived unexpectedly and demanded a private interview with Duchess Anne. He succeeded where others had failed, and three days later the betrothal was proclaimed; Marshal von Polhain received an invitation to the wedding.

All Europe was startled, for this marriage entailed not only the repudiation of Maximilian by Anne, but also that of Maximilian's daughter Margaret of Austria by Charles, and the child had borne the title of Queen of France all the ten years she had spent at the French court.

Austria's fierce denunciations were ignored, and couriers hurried off to Rome seeking the necessary dispensations while Charles saw to it that the marriage treaty was craftily drawn.

Anne must yield all her rights without power of revocation, though these same rights should revert to her if she outlived the King and the pair had no heir. In such case she bound herself to make no other marriage, unless with the successor to the throne of France, or the son of that successor.

Busy fingers worked a wedding garment of sable and cloth-of-gold, and also a fine jewelled head-dress which Anne intended to present as a propitiatory offering to the child, two years her junior, whom she had supplanted. But for the sudden change in her matrimonial plans Anne would have been Margaret's stepmother.

There was some difficulty in procuring the papal dispensation, but Innocent VIII withdrew his opposition when Anne took oath that the marriage was being made of her own free will, and that her sudden capitulation had not been induced by violence on the part of Charles.

A gorgeous coronation followed; Louis d'Orléans,

heir-presumptive to the throne, was called upon to
hold the crown over Anne's head, since it was too
large and heavy for her to support, and "such a
marvell of People" thronged the Paris streets to
watch this new Queen pass, with her dark plaits
hanging over her shoulders, "that one could scarcely
turn."

Ceremonial accomplished, Charles took his fifteen-
year-old bride to Amboise; the jewelled head-dress
was duly presented and Margaret went her unwilling
way. If "la gentille Demoiselle" now drops from
French history, she was to have many adventures
and a vivid career of her own, including shipwreck,
an escape from marriage with Henry VIII of England,
and two experiences of wedlock, first with a Prince
of the Asturias and secondly with Philibert, Duke of
Savoy. Nor was Anne de Beaujeu's training quite
lost, for Margaret became Regent of the Netherlands
on behalf of her nephew Charles V. The shipwreck
took place on the coast of England during her voyage
to Spain, and Margaret wrote a suitable obituary
notice for herself on her wristband in order that it
might identify her if she drowned : "Ci gît Margot,
la gentille Demoiselle qu'eût deux maris et mourut
pucelle."

Anne de Bretagne proved herself an attractive
wife, and as she gained ascendancy over the King,
his sister's influence waned ; but Madame de Beaujeu,
now Duchesse de Bourbon, owing to the death of her
brother-in-law, made no effort to retain dominance.
Her daughter Suzanne was born in the year Charles
became King *de facto*.

France owed the Regent gratitude and realised it,
although the contemporary historian, Philippe de
Comines, omits all mention of the eight years of her
rule—perhaps in revenge for the fact that he suffered
several months' imprisonment under Anne (in one of
the cages invented by Cardinal de Balue) as a punishment for conspiracy against her. On the other hand,

Brantôme draws a personal and vivid picture of this unique woman, although one that is not altogether flattering :

" Femme fine et delicate s'il en fut oncques, vrai image en tout de feu Louis son père, vindicative, trinquante, corrompue, pleine de dissimulation et grande hypocrisie. Splendide et magnificque, elle avait de grandes bontés à l'endroit des personnes qu'elle aimoit et prenoit en sa main ; fort spirituelle et assez bonne."

Queen Anne's first child made its *sortie du cloistre maternelle* at Amboise within a year of her marriage, when the young mother was not yet sixteen. The child was christened Charles Orland, and all its god-fathers and godmothers came to the ceremony clad in cloth-of-gold.

The heir was placed under the special protection of the Virgin and a hundred Scottish guards. Every noble in the district prepared to rise in the child's defence should danger menace him, and " all the archers available " attended his litter when he went forth to take the air.

Fatherhood stirred Charles's latent ambition, which was fanned by a request from the Duke of Milan, who asked aid in his struggle with Alfonso of Naples, and Anne followed her husband to the frontier. When the actual campaign began she went on pilgrimages from shrine to shrine, offering up prayers on behalf of the King.

For a time success followed the French arms, and the victorious monarch rode into city after city in his armour, with visor lowered and lance couched. Alfonso of Naples fled to a monastery, awed by the approach of a conqueror who came to claim the king-dom as part of his inheritance from René of Anjou.

When the King of Naples fled, the world took alarm and united to oppose Charles, who was presently forced to retreat. Rejoining Anne, he found that an outbreak of smallpox had occurred at Amboise despite the efforts that had been taken to keep the Dauphin safe from all disease.

Before Christmas the child was dead. Anne became so ill with grief that the doctors prescribed a round of court gaieties in the hope of distracting her, but when the Duc d'Orléans led a band of gay dancers around her the Queen turned away in tears, crying that the Duke leapt so lightly because he was a step nearer the throne by reason of her son's death.

By prayer, pilgrimage, and votive offering Anne besought heaven to fill her empty arms, and in the ensuing three years two more sons and a daughter were born to her, but all died in infancy, although she persistently tied amulets around the children's necks and provided them with sturdy Breton nurses.

The Queen prayed alone now, for Charles VIII was casting his smiles in other directions.

When illness brought repentance and he returned to his consort, she, " with marvellous prudence, uttered never a complaint," but her happiness was of short duration, for, when hastening to the tennis court one morning, Charles struck his head against a low archway and died within a day.   Said Comines :
" . . . ne fut jamais que petit homme de corps, peu entendu, mais il était si bon, qu'il n'est point possible de voir meilleure créature ! "

A few hours later Queen Anne found herself deserted ; the courtiers had turned to the new King, Louis d'Orléans.

NOTE.—For the continuation of the life of Anne de Bretagne see reign of Louis XII, Chapter Three, Part II.

HOUSE OF VALOIS-ORLÉANS

CHAPTER THREE

LOUIS XII (1498–1515)

I

Louis XII and Jeanne " la Bienheureuse."

" I was not good enough for man, and so I was given to God ! "

II

Louis XII and Anne de Bretagne.

" Never Queen like her enriched all France ! "

III

Louis XII and Mary Tudor.

" The Fairest Princess in all Europe ! "

LOUIS XII

(second cousin once removed to late King)

Born at Blois	.	June 27, 1463
Married (1)	.	Sept. 8, 1474
Ascended	.	Aug., 1498
Married (2)	.	Dec. 16, 1491
Married (3)	.	Oct. 9, 1514
Died	.	Jan. 1, 1515

CONTEMPORARY SOVEREIGNS

ENGLAND: Henry VII and VIII.
SCOTLAND: James IV and V.
SPAIN: Ferdinand and Isabella, Philippe le Bel, and Juana " the Mad."

POPES

Alexander VI, Pius III, Julius II, and Leo X (Medici).

Descent

House of Valois.	House of Valois-Orléans.
┌─CHARLES V─┐	
CHARLES VI	LOUIS D'ORLÉANS
CHARLES VII	CHARLES D'ORLÉANS
LOUIS XI	LOUIS XII
JEANNE	

CONSORTS

(1)

LOUIS XI

m. CHARLOTTE OF SAVOY

JEANNE

Born at Nogent	.	May 15, 1464
Married	.	Sept. 8, 1474
Marriage annulled		1498
Died	.	Feb. 1, 1505
Beatified	.	May 11, 1739

(2)

ANNE DE BRETAGNE

(3)

HENRY VII OF ENGLAND
m. ELIZABETH OF YORK

MARY TUDOR

Born at Richmond		Mar. 1, 1496
Married at Abbeville	.	Oct. 9, 1514
Crowned at St. Denis	.	Nov. 5, 1514
Widowed	.	Jan. 1, 1515

NOTE.—Married secondly the Duke of Suffolk, returned to England and had four children. Her granddaughter was Lady Jane Grey, the " nine-days-Queen."

JEANNE DE VALOIS.

LOUIS XII.

29]

CHAPTER THREE

LOUIS XII (1498–1515)

I

LOUIS D'ORLÉANS, who succeeded Charles VIII, was scion of a collateral branch of the royal line of France, being grand-nephew of Charles VI, who had reigned a century before.

During the rule of Louis XI, young Louis d'Orléans had been betrothed to that King's daughter Jeanne, she being four days old.

In the usual course of events the little Princess would have been handed over for upbringing to her future parents-in-law, Marie de Clèves and Charles d'Orléans, poet and dreamer, who, having spent twenty-five years as a prisoner in England after Agincourt, was now, at sixty-nine, the father of two-year-old Louis. But the King had no love for this collateral branch, so, having secured his daughter's future by marrying her to the then heir-presumptive, he gave her into the charge of the Seigneur de Linières.

A mediæval fortress, surrounded by a moat and double enceinte of walls seven feet thick, with damp, dark living-rooms and mere slits for windows, can hardly have been a suitable abode for a delicate child, but the Seigneur and his wife were kind to their little charge and supplemented the meagre sum of twelve hundred francs a year which was all the King allowed for the support of this pitiful little daughter, who was visibly deformed. No one cared to dress her prettily, and her garments, which were of the coarsest materials, were often threadbare.

When five years old, Jeanne was told that she

might select her own Confessor, whereupon the wise
infant asked for a full day in which to consider the
matter guided by prayer! A few years later a
Reader was added to her entourage so that the child
might be well grounded in the lives of the Saints.
Since she had strong religious tendencies, it is not
surprising that this little Jeanne, like the more famous
Jeanne d'Arc, was soon finding happiness in beatific
visions.

But the trend of foreign affairs now influenced the
child's life. In England, Margaret of Anjou was
fighting for her son's throne, and, hoping to secure an
ally, offered the Prince of Wales as a bridegroom for
the mysterious little Princess hidden away in the
Seigneur de Linières' moated castle.

The offer was not considered worthy of serious consideration, but at least it reminded the King of his
daughter's existence. As a consequence she was
brought to court and the Duc d'Orléans received an
unwelcome order to marry her and fulfil the contract
made nine years before.

Young Louis, who was eleven and precocious,
mentioned that he would prefer Jeanne's elder sister,
who was twelve and pretty, but was told that he must
accept Jeanne or become a tonsured monk. The
boy, who stood too near the throne for his own safety,
understood that the threat was a menace.

" Oh, Notre Dame! faut-il que mon fils ait une
femme ainsi déformée! " cried Marie de Clèves on first
seeing Jeanne, who had one shoulder higher than the
other, one hip lower, and a humped back : the close-
fitting garments of the day cruelly enhanced every
defect.

Even the King made the sign of the cross at the
sight of his daughter, admitting that he had not known
she was " si mal." Indeed, it seemed incredible that
any human being could be so ugly—but he would not
be turned from his purpose.

Jeanne learnt to hide herself behind the robes of her

Confessor when her father approached. She knew
her destiny and was awestruck, seeing Louis d'Orléans
as a young god. He was a fearless rider skilled in
arms and " in every game and pastime of youth the
gentlest, kindest, and most gracious . . . indeed all
he did was pleasant and agreeable. . . ."

" I am no bride for so beautiful a prince," Jeanne
mourned, but the wedding contract was signed and
the ceremony took place ; both children went weeping
to their marriage.

By the King's orders the two were sent to Blois
and bidden to live as man and wife despite their
youth. The alternatives offered to Louis were death
by drowning or life in a monastery.

" Qu'ils n'auraient pas beaucoup d'embarras à
nourrir les enfants qui naîtront de leur union ! . . ."
wrote the King in cynical mood.

During the years of enforced companionship,
Jeanne never lost her admiration for Louis, despite
his studied neglect, and when he was captured and
imprisoned by Anne de Beaujeu in the name of
Charles VIII, Jeanne interceded for him :

" My sister," she wrote, " I humbly beg your help.
I am thinking constantly of the deliverance of my
husband, and I thought it best to put in writing the
form of asking for peace and the release of my lord
that it might be written to the King, and you will
see to it. I beg of you to help me that things may
turn out well, and my said husband and I will always
be grateful to you.

" Your good sister, Jeanne de France."

Anne stood firm, but Charles VIII listened to his
younger sister's plea and freed Louis, who failed to
offer Jeanne thanks for her successful advocacy,
though later he permitted her to nurse him through
smallpox. The two were at Linières when news of
the death of Charles told Louis that he himself was
now King and free to move for divorce from Jeanne

4

and marriage to another woman. So strong was his
desire that steps were taken to advance the new
marriage even while messengers rode post haste towards Rome.

His Holiness Alexander VI (Roderigo Borgia by
birth) appointed three commissioners to consider the
application, and presently Cæsar Borgia, all brilliant
in red and gold and with a band of rubies round his
cap, came riding into France, and fifty gentlemen
behind him almost as gorgeous as himself.

Jeanne faced the ordeal of interrogation with
dignity, averring that although she was ignorant of
the laws of marriage, the contract had been made in
good faith ; " but," she added gravely, " I know that
I am neither as handsome nor as well shaped as the
greater number of my sex. . . ."

The bishops bent their heads over the forms prepared by Louis XII, who asked for an annulment of
his marriage on the threefold grounds of constraint,
lack of consummation, and consanguinity, it being
argued that since Jeanne's father had officiated as
godfather to Louis d'Orléans this had made the pair
spiritual brother and sister.

When a Bull pronounced the marriage void Cæsar
Borgia was regally rewarded ; he received a title,
a pension, and the offer of a bride from the royal
circle.

To Jeanne also a pension was allotted, though
naturally this was on a more modest scale than that
awarded to the Borgia.

" I was not good enough for man, so was given to
God ! " said this King's consort who had never been
acknowledged Queen. She wrapped her misshapen
body in the grey robes of a nun and founded the Order
of the Annunciation, which, beginning with six poor
girls, was to grow in importance and win approval
from fourteen popes.

Being too modest to be Mother Superior, Jeanne
preferred to be known as the *mère ancille*. " She

spent her time in prayers and orisons and in serving God and His poor without giving any sign of the wrong done her . . . in all of which she was wise and virtuous, and made no scandal nor uproar, nor demand for justice because a King can do much and just what he will. Feeling herself strong in continence and chastity, she retired towards God and espoused herself to Him so truly that never another husband nor a better could she have. . . ."

Miracles were attributed to Jeanne both before and after her death, in commemoration of which Pope Julius II granted indulgence to all who said the Rosary which she had composed on the ten virtues of the Virgin.

"She was so plain in body that her husband repudiated her, so beautiful in soul that she became the Bride of Christ"—Jeanne "la Bienheureuse."

During one of the Wars of Religion Jeanne's tomb was broken open by a Huguenot mob, which fled in terror from the sight of a perfect face, believing that the white lips moved, but bolder rioters later sacked the convent and burnt the body.

Two hundred years after Jeanne's death she was formally beatified. A charming statue of her is still to be seen at Bourges, and in this the beauty of the soul has been permitted to transcend some of the deformities of the frail body.

LOUIS XII AND ANNE DE BRETAGNE

" Never Queen like her enriched all France ! "

ANNE DE BRETAGNE was barely twenty-one years old when the death of her first husband, Charles VIII, left her widowed. Had her baby sons lived, she would have ruled as Regent; as it was, finding herself no longer of importance at the court of France, she decided to return to her own duchy so soon as the ceremonial mourning permitted her to leave.

In the intervening weeks she and the new King, Louis XII, met of necessity and renewed a youthful friendship. They had known one another in Anne's childhood, when Louis as Duc d'Orléans had found a temporary refuge in Bretagne, and now the obvious occurred.

There had been a clause in Anne's wedding contract with Charles VIII by which she had bound herself never to marry again unless with that King's successor, and at twenty-one she had no wish to renounce the fullness of life and lay aside a crown ; nor was Louis prepared to see Bretagne as an independent duchy once again, if marriage with Anne could save it to France.

Unfortunately, he had an official wife in Jeanne de France. But since Charles VIII had renounced Margaret of Austria for the sake of Anne's bright eyes (or else her duchy), why should deformed Jeanne be permitted to stand in the way ? So couriers rode to Rome, and Anne listened without surprise to Louis's protestations : " He could not keep from loving her, all married as he was, for it is difficult to quench a great fire when once it has begun to burn. . . ."

The restive King awaited the papal decree and
Anne journeyed to Bretagne to receive the condolences that were her due while she planned her second
trousseau. When Louis followed, the duchy offered
the pair a magnificent wedding and France gave a
royal welcome to the Duchess who had now become
her Queen for the second time.

At her former marriage Anne had been an acquies-
cent girl; now she made rigid terms in regard to her
own sovereign rights, and saw to it that her dowry was
doubled.

History was to repeat itself in that Louis was as
often away at the wars as Charles VIII had been, but
nine months after her wedding Anne found new
happiness in the birth of a living child.

By horse and boat the King came hastening to
Amboise in his eagerness to attend the baptism, and
the infant was dedicated to Ste. Claude.

" There is good hope of having a son, since one has
a living daughter! " cried Louis, and, determined to
increase the inheritance of the heir as yet unborn,
swept into Italy, took Milan, and quarrelled with
Ferdinand of Aragon over the division of Naples.

In the intervals of military achievement he returned
to Anne and found time to organise splendid tournaments, in one of which seven gentlemen of His Majesty's
household rode against seven of Her Majesty's knights,
while a beautiful demoiselle sat on every pillion.

But an undercurrent of intrigue kept the court from
being peaceful, for, as the years passed and Anne gave
the King no son, Louise of Savoy, mother of François
d'Angoulême, the heir-presumptive, came into greater
prominence.

On one occasion when a frightened courier brought
an unauthentic message that Louis XII was dying,
Anne had a sharp lesson and was forced to realise the
uncertain tenure of her position ; for the Maréchal de
Gie, erstwhile tutor to François, seized authority,
stationed 10,000 archers along the banks of the Loire

(so that Princess Claude might not be carried away by her mother), and laid an embargo upon the sailing of various barge-loads of treasure that Anne endeavoured to send into Bretagne—merely as a precautionary measure.

Louis recovered, and vengeful Anne laid the Maréchal under arrest ; but it was thought wise to strengthen her position by a second coronation.

On the King's orders, Paris provided joyous and honourable entertainment in the way of fêtes, tournaments, and morality plays, these last being made the vehicle for some criticism of royalty.

Anne enjoyed it all, fortified by daily letters concerning the welfare of Madame Claude.

" Votre fille fait bonne chère et se fait bien nourrir," wrote the good guardian in frequent repetition, and the time sped swiftly by while Anne, developing feminism, set poets to the writing of verses in praise of women, watched artists illustrating her Book of Hours, and saw to it that her maids-of-honour made suitable marriages. She would pawn her jewels to provide a penniless demoiselle with a dower, and held a dispensation which enabled her to bless weddings at any moment.

Then Louis fell ill, and Anne carried him away from the unhealthy capital and back to Blois, courageously uttering " joyeuses paroles " when beside him, if she wept in private.

" It is an admirable thing to see her grief ! " reported the ladies-in-waiting.

Processions walked the streets, candles were lit on high altars, relics were exposed, the courtiers vowed to go on pilgrimage each to his own special saint, and the common people went naked into the churches to be scourged in the hope of " interesting Heaven towards the King's recovery "—and suddenly the fever abated. . . . " So the King was preserved by his own merits and the prayers of his people ! " reported a court chronicler.

Shortly afterwards a deputation arrived to express the nation's joy at the recovery of this sovereign who was famed for having wept when compelled to levy additional taxes. Having hailed him as " the Father of his People," the deputies ventured on delicate ground and suggested François d'Angoulême as suitable bridegroom for the King's only daughter.

Louis XII lent a favourable ear, but not so Anne. Hitherto the King had rarely opposed her wishes, being of the opinion that " something must be conceded to a chaste woman," but now he took a firm stand, and in a matter that Anne considered peculiarly her own. As a consequence she withdrew to her own duchy and remained there till the Chancellor, Cardinal d'Amboise, wrote urging an immediate return to soothe the angry King and prevent further scandal :

" Would to God I were with you to tell you what is said about your long absence ! "

Discretion sent Anne back to her duties, and if the King departed almost immediately to fight further battles, he left the Queen with hope of an heir. Alas ! In the New Year Louise of Savoy could write in her Journal :

" Anne, Queen of France, had a son on St. Agnes Eve, but he cannot prevent the exaltation of my César . . . 'Il avait faute de vie !' "

Once again Anne saw the courtiers turning away from her and towards the mother of the heir-presumptive ; once again she started on her round from shrine to shrine, while her maids-of-honour walked behind her, barefooted in the mud.

The King returned in time for her next confinement ; indeed, he sat beside her through the hours of struggle, which was thought " very virtuous " of him—but the child was a girl.

A year later came another stillborn son, and Anne saw her woman's tragedy as the result of the excommunication of Louis XII by Pope Julius.

France too was in danger, for a Holy League had
been formed to fight against the overweening suprem-
acy of the French King, and when Louis, seeking for
support, revived the Auld Alliance with the Scots,
Henry VIII landed at Calais.

Hoping to encourage James IV to stronger efforts
on behalf of France, Anne dubbed the Scottish King
her knight and sent him a ring with the request that
he would advance at least three feet on English soil
and so divert the martial efforts of Henry VIII.

Her attempt stirred the Queen of Scots to jealousy.
What right had this French woman who had been
" twice married by means of divorces " to approach
her husband ? asked Queen Margaret. But James
went forth to death on Flodden Field (Sept. 9, 1513).

Anne's other incursion into public affairs was more
successful. She spent Breton money in the building
of a warship so large that it would carry 1,200 fighting
men besides the crew, and sent it to win undying
fame. *La Cordelière* encountered an English fleet,
beat off twelve great vessels with such vigour that
only one dared venture a counter-attack, and, afire
herself, grappled with the *Regent of England* and
sank her to the bottom of the sea.

Perhaps Anne's death (Jan. 9, 1514) helped to bring
peace to France, for it enabled Henry VIII to insert a
pleasing clause in the Treaty of London (Aug. 7, 1514).
She died " an honourable and virtuous Queen, and
very wise ; the true mother of the poor ; the support
of gentlemen ; the haven of ladies, demoiselles, and
honest girls, and the refuge of learned men, leaving all
the people of France to surfeit themselves in despair
and regret," wrote one of royalist sentiment.

The King went " sore afflicted for eight days " and
feeling so sure that he was doomed to follow Anne immediately that he ordered the preparation of a grave
large enough for two.

The funeral ceremonies were protracted, the oration
which began at Blois being continued in Paris and at

St. Denis, where groaning officers of the household
carried Anne's coffin into the cathedral.

" The most Christian Queen-Duchess our Sovereign
Lady and Mistress is dead. The Queen is dead ! "
cried the Breton King-at-Arms, and three officials
advanced bearing the Rod of Justice, sceptre, and
crown. Kissing the insignia, they placed it on the
coffin.

At the end of the funeral feast the Grand-Master
broke his rod to signify that the household staff was
free to seek other service.

" The most Christian Queen and Duchess, our
Sovereign Lady, is dead ! " cried the King-at-Arms
once more. . . . " Let each provide for himself."

> Here lies Anne, wife of two Great Kings, yet
> Greater a hundredfold herself, as Queen twice-crowned. . . .

So ran the epitaph.

" Her death was sorrow to many, but (it was
whispered) there was one who was glad, and that was
Monseigneur d'Angoulême ! "

LOUIS XII AND MARY TUDOR

" The Fairest Princess in all Europe ! "

LOUIS XII was an old man ("fort antique et débile," according to Louise of Savoy) at the death of Anne de Bretagne, although his years were but fifty-two. Worse still, he had no heir, but only a daughter who was barred from the throne by French law.

Seeking a consort who would provide a remedy, Louis remembered Margaret of Austria, who had been discarded by Charles VIII in order that he might marry the woman Louis had now seen buried. But Margaret was the childless widow of two husbands, so it might be preferable to wed her young niece Éléonore.

Negotiations began with Spain, and scribes prepared a treaty in which a blank was left for the insertion of the name of the princess upon whom was to fall the honour of marriage with his Most Christian Majesty.

Meanwhile the Battle of the Spurs was fought (Aug. 16, 1513), and on Wolsey's instigation Henry VIII of England offered to bestow his sister Mary Tudor upon Louis XII as part of the subsequent peace settlement (Treaty of London, 1514). True, she had been contracted, and recontracted, to the Archduke Charles, but neither Henry nor Louis were sovereigns who would let such scraps of paper prevent more advantageous designs. So the matter proceeded.

Never, since the times of the Carlovingians, when a roving monarch had fetched a Kentish maid to France, had a French sovereign married an English

MARY TUDOR, QUEEN OF FRANCE.

bride, and now there were forebodings. Nor was England better pleased than France, for there Louis was held to be in his dotage, while all true Englishmen felt sure that Mary was the fairest princess in Europe. Even the hypercritical Venetian ambassador described her as " a Paradise," although her eyebrows might be thought a shade too light.

The Tudor Princess was eighteen, tall, fair, graceful, and clear complexioned. She was all obedience when Henry VIII demanded the renunciation of her betrothal to the Archduke Charles, but offered strenuous opposition to marriage with Louis, since she had lost her heart to Charles Brandon, Duke of Suffolk.

An unexpected ally appeared in the guise of Margaret of Austria, who warned Henry that his sister, if sent to France, might meet with the same treatment she had experienced after having wedded a French King, but the Tudor answered grimly that he had " taken sufficient precautions in this matter," and brought Mary to acquiescence by promising that she might please herself next time—and marriage with Louis XII could not last long.

Shortly afterwards a commission arrived to advance matters and to express the hope that the alliance would be profitable to all Christendom, also to insist that Henry should fulfil his promise in regard to Tournay, which was still held by an English garrison :

" Tournay must be placed in such security that on the marriage being accomplished it can be given up to his Most Christian Majesty without dissimulation," [1] said the ambassador, and hinted that the King of England seemed to be endeavouring to marry Mary off without a dowry, " which might be turned thereafter to her reproach. . . ."

Meanwhile Henry was conducting diplomatic negotiations with Leo X (for there was no denying that Mary Tudor had been affianced to the Archduke Charles), and explaining her betrothal to Louis XII as

[1] State Papers, Foreign, 1514.

for the good of Christendom. Once allied, England and France could turn their armies upon the Infidel.

These details being adjusted, there followed a proxy marriage at Greenwich, after which Mary Tudor was put to bed in the presence of many courtiers. The Marquis of Rothelin "in his doublet and with a pair of red hose but one leg naked went into the bed too and touched the Princess with his naked limb," after which it was announced that the marriage had been consummated, and there was great rejoicing both in England and in France, where Louis had gone through a very similar ceremony at which the Earl of Worcester officiated as bride.

To make all trebly sure, the deeds of marriage were then ratified in both countries.

While Mary prepared her trousseau, which included " gowns made after the fashion of France, of Milan, and of England, together with jackets of first, second, and third quality, wagons and chests, bedding, furniture, curtain stuffs, cushions, sheets, and covers," Louis sorted his jewels, for if Mary was to receive much, she was to have the gifts at different times in order that the King might have his reward in " divers kisses."

She sailed at last, escorted by Suffolk, had a stormy crossing, and was carried ashore at Boulogne. Unwilling François d'Angoulême came to meet her, bearing messages from the King. He was twenty, she eighteen ; they seem to have liked one another very much.

François was to appear the fairer in contrast to Louis, for all had not seen the King in as favourable a light as had his first bride by compulsion, Jeanne de France, and now self-indulgence had set its seal upon him. He looked crafty, was gouty, and had moist lips, a very low forehead, a large, blunt, ill-shapen nose, and walked with a slouching gait.

But the Earl of Worcester was content that Mary would have a good life with him " by the grace of

God," and found pleasure in drafting the official
reports of her wedding.

" Oct. 9th. Item. The Sunday in the morning
all was performed according to the said appointment,
and the matrimony was solemnised. . . . The Queen
that day kept her chamber. On this same day the
King gave her a marvellous great pointed diamond,
with a ruby almost two inches long. . . . The next
day he gave her a ruby . . . the next a great round
pearl."

Mary too could report the King's approval :
" Indeed, my lord makes as much of me as it is
possible for any man to make of a lady. . . ."

So soon as Louis's gout permitted him to travel, the
court left Abbeville for Paris, where Mary was crowned
and the jousts began with such energy that " there
were at divers times both man and horse overthrown
and slain."

The English representatives ran on the first day
only, for afterwards, as they explained to their King,
" there were no noblemen to put to us, but only poor
men of arms and Scots. . . ." However, all went
well, despite this lack, " and the Queen increases daily
in the favour of her lord."

Indeed, Louis changed all his habits to please this
too fascinating young wife, even to the hour of his
dinner (formerly at 8 a.m.), and now rarely went to
bed before midnight, despite the protests of his
doctors.

The King boasted that he would yet live to see the
birth of an heir to his throne, and the Angoulême party
went in hourly fear, for few had faith in Mary's virtue.

Suffolk, François himself, and a score more (all
equally smitten) surrounded Mary, dancing, laughing,
and making merry, while anxious Louise of Savoy
watched this reckless, too attractive Queen, and did
what she could to safeguard her son's prospects.
The King's daughter, Madame Claude (daughter of
Anne de Bretagne), became Mary's perpetual com-

panion by day, and the Baronne d'Aumont attended
her at night.

"Il ne faut qu'un accident pour que vous restiez
Comte d'Angoulême toute votre vie!" said an aged
courtier warningly to François.

On November 26 a deputation of learned men
arrived from the Sorbonne to congratulate Mary upon
her marriage and lay stress on the favourable prospects
before her. Since the time of Clovis the Hairy in the
fifth century no King of France had been killed in
battle, nor were French sovereigns slain by their own
people nor chased out of the Kingdom. It was hoped
that Mary would remain Queen-Consort for many
years.

The following day Louis took to his bed; a month
later he was well enough to write to Henry VIII
concerning his contentment with that King's sister,
but on January 1 (1515) he died, and heralds went
through the streets uttering their lugubrious cry:
"Le bon roi Loys, père du peuple, est mort!"

It was not yet three months since Mary's marriage
day, nor two since her crowning, and now she was
free to wed "as it pleaseth me!"

Suitors in fact or fancy swarmed around her even
before the King's funeral obsequies were accomplished,
and Louise's anxieties increased daily.

Mary feared that Henry VIII intended to manœuvre
her into a marriage with Charles V (the archduke to
whom she had been contracted in her childhood),
though she vowed that she would sooner be torn in
pieces, and Charles, having realised that Mary was his
senior by four years, disdainfully announced that he
required a wife, not a mother.

The Dukes of Savoy, Lorraine, and Bavaria made
tentative moves, as did the Prince of Portugal, while
the widowed Emperor Maximilian hesitated between
the attractions of this youthful Queen-Dowager and
his chance of becoming a pope.

François too hovered about her till, in self-defence,

she was driven to confess her love for Suffolk.   Then, though the new King stood aside with all the gallantry of a French gentleman, other troubles cropped up.

France lodged a demand for Tournay, still held by Henry VIII, and pointed out that the jewels Louis had showered upon his bride belonged to the crown, while Henry, ignoring the question of Tournay, demanded the immediate return of his sister, the jewels, and all her goods and furnishings with a fair round sum of money to compensate him for his expenditure upon her trousseau and her passage.

While the kings and diplomatists strove, Mary took action worthy of a Tudor.

" Sir," she wrote to her royal brother, " I put my Lord Suffolk in choice whether he would accomplish the marriage within four days, or else that he would never enjoy me," and she subscribed herself as a " sorrowful, loving, and humble sister."

Suffolk wrote by the same courier ". . . and the Queen would never let me be in rest till I had agreed to her to be married . . . and so I have married her heartily."

Henry VIII of England " took the news both grievously and displeasantly."

Note.—For the story of Mary Tudor as Duchess of Suffolk see *Royal Marys*, by E. Thornton Cook (Murray).

HOUSE OF ANGOULÊME
CHAPTER FOUR
FRANÇOIS I (1515–1547)

I

FRANÇOIS I AND CLAUDE DE FRANCE
" Candida Candidis."

II

FRANÇOIS I AND ÉLÉONORE OF AUSTRIA.
" Éléonore, la très obéissante femme du Roy de France."

FRANÇOIS I
(first cousin once removed and son-in-law to Louis XII)

Born at Cognac	. .	1494
Married (1)	. . .	1514
Ascended	. . .	1515
Crowned	. . .	1515
Married (2)	. . .	1530
Died at Rambouillet	.	1547

CONTEMPORARY SOVEREIGNS

ENGLAND : Henry VIII, Edward VI.
SCOTLAND : James V, Mary Stuart.
SPAIN : Ferdinand, Charles V.

POPES

Leo X, Adrian VI, Clement VII, Paul III.

Descent
CHARLES V

CONSORTS
(1)
CLAUDE DE FRANCE

Born at Romorantin	.	1499
Married .	. .	1514
Died at Blois .	. .	1524

Issue :

Louise	. .	1515–17
Charlotte	. .	1516–24
François	. .	1517–36
Henri (II)	. .	1518–59
Madeleine	. .	1520–37
(m. K. of Scots)		
Charles	. .	1521–45
Marguerite	. .	1523–59

(2)
ÉLÉONORE OF AUSTRIA

Born at Louvain	. .	1498
Married (1) Emanuel of		
Portugal	. . .	1519
Widowed	. . .	1521
Married (2)	. . .	1530
Died at Talavera, nr.		
Badajos	. . .	1558

Issue : two daughters by Emanuel.

```
                  CHARLES V
         ┌────────────┴────────────┐
CHARLES VI        LOUIS D'ORLÉANS
                  ┌──────────────────┴───────────┐
          CHARLES D'ORLÉANS          JEAN D'ORLÉANS
             (poet)                  (Comte d'Angouleme)
               │                              │
           LOUIS XII              CHARLES D'ORLÉANS m.
                                    LOUISE OF SAVOY
                                              │
          CLAUDE    m.    FRANÇOIS  MARGUERITE
                                   m. K. OF NAVARRE
─────────────────────────────────────────────────────────
MAXIMILIAN I m. MARIE DE BOUR-   FERDINAND   OF   ARAGON   m.
         GOGNE                    ISABELLA OF CASTILLE
    ┌──────────┴──────────┐               │
MAR. OF AUSTRIA   PHIL. LE BEL  m.  JUANA " THE MAD "
                      │                   │
                  CHARLES V     ÉLÉONORE (and others)
```

FRANCOIS I.

CLAUDE, WIFE OF FRANÇOIS I.

ÉLÉONORE OF AUSTRIA.

CHAPTER FOUR

FRANÇOIS I (1515–1547)

I

WHEN Madame Claude de France, daughter of Anne de Bretagne, was a demure little maid of six years of age, a deputation waited upon her father, Louis XII, urging him to betroth the child to Monsieur François d'Angoulême, since he was heir-presumptive and in all respects a Frenchman.

The King was willing, since the marriage might secure the throne to his daughter, but there were difficulties, as the child had been affianced some years before to Charles (grandson of the Emperor Maximilian), and in virtue of her engagement, Louis had secured certain rights over Milan. However, after weighing the advantages, he cut the Gordian knot, " for reasons it would take too long to explain," as he wrote to Charles, and the new betrothal was celebrated.

A picturesque feature of the ceremony was the assembling of the Scottish archers that their captain might swear on the share he hoped to have in Paradise, or the damnation of his soul, that he and his men would serve the affianced pair to the death.

The match was a fine one for François, even if Louis had other children, for Claude had been declared Duchesse de Bretagne and Milan and was suzerain of various other territories.

Except for the incident of the Scottish archers, the little Princess had no touch of glamour to remember in connection with her betrothal, and when she went submissively to her wedding a few years later the

entire court was shrouded in black garments, even the
bride's gown being " honestly cut in mourning shape,"
for the ceremony took place on May 18, 1514, only
eighteen weeks after the death of Anne de Bretagne.

Those who were superstitious felt that the mother's
ghost was brooding over the ceremony, for Anne
would have preferred a very different son-in-law.

" Elle n'est pas belle," said the King, speaking of
his daughter, " mais sa vertu touchera le Comte, et il
ne pourra s'empêcher de lui rendre justice." But it
would have taken more than the virtue of a docile
princess to make François d'Angoulême a faithful
husband.

He had equipped himself for the ceremony by
acquiring a bed, a bolster, and a blanket, and these
are the only gifts recorded as being made to the
bride.

Claude's first act was to cede her duchies to her
husband, to the indignation of the Bretons, whom
François ignored when he assumed the title of Duc,
placed his new-made wife in his mother's charge, and
went a-hunting. On the succeeding New Year's morning, a merry band of courtiers drew back François's
bed-curtains crying that they had brought him *belles
étrennes*. Louis XII was dead, and François I was
King of France.

A few weeks later Louise of Savoy could make the
long-desired entry in her diary :

" The day of the Conversion of St. Paul, Jan. 25
(1515), my son was anointed and crowned in the Church
at Rheims, and for this I am very grateful to divine
mercy. . . . I now feel compensated for all the
adversities and annoyances which came to me in the
flower of my youth . . . through which humility has
kept me company and patience never abandoned
me. . . ."

On the royal progress that followed the coronation
fifty wagons were required to transport the kitchen
staff alone. Banquet succeeded banquet, and at each

François drank to the success of the French arms and
swore " Foy de gentilhomme ! " that by his valour
France should become yet more powerful.

Already he was dreaming of the conquest of Milan,
to which he had a shadowy claim through his great-
grandmother,[1] but there was much to do before he
could march his army across the Alps. " Our very
dear and beloved Mother " Louise of Savoy was to be
created Duchesse d'Angoulême and appointed Regent, " she being the person in whom we have a full
and perfect confidence," and his sister Marguerite must
be invested with the dignity of " Madame."

These matters adjusted, Charles de Montpensier
(who by his marriage with Suzanne, daughter of Anne
de Beaujeu, had become Duc de Bourbon and the
most powerful noble in the kingdom) was installed as
Constable of France. He stirred the hearts of both
Louise and her daughter when he came to court on the
eve of the army's departure wearing a silver sash over
his armour and with crimson plumes waving from his
casque.

The stupendous march began, and by pass and
defile François led his men through the Swiss snows.
Late summer found the French debouching upon the
Italian plains and the enemy " within cast of a tennis
ball."

The Battle of Marignano (Sept. 13–14, 1515) raged
till the light of the moon failed, when the intermingled,
exhausted armies rested, and the King snatched a few
hours' fitful sleep stretched on a gun-carriage. Next
morning the Swiss yielded, and presently messengers
rode through France carrying news of so great a
victory that all Christendom marvelled. England
discredited the first reports, but Louise of Savoy
waited no corroboration before she opened her diary
to write :

" My son, glorious and triumphant César . . . the
subjugator of the Helvetians ! . . ."

[1] Valentina Visconti, daughter of Gian Galeazzo, Duke of Milan.

It was François's splendid hour. What matter that he had been thrice wounded? At twenty-one he had defeated an army hitherto held unconquerable, and the famous Bayard had knighted him on the field of battle.

Leaving the Duc de Bourbon in Italy, François returned to France, where Queen Claude had given birth to the first of her "fine and generous progeny," and was now sitting spinning among the group of modest maidens selected by Louise of Savoy as suitable companions for her daughter-in-law.

The King, with his mother and sister, formed what François called a trinity of love, Marguerite being " le petit point de ce parfait triangle " ; so Claude's place was in the background. Only the discerning saw her as " belle, avec toujours des roses dans l'esprit et jamais d'épine dans le cœur."

The court became gayer and more brilliant. Leonardo da Vinci and other great men of the day circled around Madame Marguerite, and beautiful women were always welcomed by the ardent young King, whose valour was a never-failing subject for verse.

François had selected a salamander among flames as his device, signifying that he was never happier than when in danger.

It was not until Claude lay in childbed for the third time, with the King's mother close at hand to record the hour, indeed the very moment, of birth of yet another child to " mon fils, glorieux et triomphant César," that France welcomed a Dauphin.

Leo X sent his nephew Lorenzo de Medici to stand proxy at the gorgeous baptism, and the Florentine brought a string of thirty-six pack-horses laden with gifts for the Queen, among which was a marvellous bedstead of tortoise-shell inlaid with mother-of-pearl.

With two eligible children, François thought it well to begin matrimonial negotiations. Louise, the elder, had been offered to the oft-robbed Charles V, France offering to pay an annuity of a hundred thousand crowns till she was marriageable, and a reduced amount after the ceremony while she remained childless ; Louise having died inconveniently her sister Charlotte was offered in her stead, and Princess Mary of England was selected as a bride for the Dauphin now being rocked in his cradle. Presently French and English envoys sat side by side in St. Paul's Cathedral and in Notre-Dame in honour of yet another treaty of marriage which was to bind the two nations in perpetual amity.

With peace so established in Christendom, the world talked of a Crusade against the Infidels, until the death of the Emperor Maximilian (Jan. 15, 1519) flung François, Henry VIII, and Charles V into rivalry for the Imperial Crown.   Lavish in promises and the expenditure of good golden crowns, François hoped for success, but the Electoral Diet was swayed by the eloquence of the Archbishop of Mayence, and the King of France tried to forget his defeat as he floated down the Seine in a gilded barge with Madame de Châteaubriand.

Claude fulfilled her duty once again, Sir Thomas Boleyn arrived to represent Henry VIII as proxy grandfather, and plans were laid for a meeting between the Kings of France and England.   A site was selected between Guisnes and Ardres and François made a futile suggestion of mutual economy, but this being set aside by Henry, the French King ordered gold and silver threads to be woven into the material of which his pavilions were constructed and had them hung with cloth-of-gold.

Among other wonder structures the English brought a palace of glass all in sections (alas ! it was destroyed by French winds), and a chapel which looked like stone, though inquisitive French fingers discovered that it was only canvas.

Since Katherine of Aragon was accompanying Henry, Claude was fetched from her spinning wheel to play her part as Queen of France, though she was anticipating the birth of her fifth child within six weeks.

The Field-of-the-Cloth-of-Gold was true to its name, and the tents provided for the Queens were almost more splendid than those of the Kings; the very foot cloths before their thrones gleamed with jewels.

But beneath the gorgeous pageantry an undercurrent of anxiety was evident. No man had complete faith in the sworn treaty of amity, and strict rules were drawn up concerning the number of attendants that were to accompany each King.

François rode out first, but Henry mounted his charger almost instantly and came curvetting towards him; then each stopped suddenly, for keen eyes discovered that the contingent following François was larger than had been agreed!

In the tense pause the Earl of Shrewsbury bent to his monarch's ear, whispering that he felt sure the French feared the English more than the English the French, and Henry made a bold gesture.

"On afore!" he cried, the cavalcades moved again, and a moment later the two Kings met and embraced. One was resplendent in crimson velvet, the other gleamed in silver damask, but the Constable de Bourbon outvied both. "Had I such a subject, he would not long carry his head on his shoulders," said bluff King Henry VIII.

Distrust still lingered, and next day, when it was necessary that visits of ceremony should be paid to the respective Queens, François attended on Katherine of Aragon at exactly the same moment that Henry approached Queen Claude, so that each might act as hostage for the other.

Now came the tournament. The Kings did not tilt at one another, which was as well, for Henry struck his assailant with such vigour that the unfortunate knight never rose again and the King's horse died of exhaustion. However, the two ventured on a royal wrestling match, and, to the delight of the French, François laid the English monarch on his back! Courtiers had some difficulty in preventing a renewal of the contest.

Next morning debonair François flung aside caution and rode boldly into the English lines and demanded to see the King. Indeed, according to Michelet, " Il voulait lui servir de valet de chambre, et lui chauffer la chemise." Nor were the Queens more reserved, and as the two sat together Katherine may have found it in her heart to pity this neglected young wife who knew so little of the grandeur that should have been hers. But Claude had sons, and Katherine, had she known it, was doomed for lack of them.

The concluding ceremony was Wolsey's hour. He celebrated High Mass, with the Kings and Queens kneeling before him, in the tapestry-hung canvas chapel, where the altar was ablaze with lights and jewels. Katherine and Claude occasioned a momentary scandal by exchanging an emotional embrace during the ceremony, but the *faux pas* was forgotten in the excitement of watching the signing of the Peace Treaty. So the betrothal of the Dauphin of France and Mary of England was advanced a further step, though in the stars it was written that it should never come to fruition.

Tranquillity was of short duration in France. Soon, Louise of Savoy brought suit against the Constable de Bourbon, hoping to secure the estates which had been left to him by her cousin Suzanne, and François began to plan another Italian campaign, though his coffers were empty.

The taxes were increased till the people groaned ; offices of State were sold to the highest bidder ; soldiers went unpaid, and desertions became frequent.

Once more Claude, a King's consort and a King's daughter, was set aside and Louise assumed the Regency.

" I know for a surety that she will wisely and
virtuously acquit herself of the same," announced
the King.

Perhaps it was as well that the Queen had not been
appointed to the office that should have been hers, for
she died suddenly (July 26, 1524), as quietly as she had
lived, and a sorrowing people hastened to the churches,
not to pray for Claude's soul, but to beg her inter-
cession.

A bold chronicler wrote that the Queen's days had
been shortened by the King's evil life, and added that
she had " strengthened her soul by her sound mind,
gentle patience, and great wisdom, all of which had
helped her to endure her troubles uncomplainingly."

A pretty tribute to her still endures, for the sweetest
plum in France is known as " la Reine Claude."

But the death of a queen, even one who has given
the country seven children in nine years, could not
be allowed to delay François's plans for the conquest of
Italy.

The army moved once more, and the King rode at
its head, a brocaded surcoat covering his mail, and
the red salamander half hidden by the waving brown
and yellow plumes which surmounted his helmet.

Milan opened her gates to the conquering force,
which, made rash by victory, swept on to meet
disaster at Pavia (Feb. 24, 1525).

" Victoria ! Victoria ! España ! España ! " sounded
the triumphant cry of the Imperial forces, and nightfall
found the King of France struggling in the hands of
his captors while ill-disciplined soldiery slashed frag-
ments from his surcoat.

Panic-stricken Paris closed her gates and stretched
chains across the Seine, but Louise of Savoy showed
herself a tower of strength.

" Night and day there is not a moment lost from
your affairs," wrote Marguerite to her brother ; her
heart carried a double load of bitterness in that her

husband, the Duc d'Alençon, had fled from the field of battle.

Negotiations began for the release of François I, but Charles V seemed without mercy, and France, bereaved of her Queen, remained without a King.

FRANÇOIS I AND ÉLÉONORE OF AUSTRIA

" Éléonore, la très obéissante femme du Roy de France "

ÉLÉONORE OF AUSTRIA had a tragic youth. Her father died when she was eight years old, and the bereavement affected the reason of her mother, who insisted upon having her husband's body embalmed, and kept it always with her. The last forty years of her life were spent in the Castle of Tordesillas, with cats as her sole companions ; tradition insists that unfortunate " Juana the Mad " [1] was allowed only straw to lie on, and this in insufficient quantity.

At sixteen, Éléonore had the pale, clear complexion of her father, Philippe *le Bel*, his sparkling eyes and arched black eyebrows, with a sweet voice, exquisite teeth, and a small attractive mouth ; the " Hapsburg lip " was not noticeable. Unfortunately, while she was at this susceptible age, the Elector Palatine came riding into Spain, and Éléonore gave him her heart, to the indignation of her ambitious brother Charles V. The Elector's visit was cut short, and a few years later a protesting Éléonore was sent to marry Portugal's fifty-year-old King Emanuel. He had already wed, and lost, two of her aunts !

At twenty-three she found herself again in Spain, a widow with two little daughters. Her former lover sent an immediate proposal, but pride had killed young romance, and Éléonore would now have nothing to say to one who was not a King.

Perhaps it was as well, for had the Elector suc-

[1] She was Katherine of Aragon's sister.

ceeded in rekindling the flame of passion, the marriage
would surely have been forbidden by Charles, who
was using his charming sister as a bait, hoping to
detach the Constable Duc de Bourbon from French
interests and hinting at a plan by which the Constable
and Éléonore would become King and Queen of
Naples.

But the Battle of Pavia (Feb. 24, 1525), which flung
François I into the hands of the Emperor Charles,
altered Éléonore's destiny.

As a preliminary to the negotiations which would
restore François to his bereaved nation, the King was
required to recognise Charles's claim to Milan and
Naples, restore the sequestrated estates of the Duc de
Bourbon, pay his debts to Henry VIII, and betroth
the Dauphin to one of the Emperor's nieces—although
this Prince had been firmly contracted to Mary of
England.

The King of France vowed that he would rather
die than agree to such terms, and as a result was con-
fined in a tower of the palace of the Alcazar, where a
bed and a chair filled the small room and light entered
through a slit-like window.

News of François's plight alarmed his sister,
who wrote urging him to guard his health at all
costs :

" Do not fast in Lent," she implored. " Consider
how fish goes against you, and if you fast Madame
Louise has sworn to do so too; I should sorrow to see
you both give way."

Her anxiety increased when François fell seriously
ill and lay in such melancholy that he was near death
before Marguerite could secure a safe conduct, whereupon she hastened south to nurse her brother and
beard the Emperor. Charles had no liking for this
vigorous daughter of France, who vowed that if terms
were not made easier François would abdicate in
favour of his son, and before the expiry of her safe

conduct Marguerite found it necessary to ride for her
life till she crossed the frontier of Spain.

She had left her brother in improved health and
with fresh hope. Perhaps, if he undertook to marry
the so usefully widowed Eléonore, Charles might
listen to reason in other ways ?

Meanwhile, Louise of Savoy was making valiant
efforts on her son's behalf. She sent plenipotentiaries
to the English court authorised to conclude a defensive
alliance ; she applied to the Pope ; she attempted to
open negotiations with the Turks, and she listened to
endless orations from stiff-necked provincials. These
assured her that France's troubles had come upon her
as a result of the tolerance shown to heretics, so two
were duly burnt in front of Notre-Dame while church
bells tolled a warning to other latitudinarians.

Such efforts told. The Regent felt herself growing
old and the Dauphin was still a child ; she felt that at
whatever cost to France the King must be ransomed.

Step by step the French yielded to Charles's
demands, for though the Emperor accepted the suggestion that François should marry Éléonore, he remained unyielding on many points.

The widowed Queen of Portugal was on a pilgrimage
to the shrine of Notre-Dame de Guadeloupe when
apprised of her destiny, but she had learnt her lesson,
and wrote to place her unresisting self in her brother's
hands for disposal as he thought best.

A treaty of " sincere and perpetual peace and free
trade " was drafted, and on the eve of its presentation
François's friends stole into the tower, and before a
hastily erected altar the King swore that the signature
he intended to give on the morrow was being extracted
from him under threat of perpetual durance ; therefore he would not be bound to ratify it. With such
secret reservations the deed was signed " on knightly
faith," and under oath prohibiting its violation.
Charles stipulated that if within four months all the
provisions had not been carried out, François must

return to captivity; in the meantime twelve of the most powerful French nobles, or the King's two elder sons, were required as hostages.

Six days later the matrimonial dispensations arrived and the betrothal was accomplished with little ceremony while François was suffering from a recurrence of fever.

From now on, Éléonore invariably signed herself as " la très obéissante femme du Roy de France."

Charles V was in high good-humour, and wrote to Louise of Savoy :

" Now that I have recovered in the King your son, my good brother, and that I have given you the Queen, my sister, for a daughter, I must return to the name I formerly used, and call you my *bonne mère*."

A few days later captor and captive rode out together, and François saw his bride for the first time. Éléonore fell upon her knees at his approach, and would have kissed his hand had he not raised her " in a loving and courteous fashion."

Freedom was in sight at last—although at the eleventh hour a contretemps occurred when the guards struck for arrears of pay—and François saw Spain *en fête*. Laughing girls flung roses in his path, but the King's eyes were turned towards the frontier, where no people were allowed to assemble for periods of ten days before and after his release.

Louise of Savoy had decided that for the nation's sake the two little Princes (aged seven and eight), and not the twelve nobles, must go to Spain as hostages. It was fortunate that Queen Claude was dead ; years later François vowed that his children still carried the marks of their captivity.

Pontoons were erected on the Bidassoa half-way between Fontarabia and Hendaye ; Spanish and French warships were ordered away from the river's mouth, and father and sons met in mid-stream.

" We rely upon your good faith to perform your

promise," said the Spanish Viceroy as François, having embraced his sons, stepped into a boat.

"That which I am pledged to perform will be accomplished," answered his Most Christian Majesty. A moment later he leapt on French soil; free once more after thirteen months in captivity.

"Je suis Roy ! . . . Je suis Roy encore ! " And in his heart the treaty was already annulled.

It had been agreed that Éléonore should join her lord at Bayonne, but François found himself too impatient to await his bride, so rode on across France with his mother and sister, who had come to welcome him, bringing with them a group of charming ladies, members of the court.

The treaty was repudiated, despite thunderous protests from Charles (later, Pope Clement VII absolved the King), France was stained with blood once more, and Rome sacked before the " très obéissante femme " was again to see her faithless consort.

Indeed, François volunteered to marry Mary of England instead (if he could free himself from Charles's sister and contrive to remain a widower until the English Princess was of an age to become a wife), provided Henry VIII would join the League that was to be formed against the too powerful Emperor.

But France and Spain were both weary of war, and when Charles refused the olive branch Louise of Savoy stretched out, his aunt Margaret of Austria, now Regent of the Netherlands, grasped the opportunity. The two brought about the Peace of Cambrai (Aug. 1529), that " Paix des Dames " by which, if France lost much, she bought temporary tranquillity, and, by Éléonore's aid, the return of the Princes.

So François journeyed south once more, and at Bayonne a thousand French soldiers confronted as many Spaniards, each with a hundred special guards.

Twelve gentlemen of France passed ten leagues into Spain, while twelve Spanish dons crossed the frontier to see that all was peaceful along the French border.

Both parties returned in safety, bringing good reports, the guns of Fontarabia were dismounted as a *beau geste*, and the long-delayed wedding would have been solemnised forthwith, but unfortunately the two million crowns which were to have been paid as ransom for the Princes did not materialise in full. A tactful Spanish official feigned illness so as to give time for Anne de Montmorency, Grand Master of France, to make good the short weight, and at last the train of thirty-two mules reached Hendaye.

At six o'clock next morning Montmorency prepared to receive the Princes, and there were indignant mutterings among the French when it was discovered that the children had been again sent back into Spain on account of an alleged inaccuracy in certain papers.

Trouble was brewing when Éléonore took control and also possession of her future stepsons. Such evident eagerness for the conclusion of her matrimonial venture was considered scarcely modest, until it was remembered " that she was no virgin but a widow with two children of her own."

The members of each suite now searched the other for concealed weapons, Montmorency watched the golden crowns loaded into a boat, and while twelve Spanish nobles guarded the treasure, twelve Frenchmen fetched Éléonore and the little Princes to the centre of the stream. When the boats met the suites changed places, the Frenchmen passing one by one into the boat containing the human freight, and the Spaniards into that containing the gold.

It was evening before all was accomplished and to the sound of trumpets and the beating of drums each boat pulled for the opposite shore.

Bestowing the tired children in her own litter, Éléonore had them carried to St. Jean de Luz, and, after a night's rest, on to Bayonne in a " great chariot covered with embroidery, accompanied by her ladies all dressed in the best Spanish style."

6

François advanced to meet his bride and married her in the Abbaye de Véries at the amazing hour of 4 a.m.

A royal progress to the capital followed, for if no one wanted this Austro-Spanish Queen, all France rejoiced over the ransomed Princes.

Eléonore was crowned at St. Denis (March 5, 1531), but her moment of glory was brief, for brighter eyes than hers were attracting François, and when she snubbed the leading favourite and refused to accompany the King to meet Henry VIII at Boulogne on the ground that she should not be expected to receive Anne Boleyn, he went without her, happy among a bevy of court beauties, and calling on the Duchesse d'Estampes to play a royal part.

Nor was the peace Éléonore's marriage had brought to France of much longer duration. The terms of the Treaty of Cambrai had humiliated the country, and the King was eager to strike at his over-powerful neighbour whenever he could count upon Henry VIII as an ally, though once Éléonore's efforts delayed war by bringing about a temporarily successful meeting between her husband and her brother. In the brief interludes of peace the Queen walked in religious processions and attended the marriages of her step-children. François loved, quarrelled, outraged Christendom by recognising the Turks, sent his ships into the Solent hoping to invade England, and burnt heretics for the honour of God.

Eléonore was still aloof and a foreigner in a strange land when the King's death released her. " Les dames plus que les ans, lui causèrent la mort," was a contemporary comment. She shook the dust of France from her garments, joined her brother Charles in the Low Countries for a time, and then returned to Spain, outliving François by eleven years. She was buried in the Escurial.

CHAPTER FIVE
HENRI II (1547–1559)

HENRI II AND CATHERINE DE MEDICI

" A Queen who was of many Kings the Mother."

HENRI II
(second son of François I)

Born at St.
  Germain . March 31, 1518–19
Married at
  Marseilles Oct. 28, 1533
Ascended . March 31, 1547
Crowned at
  Rheims . July 25, 1547
Died . . July 10, 1559

CONTEMPORARY SOVEREIGNS

ENGLAND : Edward VI, Mary, and Elizabeth.
SCOTLAND : Mary Stuart.
SPAIN : Charles V, and Philip II.

POPES [1]

Paul III, Julius III, Marcellus II, Paul IV.

Descent

LOUIS D'ORLÉANS
(brother of Charles VI)
|
JEAN D'ORLÉANS
(Comte d'Angoulême)
|
CHARLES D'ORLÉANS
|
FRANÇOIS I
m. CLAUDE DE FRANCE
|
HENRI II

CONSORT
Descent

PIERO
|
LORENZO the Magnificent — GIULIANO
|
PIETRO GIOVANNI GIULIANO GIULIO
        (Leo X)   (Clem. VII)
LORENZO, D.
of Urbino,
m. MADE-
LEINE DE
LA TOUR
|
CATHERINE   Ippolito Alessandro
DE MEDICI

Born at Florence April 13, 1518–19
Married Henri
  Duc d'Orléans
  at Marseilles Oct. 28, 1533
Became Dauphine Aug. 1536
Became Queen-
  Consort . 1547
Widowed . . July 10, 1559
Became Regent
  (1) . . Dec. 5, 1560
Became Regent
  (2) . . May 30, 1574
Died at Blois . Jan. 5 1589

Issue :

1. François (II) . . 1544–60
2. Elizabeth (became
   Q. of Spain) . 1545–68
3. Claude . . . 1547–75
4. Louis . . . 1548–50
5. Charles (IX) . . 1550–74
6. Henri (III) . . 1551–89
7. Marguerite . .1552–1616
8. Hercule (later Fran-
   çois Duc d'Alen-
   çon and Anjou) . 1554–84
9–10. Twins : Jeanne
   and Victoire ;
   one died at birth
   and the second
   within the year . 1556

[1] During the *childhood* of Catherine de Medici three Popes previous to these occupied the Holy See, viz. Leo X, Adrian VI, and Clement VII.

CATHERINE DE MEDICI.

HENRI II.

67]

CHAPTER FIVE

HENRI II (1547–1559)

CATHERINE DE MEDICI was orphaned before she was a month old. As sole, direct legitimate heir of a princely. house, her life was important, so her great-uncle, Pope Leo X, sent his cousin, Cardinal (Giulio) de Medici, to take charge of her affairs in Florence. The Cardinal saw the infant " Duchessina " duly baptised (with two monks and two abbesses among her six godparents), and sent her off to papal care in Rome.

Less than three years later Leo X died, and after a brief interlude Giulio de Medici himself was elected to the Holy See, and took the name of Clement VII to illustrate his merciful disposition.

Italy was struggling to fling off the foreign yoke that weighed her down, and Rome became the centre of the maelstrom, so Pope Clement, fearing for the safety of his ward, sent Catherine back to Florence under the charge of Cardinal Passerini, together with her illegitimate cousins, Ippolito and Alessandro. The trio made their home in the Medici Palace, until news of the sack of Rome and the flight of Clement VII to a refuge in the Castle of St. Angelo encouraged an outburst of republicanism in Florence, and a mob yelled down the Via Larga cursing the young Medici. Eight-year-old Catherine was hurried into the Convent of Santa Lucia for safety's sake.

But though Florence proclaimed her freedom loudly, she lay open to attack, and the city fathers saw Catherine as a possible hostage, so the Republican

Guards claimed her late on a December night and led
her on foot through the plague-stricken streets to the
Murate.[1]

The Abbess opened wide arms to the frightened
child, and the too brief years Catherine spent in this
convent were green in her memory fifty years later;
it was the only period in the life of Catherine de
Medici when she was under the tutelage of women.

Scarcely had the " Duchessina " been established in
the Murate before Clement VII escaped from St.
Angelo. He lay in Orvieto " assailed by hunger,
skarsite, and in il-favored lodgings," but still firm in
his determination to recover Florence from the
Republicans. Here the ambassadors of Henry VIII
found him when they came to advance " the King's
secret matter," and secure papal acquiescence in the
divorcing of Katherine of Aragon, and here he listened
to those who proposed a marriage for the heiress of
the Medici with a descendant of the Bourbons.

Presently an alliance was effected between the Pope
and the Emperor Charles V, who besieged Florence,
while Catherine played and worked among the nuns
unconscious of a desperate suggestion to expose her
on the city walls in the hope that this would cause the
Imperial forces to suspend fire. One ranter urged
that she should be used to ransom Florence, or that
if the Pope would not yield to republican demands,
Catherine should be given to the lust of the banditti-
like soldiery.

Food became scarce, but somehow the nuns fed
their dangerous little guest, although even mice were
difficult to purchase. Then the harassed Com-

[1] Signifying " the walled up." Novices entered this convent not by a
gate but through a hole in the wall, which was then blocked to illustrate
that the entrant had become dead to the world. The Nunnery had
been established a hundred and fifty years before, and miraculous
happenings had rendered it famous. It was believed that St. Michael
himself had been seen on the roof, while Catherine's own great-grand-
father, Lorenzo the Magnificent, who had leapt the walls one night in
his lawless youth, had testified to finding an angel guarding the bed of
every sleeping nun.

missioners, who feared that Clement VII would contrive to regain possession of Catherine, discovered
that the Murate had become a hotbed of Medici
intrigue, and ordered the child's immediate removal.

But Catherine at eleven was no cipher. She
cropped her hair, dressed herself in the garb of a nun,
and clung to the Abbess.

" Holy Mother ! I am yours. . . . Hold me—and
who will dare drag a spouse of Christ from her haven ! "

But the republicans were not to be gainsaid. Still
in her nun's robes, Catherine was lifted on to a horse
and wept tears of mingled rage and fear until she
found herself at Santa Lucia once more. When
Florence fell she contrived to escape to the Murate,
but even as she vowed that she had a vocation and
would remain there for ever as a nun, Pope Clement
was considering the various proposals that had been
made for her hand, and summoned her to Rome.

John Stuart, Duke of Albany (brother of James III
of Scotland), who had married Catherine's maternal
aunt, saw the girl as a suitable bride for his young
King, James V, but the inaccessibility of Scotland,
with the consequent expenses of courier travel, forced
the Pope to decide against this union.

Six other names were advanced, including that of
the Duke of Richmond, before, on the instigation of
Henry VIII,[1] the King of France made a tentative
proposal on behalf of the Duc d'Orléans, and Clement
decided that the offer of a Son of France was so great
an honour that it should be accepted unconditionally.

Clement VII had had a difficult time of late. Henry
VIII was reiterating his demands for the annulment
of his marriage, while Charles V besought his Holiness
to remain firm. " Should he lose one unfruitful
island by such a course, he would assuredly gain the
obedience of many more important kingdoms ! "

---

[1] Henry was much aggrieved later because François would not make
final acceptance of Catherine conditional upon the Pope's consenting to
his divorce with Katherine of Aragon.

Marseilles had been selected as a meeting-ground for Clement VII and François I, and Catherine started on her wedding journey without being sure of the name of her husband, since the Pope still hoped to secure the King's elder son, rather than Henri d'Orléans.

Clement VII arrived in a crimson-satin-bedecked galley with an awning of cloth-of-gold ; his attendants followed in three gorgeous barges. Catherine had travelled separately, as etiquette decreed, under strong escort, and her colours were purple and gold.

The courts of Rome and France had already assembled and now put to sea while hautbois, clarion, and trumpets sounded and cannon shook the fortifications.

Awed citizens made obeisance as the Pope was carried by arrayed in his pontifical robes, while a white palfrey led by white silken cord ambled before him carrying the Holy Sacrament, and behind him rode the cardinals on their slow-paced, stately mules. Indeed, the ecclesiastical procession surpassed in glory that of the Court of France and also Catherine's, though the proceeds of a forced loan had been spent on her equipment. Of her dowry 100,000 ducats were the gift of the Holy Father,[1] made " as well on account of the singular love and affection he bears her, as in consideration of the splendour and high station of the house into which she is admitted." But even this handsome acknowledgment did not placate certain elements among the French, and when the first instalment was paid over on the marriage day there were open murmurings that it was a small price for such a mésalliance.

Catherine was naturalised by letters patent on the eve of her wedding in Marseilles Cathedral, to which she went wearing " an ermine corsage covered with pearls and diamonds." Clement VII officiated, for

[1] The gold was advanced on the security of certain papal ornaments, and this occasioned trouble some months later when Clement died inconveniently and his successor demanded these ornaments.

Rome had little faith in France and thought it
possible that if the knot were not securely tied the girl
might be returned later with a tarnished reputation
"which would fix a stain through her even on his
Holiness himself."

After all the bridegroom proved to be Henri Duc
d'Orléans, the King's second son, and scarcely any
older than Catherine, who was not yet sixteen.

" Fa figliuoli," said Pope Clement VII benignly, as,
having delivered a benediction, he drew the curtains
around the marriage bed.

On the conclusion of the wedding festivities, the
French court returned to Fontainebleau, and Catherine de Medici soon realised that her advent was unwelcome.

The Venetian Ambassador described the position in
a brief paragraph : " Monsieur d'Orléans is married to
Madame Catherine de Medici, which dissatisfies the
whole nation ; it is thought that the Pope deceived the
King in this alliance . . . however, his niece is very
submissive."

Submission was the only card that Catherine could
play. Her husband avoided her—" On y sentait la
mort " . . . and no one of the various court groups
showed any disposition to welcome the thin young
Italian whose newly adopted motto was : " J'apporte
lumière et la sérenité." Fortunately she rode well,
so could join the *petite bande* which accompanied the
King on his hunting excursions, and gradually won
his favour. Had Catherine been able to obey the
Pope's last command, she might have achieved a
definite position, but the passing years found her still
childless.

Calumnies were circulated, and when the Dauphin
died, people whispered that he had been poisoned " by
order of the Florentine," so that she might come to
wear the crown of a Queen-Consort.

Growing bolder, Catherine's enemies approached

the King, urging that the childless wife of the heir-apparent should be set aside, and she, knowing the attitude of the court, went to François in tears, offering to renounce her husband and retire into a convent if such was the King's will.

" God will give a royal line to Madame la Dauphine when she has reached the age at which the women of the Medici are wont to have children," wrote François's sister Marguerite, and Catherine was respited.

François too was gracious : " Since God has willed that you should be my daughter-in-law, and wife of the Dauphin, I do not wish to make any change, and perhaps it will please Almighty God . . . to grant the gift we so much long for."

Henri was harried to his duty, and presently the Dauphine's first child was laid in the arms of Diane de Poitiers.

Paris rejoiced over the birth of an heir and ceased to gibe at the balls on the Medici arms ; hitherto they had been decried as representing pills made by the doctor who, despite all evidence, was assumed to have been the founder of the Medici fortunes.

Having begun, the Dauphine continued, and Henri ascended the throne soon after the birth of their third child.

Catherine looked every inch a queen as she sat in royal attire and sparkling crown to receive an address from *Parlement* while the Princes of the Blood and two rows of duchesses and countesses stood behind her. Nor was she less regal when she made her State entry into Paris after her coronation, carried in an open litter and preceded by four cardinals.

But Diane de Poitiers had supplanted the young wife. She was created Duchesse de Valentinois, and awarded a salary " on account of the good, praise-worthy, and agreeable services she hath rendered to our dear and much loved companion the Queen."

Catherine bore children and yet more children, in all ten in twelve years, the last being twins of whom

one died at birth. She treasured their portraits in
her Book of Hours where they are shown lying side by
side, tightly wrapped in swaddling clothes and looking
more like cocoons than human infants. " Féconde
d'enfants malades et d'enfants morts, elle vieillit,"
says Michelet.

While Catherine gave birth to children, Henri II
waged wars ; he had never forgiven Charles V, by
whom he had been held hostage in Spain, and England's grasp on Calais and Boulogne was a perpetual
irritation to France, especially since the English had
cut an inscription on the gates boasting that the
French would never retake Calais till iron and lead
could float like cork.

In the King's absence Catherine was Regent, with
Chancellor Bertrandi as a colleague. She was shocked
at the sedition which began to show itself, and decreed
that " those who talked treason should be arrested
secretly, and put in a safe place till the King can send
word what he wants done with them." Meanwhile,
skilled men should be sent about the country to refute
evil doctrines.

Henri watered his horses in the Rhine (1552) and
returned while Catherine was writing some of her innumerable letters begging for news of him, but his
further campaigns were less successful, and when
disaster overwhelmed the main French Army at St.
Quentin (1555), the Queen rose to the occasion magnificently, delivering such a vigorous appeal for funds and
the prosecution of the war that what she asked was
voted with hardly a dissentient voice, whereupon she
thanked the deputies " in so sweet a form of speech
that she had them nearly all in tears." All Paris rang
with praise of her, and for a time forgot that this
Queen was of alien stock.

In recognition of the help Catherine had afforded
him, Henri II had a medal struck showing her head
beside his, and took to paying her evening visits instead

of going direct to Diane, as had become his custom.
He had signed the Treaty of Cateau-Cambrésis
(1559), " giving away in twenty-four hours what
thirty years of reverses could not have taken from
him," and in the ensuing peace had leisure to amuse
himself with " la Reinette d'Écosse " (who had been
sent to France to save her from the dangers rife in her
own land) and to plan the marrying of his two elder
children.

A splendid tournament was organised in honour of
the wedding of the Dauphin and the espousals of
Madame Elizabeth, and knights came from afar, for
the King himself was to ride in the jousts wearing
Diane de Poitiers's colours, while all the ladies of the
court looked on.

Henri's first opponent was the Duke of Savoy, his
second a Guise, his third young Montgomery, Captain
of the Scottish Guard. As he met the Scot, the King
lost his stirrup and a further encounter became
necessary. The two rode down the lists with levelled
lances to meet in fierce collision, and a cry of horror
arose as the King fell, pierced through the eye by
Montgomery's shattered lance.

He died ten days later, although all prisoners lying
under sentence of death were required to give their
lives immediately, in order to provide the King's
surgeons with experience in dealing with similar
wounds.

Catherine de Medici's reign was over, but her rule
was to begin with the accession of her second son.
Ignorant of the future, she adopted a new crest and
motto—a heap of quicklime on which tears were
dropping : " See, the glow lingers though the flame
be gone."

NOTE.—For the continuation of the story of Catherine see the lives of
François II, Charles IX, and Henri III.

CHAPTER SIX

FRANÇOIS II (1559–1560)

FRANÇOIS II AND MARY STUART
"La Fée Écossaise."

FRANÇOIS II
(eldest son of Henri II)

Born	. .	Jan. 19, 1544
Married	. .	April 24, 1558
Ascended	.	July 10, 1559
Died	. .	Dec. 5, 1560

CONTEMPORARY SOVEREIGNS

ENGLAND : Elizabeth.
SCOTLAND : Mary Stuart.
SPAIN : Philip II.

POPES
Paul IV, Pius IV.

Descent

FRANÇOIS I
|
HENRI II
m. CATHERINE DE MEDICI
|
FRANÇOIS II

CONSORT
Descent

JAMES V OF SCOTLAND
m. MARY OF GUISE-LORRAINE
|
MARY STUART

Born at Linlith- gow . .	Dec. 7–8, 1542
Ascended (Q. of Scots) . .	Dec. 13, 1542
Married (1) in Paris . .	April 24, 1558
Married (2) (Darn- ley) . .	1565
Married (3) (Both- well) . .	1567
Forced abdication	1567
Executed at Foth- eringay . .	1587

Issue : one son (James VI) by her second husband, Lord Darnley.

FRANÇOIS II.

MARY STUART.

CHAPTER SIX

FRANÇOIS II (1559–1560)

FRANCE was in sore need of an ally when news came out of Scotland that James V was dead and his week-old daughter Mary Stuart had been proclaimed Queen. Both Henry VIII of England and François I were quick to realise the matrimonial value of the child ; the former sent an offer of the hand of his seven-year-old son, Edward, the latter suggested Charles Duc d'Orléans, aged twenty-two, as a suitable bridegroom. François had no grandson as yet on account of Catherine de Medici's unfortunate delay in becoming a mother.

England seemed the favoured candidate, but Scotland would not send her baby Queen south, so trouble arose. Then, misliking Henry's methods, the Scottish Parliament annulled the marriage treaty and reopened negotiations with France, though English archers came pouring over the border.

The death of Henry VIII gave the harassed country momentary peace, but presently the Protector Somerset arrived demanding Edward VI's infant bride at the sword's point.

Even the Isle of Inchmahome in the Lake of Menteith, where the little Queen had been sent with four small namesakes, seemed scarcely safe, and Mary of Guise-Lorraine turned anxious eyes towards her own native land, where Henri II had succeeded François I and Catherine de Medici had begun to fill her nursery.

In Scotland's hour of peril there came a welcome message from the new King proposing a revival of the

Ancient League of Amity and Kindness which had existed between Scotland and France from time past the memory of man. Accompanying this suggestion was a proposal for the marriage of " our well-loved son the Dauphin, to our dear and much-loved sister and daughter, *la Dame Reyne d'Écosse*, provided always that the infant should be sent to continue her *nourriture* beside our dear and very saintly Companion la Reyne," who, " by ancient blood and grand lineage," possessed such an assembly of virtues and rare qualities that Henri felt sure Mary Stuart would obtain inestimable benefit by being placed under her charge.

For himself he would " affectionately solemnise her *fiançailles* when capacity and age permitted the ceremony to take place by the aid of God . . . and Scotland and France, so united in matrimonial alliance, would enjoy perpetual security and *grand repos*. . . ."

The Scottish Commissioners assembled and with true Scottish thoroughness scanned all former contracts between the two countries back to those of the time of Robert the Bruce,[1] then " bent their gude myndes and will towards the marriage of her Grace and the said Dolphin . . . and decided that it would be advisable to agree to the same for her Highness's weal and honour."

Certain stipulations were made in case the nation's sovereign lady should die without leaving heirs of her body, when " the righteous blude of Scotland " was to succeed without impediment, and also the Commissioners wished to know what Henri proposed to allow " the Dolphin for his living ? "

An agreement was reached between France and Scotland and the Estates annulled the treaty that had been made with England on the ground that " the said contract of marriage was grantit for the

[1] Keith's *History of Church and State* (Ap. Scottish Acts of Parliament).

said peice to have been observit and keipit betwixt
the two Realmes, which was not keipit, bot broken
and violet be the said King of Ingland." [1]

French troops landed in Scotland, the English retreated, and, the French fleet having embarked, the
fugitive Queen landed safely at Roscoff (Bretagne).

Henri II gave instructions that the Château de
St. Germain must be thoroughly *nettoyé*, to fit it
for Mary's reception, and that she, being a crowned
Queen if only six years old, was to take precedence
over his own children, while Catherine de Medici
prepared Madame Elizabeth (who was considerably
Mary's junior) to meet " La Reinette d'Écosse," and
be her companion on a State drive.

The two small girls made solemn friends, while the
four-year-old Dauphin lost his heart completely at
the first sight of the vivacious little maid who was to
be his bride, and his father found her " le plus parfait
enfant que je voys jamais ! " Indeed, Mary captivated the whole court even when seen in what was
considered the barbarous costume of her own savage
country.

Catherine de Medici gave careful attention to the
child's training and would dictate to her such un-
impeachable sentiments as " the true grandeur and
excellence of a prince does not consist in honours, or in
purple and gold . . . but in prudence, wisdom, and
knowledge."

Mary seems to have profited by this type of instruction, for a little later she was found writing to the less
studious Madame Elizabeth : " I have heard from
our masters, my sister and darling, that now you are
studying well, for which I greatly rejoice . . . the
gifts which we owe to nature are of short duration,
and age will deprive us of them. Fortune may likewise withdraw her favours, but that good thing which
virtue bestows is immortal."

Education on other lines was not neglected.

---

[1] Acts of Parl., Scot.

Quinces were purchased so that Mary could make jam,
and wool with which to teach the Princess how to
embroider, though if any of the needlework now carefully preserved in Scottish homes, in the belief that it
was done by the little Queen of Scots when on Inchmahome, is genuine, she had little to learn. Health,
too, was carefully watched, and when the royal children
fell ill with measles all were carefully dosed with an
infusion of " unicorns' horns."

When Mary was eleven years old she and her fiancé
made their formal entrance into court life ; everyone
declared that the Queen of Scots could turn all Frenchmen's heads with a single smile.

Mary now had a household of her own, with Scottish
attendants. She had never been allowed to forget
that she was a Queen and received regular letters
from her mother on State affairs. The regal manner
in which she could reply to Scottish deputations won
high approval. Few knew that at the behest of
Henri II the child had signed certain papers making
over Scotland as a free gift to the King of France
should she die without issue.

At home in Scotland Mary of Guise-Lorraine upheld
her daughter's rights. She had visited her once, but
dared not risk the dangers of the voyage a second
time even to be present at the wedding, which the
King hastened on, refusing to acknowledge possible
danger to fourteen-year-old François, who was still
sadly wanting in vigour.[1]

Two hundred years had passed since a Dauphin had
been married on French soil, so Paris determined on a
ceremony of unparalleled magnificence, and Scotland,
not to be outdone, ordered that a special tax should be
" uplifted " to defray the expenses of those nobles
who might venture to attend the ceremony.

[1] " The marriage was against the laws of nature. To marry the little
puppet, puffy and lymphatic, a miserable schoolboy, to the gracious,
accomplished Queen of Scotland, already a woman of the world, nearly
two years older in years, and ten in development, was to send him to
certain death " (Bouchot).

First came the official *fiançailles*, followed by a magnificent ball, then five days later (April 24, 1558), the wedding.

A canopy was erected before the door of Notre-Dame, and here the people, controlled by the Swiss Guards, watched the arrival of the gorgeous courtiers, the stately abbés, bishops, and cardinals, the Dauphin, hero of the occasion, but eclipsed by Antoine, King of Navarre, his own small brothers, and the Queen-Dauphine herself, who appeared, led by the King of France and her uncle the Duc de Lorraine, looking " like unto a lily " in her gleaming white with a train of marvellous length. Jewels flashed around her throat and shone in her golden crown, and her shining hair floated loose in the April breeze.

Following her walked Catherine de Medici, the Princess de Condé, Marguerite the King's sister Queen of Navarre, and the little Princesses Elizabeth and Claude, who had been Mary's playmates.

" Arrived at the door of the church, the King took a ring from his finger, and gave it to the Cardinal de Bourbon, Archbishop of Rouen, who married the pair with it in the presence of the Bishop of Paris, who gave, an eloquent oration. . . . Then the Duc de Guise made the nobles and gentlemen retire that the common people might see the royal spouses, and heralds threw largesse, whereby there was so great tumult that even thunder would not have been heard, and many fainted. . . . And all the while the Dukes and Lords marched along the scaffolding which was all adorned with grape-vines, emblem of fertility, and so into Notre-Dame, where the Archbishop celebrated Mass, and the bridal pair sat on a golden throne under a golden canopy. After which all went to dinner at the Bishop's house."

There was still to follow a procession, a ball, a supper, and then the *pièce de résistance* of the evening.

Twelve artificial horses came curvetting into the great Salle, so wonderfully made that they appeared

to be alive, and each was bestrode by a royal prince.
Following these came six vessels, all covered in cloth-
of-gold and crimson velvet, moving as if they floated
on water. The King of France leaned from one to
take Madame the Queen-Dauphine as passenger, the
Dauphin handed in his mother, the King of Navarre
claimed his wife . . . " and all conducted their vessels
safely to port ! "

Watching the graceful young bride, courtiers whispered that although Scotland was a thing of price,
Mary was worth still more . . . had she neither sceptre
nor crown, her divine body was worth a kingdom.

" It is impossible to describe all the triumphs and
magnificences," reported an eye-witness, " and those
who were there could not say whether the torches
and lanterns, or the jewels, gave most light . . . and
when the royal buffet was opened admiration was
still greater. . . . Then all went to bed till the
morrow. . . . Let us pray the King of Kings to keep
these Princes in joy, prosperity, and love, and that
they may ever govern their people well."

But the less optimistic shook their heads, saying :
" Les Valois étaient pourris, la race était lépreuse—et
qu'il fallait bientôt changer de dynastie." [1]

A year passed swiftly while François and Mary were
reported as living together in great love and concord.

France, frenzied with joy, celebrated the recapture
of Calais, when after a week's siege the English were
driven out of the town they had held for 200 years,
and on the death of Mary Tudor (Nov. 17, 1558) Mary
Stuart quartered the arms of England with her own.

Elizabeth Tudor sent a stern rebuke, but France
was concerned with the marriage of Madame Claude
to the Duc de Lorraine and busy welcoming the Duke
of Alva, who came as proxy for Philip of Spain to wed
Madame Elizabeth. The bridegroom as originally
arranged had been Don Carlos, Philip's son by the

[1] Michelet.

first of his wives, but after the death of Mary Tudor, and when Philip's offer " to do God a service " by wedding Elizabeth of England had been declined, an alteration of names had occurred in the contract.

While Spanish officials shook their heads over the difficulty of transporting the trousseau of a French Princess over the Pyrenees by pack-mules and bullock-wagons, the tourney in celebration of the espousals began.

Looking into the arena, Mary Stuart saw Henri II fall, pierced through the eye by his adversary's lance. Eleven days later she was Queen of France.

Even in the chamber of death Catherine de Medici, the " fille des marchands," as Mary had once called her, remembered that she no longer held first place and stood aside to offer precedence to this daughter-in-law from an alien land, who had stolen her eldest son.

But if the reign of *le petit Roy* had begun, Mary's maternal uncles the Duc de Guise and Cardinal de Lorraine stepped into power.   François II, if officially of age, was " trop jeune et de peu d'esprit."

There was need for a strong hand.   Mary of Guise-Lorraine died within a few months of her daughter's accession to the throne of France, and Scotland, goaded beyond endurance by French interference, repudiated the Ancient League.   Although Scottish Commissioners had taken oath of fidelity to François II as King of Scotland, a strong party was looking towards England for help, and Cecil drew up a memorandum :

" When Scotland shall come to the hands of a mere Scotsman in blood there may be hope of some accord, but as long as it is in the hands of the French, there is no hope of any long amity between the two realms,"

and, since Scotland was in the French King's hands, " by reason of his wife, great circumspection must be used to avoid the deceits and trumperies of the French."

Elizabeth, heretic and usurper in the eyes of the French, was as firm in her views as was her minister, and sent a demand that François and Mary should ratify the Treaty of Edinburgh, which (agreed by a Parliament assembled without Mary's consent), acknowledged Elizabeth's rights.

Nor were interior affairs less complicated. The coronation (which Mary, being Queen-Regnant, could not share) was hardly over before public indignation against the usurpation of power by Mary's over-powerful uncles made itself felt, and rumours of a conspiracy stirred the Cardinal de Lorraine to remove the youthful King and Queen from Paris.

There were arrests, condemnations, and executions of those concerned in the plot of Amboise. During a whole month " there was nothing done but decapitations, hangings, and drownings, the walls of the castle were disfigured by the heads of the slain . . . the Loire was covered with corpses." Seats were arranged in tiers so that all the members of the court could watch the execution of a batch of fifty-seven prisoners, some of whom saluted the young King and Queen before laying their heads upon the block. And always the power of the Guise-Lorraines increased.

" The House of Guise now ruleth, with whom I am in very small grace," wrote the English ambassador, " and the Queen of Scots, who is a great doer here, and taketh all upon herself, hath so small an opinion of me as I shall be able to do little service withal, therefore it may like you to use means for my revocation."

Unrest increased, till the carrying of firearms was prohibited and large boots and wide sleeves were looked at with suspicion; often they were hiding-places for concealed weapons. The word Huguenot was heard for the first time; it was used in Tours for those

of a new religion who used to meet near King Hugo's
Gate, and whereas less than thirty heretics had been
burnt during the reign of Henri II, the number so
punished increased sevenfold during the first twelve
months of François's rule.   Catherine de Medici grew
anxious at the Guises' misuse of power and the people
named Cardinal de Lorraine " the Tiger of France."
Anonymous pamphlets were circulated complaining
that he was abusing the youth of the King.

Those of the New Religion grew bolder.   They
petitioned for churches wherein they might worship,
and demanded the summoning of the Estates.   A
new conspiracy was discovered, towns were to be
seized, and the Guises arrested; it was said that the
King of Navarre and the Prince of Condé were involved.   The latter was arrested and condemned to
death.

Le petit Roy fell ill, but, despite a feverish cold, he
persisted in going on a hunting expedition, and
returned complaining of acute pain.   Queen-Mother
and Queen-Consort, Cardinal de Lorraine, and the
Duc de Guise tried to keep the knowledge of the King's
condition from the public, and with an abscess in his
ear and a gangrenous throat, François II touched for
the King's evil; but when the Venetian ambassador
was refused an audience, something of the truth was
guessed.

François gasped for life, now in violent fever
weeping in Mary's arms, now in syncope.   The
doctors, harried by the Duc de Guise (who complained
that they were doing no more for their sovereign than
for a beggar), bled, purged, and cupped his frail
anæmic frame, and wife and mother contested for the
right to remain beside the dying boy's bed.

When the inflamed ear ceased to discharge, a sudden
swelling in the temple gave warning of death.   On the
evening of December 5 (1560) the seventeen months'
reign ended.

On the very morning following the death of François, Mary Stuart was called upon to give up possession
of the crown jewels, when, " perceiving that her
mother-in-law's countenance was not kindly disposed
to her," she withdrew to a convent at Rheims, where
an aunt was Abbess, there to complete the usual
forty days' mourning. Meanwhile a pamphlet entitled *An Admonition and a Warning to Craftie, Deaf,
and Foolish Kings* found a ready sale :

> " Lest François, that unhappie childe,
>   His father's footsteps following plane,
> To Christ's crying deaf ears did yield,
>   Ane rotten ear then was his bane. . . ."

Mary Stuart mourned, but Scotland rejoiced, and
Knox pointed out how " a deaf ear that never would
hear the truth of God " had been instrumental in
giving the Queen back to her country.

The battle for the hand of the Queen of Scots began
anew. Philip of Spain, perhaps regretting his own
precipitancy in having contracted a third marriage,
offered Don Carlos in default of himself. Cardinal de
Lorraine advanced the claims of the Archduke Charles,
a Bavarian prince and the Duke of Ferrara were
added to the list, while the precocious ten-year-old
King of France who had succeeded François showed
an alarming desire to retain his too fascinating sister-
in-law. If she would but wait a year or so, he would
make her a fine husband !

But Commissioners arrived from Scotland. The
Pope bestowed on Mary the high honour of the Golden
Rose, and Catherine de Medici sped her on her way
back to her own kingdom.

Elizabeth refused to grant a safe conduct unless
Mary would acquiesce in her demands, and an English
squadron put out to sea, hoping to intercept the
widowed Queen ; but no man knew the port of her
departure.

" Some say she will not go at all," wrote the har-

assed English Ambassador, " yet all her stuff is sent
down to the sea, and there is none other bruit in her
house, but of her hasty going."

With four stalwart uncles in attendance, Mary
Stuart rode out from St. Germain for the last time,
and Cecil made another memorandum :

" Neither those in Scotland, nor we, do lyke her
going home. . . . The Queen's Majestie hath three
ships in the North Sea to preserve the fishings from
pyratts. . . . *I think they will be sorry to see her
pass!* "

" Adieu, France . . . adieu, mes beaux jours ! "
said the Queen, straining her eyes into the dawn before
the fog swallowed up her galley.

Five days later she reached Leith, despite the
watchful English ships. She was Mary Queen of
Scots once more—no longer Queen of France.

NOTE.—For Mary Stuart as Queen of Scots see *Their Majesties of
Scotland*, by E. Thornton Cook.

CHAPTER SEVEN

CHARLES IX (1560–1574)

CHARLES IX AND ELIZABETH OF AUSTRIA.

" La vertu vient habiter le palais souillé des Valois ! "
—JULES DE BERN.

CHARLES IX
(brother of François II)

Born at St. Ger-
    main-en-Laye .   June 27, 1550
Ascended .   . Dec. 5, 1560
Married at Mézières Nov. 26, 1570
Died at Vincennes May 30, 1574

CONTEMPORARY SOVEREIGNS

ENGLAND : Elizabeth.
SCOTLAND : Mary Stuart, James
    VI.
SPAIN : Philip II.

POPES

Pius IV, St. Pius V, Gregory XIII.

Descent

FRANÇOIS I
|
HENRI II
m. CATHERINE DE MEDICI
|
CHARLES

CONSORT

Descent

CHARLES V (Emperor)
|
MARY OF AUSTRIA
m. MAXIMILIAN II
|
ELIZABETH OF AUSTRIA

Born at Vienna . June 25, 1554
Married at Mézières Nov. 26, 1570
Died at Vienna . Jan. 22, 1592

Issue : one daughter, 1572–8.

[*Musée du Louvre, Paris.*

ELIZABETH OF AUSTRIA.

CHARLES IX.

91]

CHAPTER SEVEN

CHARLES (IX 1560–1574)

(The continuation of Catherine de Medici with the story of Elizabeth of Austria)

CHARLES IX was ten years old when he became King of France on the death of his brother François II ; he wept from fatigue at the weight of his crown after the five-hour-long coronation ceremony.

His mother, Catherine de Medici, had been in the background during the reign of her husband, Henri II, and in the brief interlude when her eldest son had been King she had had "no guide of him," for Mary Stuart and her too-powerful Guise-Lorraine uncles had thrust the Queen-Dowager aside. Now Catherine's hour had come, and in her determination to keep control of the young monarch she decreed that he should sleep in her room ; no alien influence should steal this king from her in his boyhood.

Four days after Charles's accession a royal proclamation told the world that the new King had begged his "very dear and well-beloved mother to take in hand the administration of the realm. . . ."

In turn the Queen-Mother made her pronouncement. She would bring up the King for the honour of God and the good of his people. Once again a foreign princess was Regent of France,[1] and the hour was critical, for Guise and Bourbon stood behind the throne in rivalry, while the Reformed Religion had established itself in France despite the efforts of the previous kings. "The realm was full of sedition, for

[1] Her predecessor was the thirteenth-century Blanche of Castille, mother of St. Louis.

which religion was alleged to be the principal cause . . .
a thing almost incredible."

Across the seas Elizabeth of England watched, ever
hopeful of recovering Calais ; and Philip of Spain sent
messages urging that the dangerous doctrines which
had taken root in France should be eradicated before
they spread to other countries.

Catherine would not take action, although she
sanctioned a letter to Geneva asking for the recall of
those preachers who were making trouble in her son's
kingdom : " The times no longer permit us to deal
forth death and rigorous justice as in the past," she
told Philip, " for the evil has grown too much."

In the hope of maintaining a balance of power
between the antagonistic forces, she ordered the
release of Condé, leader of the Huguenots, who had
been sentenced to death under François II, but as the
Prince took back his sword he cursed the Duc de
Guise.

Charles IX had succeeded in December (1560), and
in the following August Catherine summoned the
Estates which had not met for eighty years ; its
members grudgingly agreed to accept the Regency.
Two months later the Queen-Regent took the little
King to open the Conference of Poissy, hoping that
there Calvin and the Cardinal de Lorraine would meet
to thresh out their differences and frame a religious
compromise that would give peace to Christendom.

Spain was scandalised by Catherine's tolerance of
such an assembly and wrote by the hand of Elizabeth [1] : " The King, my lord, begs you to chastise all
rebels without delay. If you fear to do so on account
of their number and rank . . . your majesty should
apply to him for aid. . . . We will willingly lend
you our wealth, our armies, and all we possess, to
maintain the cause of religion. Punish and they
will not persist ! . . ."

[1] She had been sent to marry Philip II soon after the death of her
father, Henri II.

The Duc de Guise lodged his protest also, challenging Catherine to " cease drinking from two fountains " and identify herself with the Catholic party without further procrastination.

Religious controversy invaded the palace, and Charles, his brother Henri d'Anjou, and their small sister Margot nearly came to blows over their respective faiths.

Still striving for conciliation, Catherine called an Assembly of Notables and issued the Edict of January (Jan. 1561-2), which gave restricted liberty of worship to Protestants. When the *Parlement de Paris* refused to register the decree, she mounted her horse " and rode at so furious a gallop that it seemed as if she would ride into the Council Chamber." She forced the edict through, and it appeared, though not in a form she approved : " Published, read, and registered in our *Parlement de Paris* by reason of the importunity of those who profess the so-called Reformed Religion, and this only provisionally, while awaiting the majority of the King."

Neither party was content, and passions rose higher, culminating a few months later in the siege of Vassy. When passing through the village the Duc de Guise found a heretical service in progress ; his servants interrupted the meeting, and an affray ensued in which forty-five Huguenots were killed. Those of the reformed religion demanded justice, but the Duke found himself a hero in the eyes of the Parisians. So began the first of the nine civil wars that were to ravage France in the space of a single generation.

Each party committed barbarities. Men, women, and children died for their faith, shrines were desecrated, and tombs destroyed. Antoine, King of Navarre, fell before Rouen ; Guise was killed. Admiral Coligny was accused of having instigated the murder, and the captured assassin warned Catherine that her death, and that of her children, had been decreed by the Huguenots.

Looking abroad for help Catherine brought in Swiss and German mercenaries and the Huguenots sent a signed blank sheet of paper to Elizabeth of England, offering to give Havre-de-Grâce into her hands " until Calais be restored " if she would render assistance.

The Edict of Amboise (March 19, 1563) brought the country four years of precarious peace : " The ashes of the fire which has just gone out are still so hot that the least spark will make them leap into bigger flames than we have yet seen," said Catherine to the Spanish ambassador—but in the lull she decided to declare Charles of age for political reasons, although he had barely entered his fourteenth year. He held a *Lit de Justice*[1] at Rouen announcing that, having attained his majority, he would allow no one to disobey him, and soon afterwards the court started on a tour of France in order that the people might see their King. Progress was slow and difficult, for the travellers numbered eight hundred.

Now, too, Catherine began to take steps towards marrying her son. If Queen Elizabeth would but marry him, he could wear a dual crown !

The English Ambassador demurred, pointing out that Charles was extremely young, but the Regent answered suavely :

" If Queen Elizabeth will put up with the youth of my son, I will put up with the Queen's age," and she looked towards her son, who spoke up bravely :

" I should be very glad if your mistress would be as well pleased with my age as I am pleased with hers ! " (Elizabeth was thirty-one.)

Marriages were much in Catherine's mind during the tour, for she had with her the Duc d'Anjou (whom she hoped to wed to the widowed and insane Juana of

---

[1] *Lit de Justice* originated with Philip the Tall in the fourteenth century, and was the seat or throne on which he sat at the extraordinary meeting of *Parlement*. It was a bed-like contrivance set under a canopy, and had five large cushions, one to sit on, one to lean against, and the remainder to support his arms and legs.

Portugal), and her daughter Margot, whose portrait had been sent to Don Carlos of Spain.

She had hoped to discuss these affairs with Philip II near Bayonne, but he refused to meet her, although he permitted his consort Elizabeth to do so, provided that Catherine did not bring the heretical Queen of Navarre in her train—and provided too that Elizabeth did not seize upon the occasion as an excuse for foolish expenditure. Her ladies must be told that their ordinary robes (which should last them nine months longer) were quite sufficient ; new ones were not required.

These points settled, Philip placed his wife under the charge of the Duke of Alva and retired to a monastery for meditation.

The meeting took place, hedged about by etiquette.

" I am always your daughter, and the same you sent to Spain ! " Elizabeth assured her mother, but Catherine was disappointed to find that the Queen had little influence, while Alva set the marriage schemes aside, saying it would be time enough to talk of such matters when the Decrees of the Council of Trent[1] had suppressed heresy in France.

The Duke found Catherine " more than cold in all matters pertaining to the Holy Religion," and bewildered King Charles by telling him that he was chosen of God to put his hand to a work of great chastisement.

The court returned to Paris through a France decimated with plague. In some cities naked corpses could be seen daily, lying by the wayside awaiting collection at sunset. Everywhere graves had become so expensive that the bodies of the poorer people were often flung into the rivers, " to the ruin of the fishermen." [2]

[1] The Decrees had alarmed Catherine de Medici, who, having perused them, wrote over the signature of Charles IX : " The Fathers seem to want to pass articles which will file the nails of Kings and let their own grow."

[2] Calendar of State Papers, Eliz., Foreign, 1564–5.

Once again Catherine found herself engulfed in quarrels, and her son the centre of plots. Taking drastic action, she ordered a solemn meeting for reform and conciliation, where she obliged the widow of the murdered Duc de Guise to give Admiral Coligny a kiss of peace, but others of the family stood sullenly aside, and the Queen-Mother knew that the fire was not quenched.

Spain too was showing her claws, for Philip, when refused permission to march his army across France to the Low Countries, retaliated by annihilating a French settlement in Florida.

France began arming, rumours spread, the nervous tension snapped, and the second civil war began (Sept. 1567) with an attempt to capture the King, who had to be hurried out of Meaux guarded by Swiss mercenaries, an indignity he never forgot.

Now the Catholics were victorious, and now the Huguenots. Catherine pawned the crown jewels, turned to Rome for help, and tried to forget her grief at the news of the death of her daughter, the Queen of Spain, in rejoicing with Anjou over the victory of Jarnac (1569).

German troops invaded the country to assist the Protestants, and Spaniards, sent by Philip, strengthened the power of the Catholics. Violence increased, and a wave of horror swept the country when the bones of St. Louis, and the heart of François I, were burnt and scattered.

All Paris turned against " cette Jézabel immorale," the Queen-Mother, who had stood hesitating too long " with an olive branch in each hand " ; many a man swore that he could wish her tied in a sack and thrown into the Seine.

An exhausted country tolerated the Peace of St. Germain-en-Laye (Aug. 1570), although Pope Pius V saw it as a surrender to the Huguenots. His nuncio demanded an audience to assure Charles and his mother that the heretics were determined to pull

down the throne as well as the altar, and that ex-
termination was the only cure. Catherine replied
so tactfully that a letter went forth to Rome in which
the nuncio " hoped that he would have good news for
his Holiness soon."

Once again Catherine was free to deal with more
personal matters. Perhaps the recently widowed
King of Spain would accept his dead consort's sister
Margot as a fourth wife ?   Elizabeth of England, too,
was still unmarried, although Catherine had offered
her both Charles IX and Henri d'Anjou ; she now
advanced the name of her youngest son, the Duc
d'Alençon, who had " a fine mind, a countenance
beyond his years, and was not so obstinate as Henri."

While Elizabeth coquetted with the idea the Queen-
Mother developed her plans for marrying Charles and
sought a suitable bride for him among the fourteen
children of the tolerant Emperor Maximilian. Her
first choice was Anne, but the girl was married suddenly to her uncle, Philip of Spain (so spoiling Margot's
chance), and Catherine made a hasty proposal for the
second daughter, Elizabeth.

Fortunately Charles, if twenty years old, was still
amenable and willing to accept Elizabeth as readily as
Anne.

" She will not give me a single headache," he said as
he studied a portrait of the fair-faced, sixteen-year-old
Princess, and his mistress, Marie Touchet, pushed it
aside in relief : " L'Allemande ne me fait pas peur."

The King's brothers Anjou and Alençon rode to
meet Elizabeth at Sedan ; there followed a proxy
marriage at Spiers, and a ceremonial wedding at
Mézières, where Charles (who had travelled incognito)
saw his bride arrive in a State carriage with four white
horses and descend into a sea of mud, for the country
had been deluged by rain and flood.

All France was pleasurably excited, since no
romantic marriage of a reigning sovereign had taken
place since Charles VIII wedded Anne de Bretagne.

François II had married when Dauphin, Henri II as a second son, François I's wives had been thrust upon him, and of the wives of Louis XII the first had been repudiated, the second was a widow, and the third had been wed when the King had one foot in the grave. The glamour of youth hung about Charles and Elizabeth ; in addition, she had a reputation for piety, an excellent thing in a woman.

It was said that even as a child she had persisted in praying at regular hours throughout the night, and when her elders made difficulties, the resolute little Princess tied a ribbon to her wrist and hung it through the keyhole, so that a devoted attendant might awaken her at prayer time.

Now she showed herself gentle, sweet, and soft in speech, though she often let smiles take the place of words. France was quick to hail her as " the most virtuous Queen to reign since Kings and Queens began."

The Emperor Maximilian had tried to prepare his daughter for her new life by telling her that she was going to the most beautiful and powerful kingdom in the world, although one broken and dismembered. It was a mild description of the state of France, for scarcely was the young Queen's coronation accomplished before the plots and counter-plots began again.

Catherine de Medici turned from the planning of a little farm, where she could pass her time in honest pleasure, to the balancing of one party against the other, so that her son might remain on his throne, and to the keeping of peace between the brothers. Charles was dangerously jealous of Anjou's military renown, and the English Queen was still " forbearing her assent " to her marriage with Alençon, not only by reason of inequality of age, but because someone had sent her a description of his person. It seemed that he was " double-nosed, and has great blemish of his face by the smallpox." She did not know " how she

could bear with this inconvenience, however other-
wise he was for stature, shape of body, and gift of
mind," as the Envoy Sir Thomas Smith explained to
Catherine. She, despite her other anxieties, gave
thought to her daughter-in-law Mary Queen of
Scots, now a prisoner in Elizabeth's hands, and was
" wishful of her liberty and that she might be restored."

Sir Thomas spoke of " the evil practised by Mary
against his august Mistress . . . and the Queen-
Mother desired that if they found her so dangerous
they would send her to France. . . ."

" Will you have her head or her body ? " asked Sir
Thomas.

" Tush ! " answered Catherine de Medici. " We
would have her alive . . . but the Queen my sister of
England is so marvellous and gentle that I know well
she will do her no harm,"[1] she added, ending the
interview.

While Charles's consort played her little part as
Queen of France, and was always ready with a smile
of welcome when the King came to her from one of his
vigorous bouts with hammer and anvil, or exhausted
by the wild blowing of a hunter's horn, Catherine de
Medici considered uniting Huguenot and Catholic by
marrying her daughter Margot to Henry of Navarre,
since Philip of Spain was no longer available.

Few saw good in the plan, but Catherine forced the
matter forward and designed a commemorative plaque
with a suitable inscription—" Discord bound by this
bond."

Huguenots and Catholics assembled for the ceremony, each watching the other with suspicion, and
when news that Admiral Coligny had been shot flashed
through Paris it was as a spark to tinder.

" It is I who have been wounded ! " cried the indignant King.

" It is all France," said Catherine de Medici.

[1] Calendar of State Papers, Eliz., Foreign, 1572–4, pp. 24–5.

The furious, stricken Huguenots saw the deed as
Guise vengeance, and each side looked to its arms
while couriers hurried to half the courts in Europe.
The nuncio reported that the attempted murder was
the direct result of the Queen-Mother's jealousy of the
influence Coligny had secured over her son ; the
Venetian Ambassador saw the hands of both Catherine
and Anjou in the act.

The wounded Admiral asked for his sovereign :
" Mon père," said Charles IX as he bent over the
bed, " you had the stroke, but I have the perpetual
pain ! " He stayed till Catherine intervened ; she
would not rest until she had forced Charles to repeat
what Coligny had said to him.

" He told me to reign alone ! " said the King, and
in an emotional paroxysm vowed that he would
wreak such justice on the Admiral's murderers that
every soul in his kingdom should thereby take
example.

Every hour new rumours swept the city, and in the
Louvre Catherine listened to her little group of
counsellors.

Plans were hastily laid. At midnight the King was
called and told that the Huguenots were moving ;
within a day, almost within an hour, the Louvre itself
might be attacked. If he would save his life and that
of the royal family he must act, and quickly. . . .
" Quoi ! vous n'osez vous défaire de gens qui ont si
peu ménagé votre autorité et votre personne ! "

The city gates must be closed so that none should
escape ; candles must be lit in every window so that
foe might see foe ; those of the true faith must tie a
white scarf around their arms and wear the cross in
their hats.

" Kill ! Kill ! " cried Charles, driven to bay. " Kill
all so that not one shall be left to reproach me ! "

St. Bartholomew's Day began (Aug. 24, 1572) and
Henri Duc de Guise rode forth. For fear that Charles
should vacillate, the ringing of the signal bell of St.

Germain-l'Auxerrois was advanced from 3 a.m. to 2 a.m.

Huguenots came flocking towards the palace and were struck down by the guards, who saw them as the forerunners of those who intended to murder the King.

As blood-mad as the city, Charles seized an arquebus and fired on his people as they fled.

" Let blood ! Let blood ! " shouted the Maréchal de Tavannes.[1]

Corpses were piled beneath the palace walls and floated down the Seine. Even the wounded Coligny was not spared : a band of fanatics stabbed him through with their swords and flung his body out of the window to the waiting Duc de Guise ; someone carried his head to Catherine de Medici, believing that she would wish to send it to Cardinal de Lorraine in Rome.

Young Queen Elizabeth, seven months gone with child, was told of the night's occurrences when she awoke at her usual hour next morning.

" Does my husband know of this thing ? " she asked, and cried out at the answer. " Mon Dieu ! What counsellors can they be who have given him such advice ! "

The massacre continued while Elizabeth prayed for Charles's soul and Catherine wrote hasty despatches. England, Spain, Italy, Austria, Poland, all must be told of the recent happenings, each in the vein most suited to that country's religious or political bias.

Orders went out in the King's name bidding other cities follow the example of Paris and exterminate the heretics.[2] Twenty obeyed.

Charles summoned the *Parlement de Paris* and

---

[1] Years later, when lying on his deathbed, Tavannes was asked if he did not repent the massacre of St. Bartholomew's Day : " Repent ! " came the quick answer. " I am happier in my conscience over my part in that day than over any other act in my life. . . . I count upon it to weigh in the balance against all my mortal sins."

[2] Contemporary report put the number of the massacred as high as 100,000, but modern writers accept 7,000 as a more accurate figure.

proclaimed his personal responsibility for the massacre. That body, after due deliberation, condemned the dead Admiral as a traitor . . . " he having been found guilty of high treason against the King's authority." It decreed that Coligny's name and memory were to be suppressed, and his corpse, after being hanged for twenty-four hours on the Place de Grève, was to be suspended on a gibbet at Montfaucon.¹ His estates were forfeited and his name was declared ignoble. On every anniversary of St. Bartholomew, while thanksgiving prayers were offered for the overthrow of the conspiracy, the Admiral's arms were to be dragged through the streets at the horse's tail.

Although a minority was horrified by what had occurred, and, disbelieving the story of a Huguenot plot, risked their lives by hiding their friends of the reformed faith, the majority rejoiced that henceforward there would be but one religion in all France, and a pæan of praise arose to St. Bartholomew in that " he had lent his knife for the salutary sacrifice."

A pamphlet which exhorted Charles to proceed in the course he had begun was widely read, and pulpits resounded with praise of this King who, in a single day, and by a single act, had banished heresy and chastised according to their merits those who had worked towards the undoing of Church and throne.

But the reaction of the outer world was not entirely to the satisfaction of the French court. If Naples voted a congratulatory address to Charles, Ivan the Terrible lodged a protest, and the Emperor Maximilian wrote that " in countenancing so great a butchery " Charles IX and the Queen-Mother had done the " most ill-advised and evil thing in the world."

¹ Charles turned aside from a hunting expedition to see the body of the man he had called " mon père " hanging by its feet from the gallows. . . . " The King has become so bloody that it is impossible to stay his thirst . . . it is much lamented to see his cruelty. . . . Many be sorry that so monstrous a murder was ever invented." (Contemporary Journal.)

Spain and Rome alone offered entire approval. Philip's messengers, bringing an address to Charles and Elizabeth on the birth of their daughter, brought also a substantial offering for the murderers of Coligny. It was reported that the King of Spain had laughed for the first time in his life on hearing of the massacre, and all Spaniards believed that " this politic and ingenious act " had been planned on the advice of Alva when he had discussed the state of France with Catherine at Bayonne seven years before.

In Rome, Cardinal de Lorraine created the impression that the resolution to strike at the heretics had been taken before he left Paris, and consequently credit for the deed belonged to him, and to his nephew the Duc de Guise, though a modicum of praise was due to Charles IX " for the holy deceit and pious dissimulation " with which the affair had been carried through. The Holy City was illuminated, and a Te Deum was sung in St. Peter's—some said in celebration of St. Bartholomew's Day, but others believed that the rejoicing was because a Huguenot plot had been frustrated, and Charles's life was safe.

Scotland swung to the other side, expressed her opinion frankly despite the " auld alliance," and, fearing similar outbreaks within her own borders, issued an order under signature of the King's Majesty :

" In respect of the great murders and more than beastlie cruelties used in divers parts of Europe, suggested, no doubt, by the unhappy and devilish Council of Trent . . ." every Kirk was directed to appoint commissioners, these to consider measures " to defend Christ's Evangel from the rage and lawless cruelties of bludie and treasonable papists. . . ."

England was less outspoken, but Elizabeth was the recipient of warnings that if she did not take revenge for the massacre of St. Bartholomew there was nothing to expect but the destruction of all the Protestants in Europe.

She robed herself in mourning to receive the French

Ambassador, and protested that the deed was against all law, divine and human ; but she listened to his diplomatic report on "the accident in Paris," and although she refused to permit the Duc d'Alençon to visit her at the moment, she did not break off matrimonial negotiations. After all, the young aspirant's pockmarks, if " thick," were not " great."

In France the other Elizabeth went about her court like a wraith, but Catherine de Medici was said to look ten years younger.

Yet another civil war was raging, with the town of Rochelle as a storm centre, although an Edict of Pacification had been published decreeing that " the memory of all things that have happened since August 24 shall be extinguished—they shall not reproach each other in dispute, nor use offensive words, but live peacefully together." But France had time to dream of freeing Mary Stuart, and presently the English Ambassador was writing a warning that he had given a passport to one who carried a box of linen to the Queen of Scots ; it might be that what was written on the linen would make valuable reading. Perhaps Elizabeth, " under cover of seeing the fashion of the ruffs, might cause the pieces to be held before the fire . . . when the writing will appear."

But more important than the freeing of Mary, in Catherine's mind at least, was the future of her favourite son, Henri d'Anjou. Some months since, his name had been put forward as a candidate for the vacant crown of Poland. Unfortunately, the shock of St. Bartholomew's massacre had lessened his chance ; yet Charles was vowing that Anjou must leave the country.

It was a relief when a deputation of Polish noblemen arrived to ask the Prince's acceptance of the crown and Paris could be distracted by a fête at which sixteen beautiful ladies, representing the sixteen provinces, danced gracefully, " all dressed with the utmost propriety," and mummers showed the three brothers, Charles wearing the crown of France, Henri that of Poland, and François d'Alençon waiting with poised head ready to receive that of England from the hands of an angel whose features were those of Elizabeth.

The court rode with the newly appointed King of Poland on the first stage of his journey, and Catherine, finding parting difficult, went farther than the rest :

" Allez, mon fils, vous n'y demeurerez pas longtemps ! " was her consolatory farewell.

Upon her return she found Alençon and her son-in-law Henri of Navarre intriguing with the Huguenots, and Charles ill ; opinion was divided as to whether the King's sufferings were caused by poison or magic, but a conspiracy was discovered which involved the Duc d'Alençon, La Mole and Coconas (two of his friends), and among La Mole's possessions was found a wax figure with its heart transfixed by a dart—sure evidence that he was endeavouring to destroy the King by sorcery.

The most celebrated alchemist of the day explained that the incriminating figure was not that of Charles, but of La Mole's obdurate lady love, whose heart he was besieging by enchantment ; but the two conspirators were condemned. The King watched them put to death on the gallows and had torches held aloft that he might see their writhings, but his sister Margot had La Mole's head brought to her and buried it by night.

Three days later Charles had a hæmorrhage of the lungs. The young Queen of France walked barefooted on a pilgrimage from Vincennes to La Sainte Chapelle to intercede for her husband, and begged those who passed her on the way to add their prayers to hers ; but his sickness increased. Elizabeth returned to sit beside him, " not speaking, but keeping her eyes fixed upon him. She loved and honoured

him extremely, although she knew his amorous
complexion. . . ."

Between Charles's paroxysms he recognised his
wife, and with a sudden spurt of energy gave her into
the charge of Henri of Navarre : " Je me fie en vous
de ma femme et ma fille. Je vous les recommende et
Dieu et vous les gardera ! " he murmured ; then,
turning to Elizabeth, began a warning sentence :
" Méfiez vous de . . ."

" Monsieur ! Ne dites pas cela ! " interrupted
Catherine de Medici.

" C'est la vérité ! " said the dying King.

But in the last hour Charles forgot Elizabeth and
remembered only Marie Touchet, the mother of his
son.

Sorbin, a court preacher, won fame by his *Histoire
. . . de la vie, mœurs et vertus du Roy très chrétien et
débonnair Charles IX, vrayment piteux, propagateur
de la Foy Catholique, et amateur des bons esprits et de
toutes les actions vertueuses.* It was left to Elizabeth
to pray for the King's soul : " When the curtains
were drawn around her bed she would kneel in her
shift and pray to God an hour and a half. . . ."
One of her ladies, hearing the Queen sighing, looked
between her curtains and remonstrated, after which
Elizabeth tried to conceal her devotions, but her
shadow betrayed her.

More fortunate than some Queens (because considered of little account), Elizabeth of Austria found
that Charles's death had brought her freedom. She
had given the King only a daughter ; had she had a
son, as her ladies reminded her, her grandeur now
would have been increased.

" Do not say to me such grievous things ! " cried
the widowed Queen. " As if France had not troubles
enough without my completing her ruin. . . . Had
I a son, there would be divisions, struggles, seditions,
and more wars. . . . Had I a son, I should be

miserable to think I had conceived him, and so
caused a thousand maledictions from the people whose
voice is that of God."

When etiquette permitted, Elizabeth visited Amboise to say farewell to her three-year-old daughter
Marie-Elizabeth, who must be left behind when her
mother returned to Austria.

" Madame, I do not know you," said the little
Princess briefly.

Religion offered solace, and Elizabeth went to
found the Convent of Ste. Claire in Vienna, wherein
she lived the life of a nun of the Third Order of
Franciscans, although she never forgot the court
of France. When her sister-in-law Margot Queen
of Navarre fell on evil days, Elizabeth sent her half
her dowry.

Nor did the world forget Elizabeth, for Philip of
Spain endeavoured to secure her as a successor to her
sister, who had been his fourth wife. " But such
was the great constancy and noble firmness of this
virtuous Queen towards the venerated bones of her
husband the King, which she honoured incessantly
with tears and regrets, till (not being able to furnish
more, for a fountain must in the end dry up) she
succumbed and died. . . . Loss most inestimable !
For she might have served longer as an emblem of
fortitude to the honest ladies of Christendom ! "

CHAPTER EIGHT
HENRI III (1574–1589)

Henri III and Louise de Vaudemont et Lorraine

" Priez Dieu pour elle ! "

HENRI III
(brother of Charles IX)

Born at Fontaine-
  bleau   .   Sept. 19–20, 1551
Ascended .   . May 30, 1574
Crowned at
  Rheims .   . Feb. 13, 1575
Married at
  Rheims .   . Feb. 14, 1575
Assassinated . Aug. 1, 1589

CONTEMPORARY SOVEREIGNS

ENGLAND : Elizabeth.
SCOTLAND : James VI.
SPAIN : Philip II.

POPES

Gregory XIII and Sixtus V.

Descent

FRANÇOIS I
|
HENRI II
m. CATHERINE DE MEDICI
|
HENRI III

CONSORT
Descent

NICOLAS, COMTE DE VAUDEMONT
  m. MARGUERITE D'EGMONT
|
LOUISE DE LORRAINE

Born at Nomeny   April 30, 1554
Married at
  Rheims .   . Feb. 14, 1575
Died at Moulins . Jan. 29, 1601

Issue : one stillborn son.

LOUISE OF LORRAINE.

HENRI III.

CHAPTER EIGHT

HENRI III (1574–1589)

(The end of Catherine de Medici, with the story of Louise de Vaudemont.)

HENRI D'ANJOU, heir to the French throne on the death of his brother Charles IX, was in Poland at the demise of the crown, having been elected King of that country some six months previously.

While the court seethed with the crop of rumours usual on the death of a French King, and accused Catherine de Medici of complicity in poisoning her son—had she not put pink candles in his room?—the Queen-Mother wrote her " piteous news " to his successor Henri III.

She told him that she was Regent of France for the second time, and that Charles had died " the best Christian that ever was . . . the last words he said being ' my mother ' ! "

For consolation in her sorrow she looked forward to seeing Henri soon, and in good health, " for if I should lose you I would have myself buried with you, alive, because I could not bear this loss also."

To ensure delivery, the Regent sent duplicate letters by messengers travelling by different routes, but after a journey of two weeks both men reached Cracow within a few hours of each other.

The fifth civil war was in progress; d'Alençon and the King of Navarre were suspect, and it was necessary to keep them straitly; the treasury was empty and credit stood low. It had cost a hundred and fifty thousand crowns to bury Charles IX, and Catherine knew that almost as much would have to be found to

9   III

pay Henri's immediate expenses. The Regent felt her burden weighty.

It was planned that so soon as the new King set foot on French soil a salvo of artillery should be fired, which, taken up by each succeeding fort, would carry the news throughout the length of France ; but Henri III seemed in no hurry to assume his duties as sovereign.

The King had left Poland with all speed, " by stealth as commonly reported, escaping out of the castle window in the night," and was pursued to the frontier by his indignant subjects when it was discovered that he had taken the crown jewels ; but Catherine could get little definite news.

Not daring to face the German Princes, since they still held him primarily guilty for the St. Bartholomew massacre, Henri travelled through Italy and dallied in Venice, where his moral ruin was completed.

Avignon welcomed him at last, whence he could not get away, . . . " the stream was running too swiftly for him to come up it and he dared not travel by land . . . since them of the religion will let no King's men pass."

While he waited, an access of piety sent Henri to join the flagellants and do penance for his many sins by beating himself as he walked in procession. Cardinal de Lorraine, who was in attendance, died as the result of similar penitential efforts. In a violent storm which broke out almost immediately the Catholics saw a sign of the misfortunes which would fall on France owing to the loss of the Cardinal, but the Huguenots rejoiced, saying that Hell had let loose her furies to greet him.

When news of Henri's approach to Lyons reached Catherine, she ordered her coach and, taking Margot with her, and also Alençon and Navarre (both still under guard), joined her favourite son in time to share his state entry, after which the royal party proceeded to Rheims, where Henri was *sacré*.

Long before this France had begun to discuss the question of a consort for her new King. Some had thought it probable that he would offer to marry Charles's widow, but Henri turned a deaf ear to the suggestion, as he had done when a marriage with the very plain daughter of his predecessor on the Polish throne had been urged.

The youthful Princesse de Condé had held him in her toils for some time ; indeed with a careful secretary in attendance to open a small puncture in his arm, he had written to her in letters of blood, and on her premature decease he had worn a silver death's-head on every article of his attire, even to his well-tied shoe-strings ; but now, so far as the world knew, he was fancy free.

Amazement was the greater when on the very day succeeding the coronation Henry announced his intention of celebrating his wedding without even giving time for the usual gift money to be collected from the public.

The bride was Louise de Vaudemont, a girl of eighteen, who had caught Henri's straying fancy when he was on his way to Poland.

No one was more surprised than Louise herself. She was a niece of the dead Cardinal de Lorraine and had been carefully brought up by succeeding step-mothers, the first of whom had surrounded her with sacred images, holy pictures, and medals, while educating her from devout books and legends before introducing her to life in a small ducal court.

News of her proposed elevation reached the selected bride on her return from one of the pilgrimages that were her chief dissipation. While still in bed she was startled by the entrance of the reigning stepmother, and, foreseeing trouble, hastened to apologise for not having attended that stepmother's levee.

" It is I, Madame, who should be at yours," answered the Comtesse de Vaudemont, sweeping three low curtsies. " I come to tell you the glorious news that you are to be Queen of France, and to beg patronage for myself and my children. Pardon me for not having treated you with more respect in the past."

Louise had not grasped the purport of this amazing information when her father ushered in the French Envoy who brought official confirmation of the Countess's statement. The bride was dressed and escorted to Mass with all the state that should surround a prospective Queen of France, " and the betrothal was easily arranged because by father, by daughter, no such luck was expected."

The marriage and coronation followed with incredible speed. Scandal-loving tongues whispered that during the initial ceremony Henri showed himself attracted by the vivacity of one of Louise's cousins, and would fain have substituted her for his bride, but a sober-minded chronicler discredits the report on the ground that Henri showed himself a faithful husband *pour quelque temps*.

Paris organised a magnificent fête to celebrate the entry of the King and Queen, and sentimentalists rhapsodised over Louise's beauty.

" C'est la Vénus de Praxitèle !—mais non, c'est le portrait de Louise de Lorraine," cries Brantôme after enumerating the Queen's perfections one by one (though even he admitted that a touch more of the *lumière de l'esprit* was required to make her perfect).

Other men saw her with different eyes, for Sir Thomas Smith wrote to Elizabeth of England on returning from an audience :

" In the Queen's chamber there were ladies young and old, fair and foul, to the number of nine or ten. Of these, truly your Majesty, of favour there is more beauty in your Majesty's little finger than there is in any one lady here—or all of them." He had heard the new French Queen commended as very fair and of good presence. Of his own opinion she was " clear-skinned, but without colour ; of stature convenient—

if she be not heightened by pantoufles. . . . She
stoops, bears her head somewhat forward, but for
presence, or the majesty of a princess, she has none.
. . . Her attire was black, as that of the rest of the
ladies, but of no comeliness and therefore not worth
describing to your Majesty. . . .

" The King is of good stature, but has an indifferent
person. The hair of his head is black and something
long. He turns a roll up (I think with a hot iron),
but from the roots to the crown of his head it is very
smooth." [1]

A year after Henri's wedding Catherine's persistent
efforts secured peace once more, but there were uneasy
murmurings, since the Paix de Monsieur (Beaulieu,
1576) was considered too favourable to the Protestants. Not only did it permit free exercise of the
Reformed Religion, but granted exemption from
taxation to the families of certain victims of the
St. Bartholomew massacre, so the League of the Holy
Trinity was formed for the defence of Catholicism.
This spread rapidly, and Catherine de Medici, always
on the alert where the interest of her children was
concerned, saw in it a sinister effort to overthrow the
Valois and place the Duc de Guise on her son's throne.

The flames were fed once more when the Estates
decided that " all must be united in one religion by
the best means the King can employ," and the King of
Navarre showed himself as leader of the Huguenots.

Smith saw England's opportunity, and sent a secret
messenger to inform Elizabeth of a fine opportunity to
retake Calais " by stealth. . . . There are not above
200 men in garrison and most of these are town
dwellers and unable men." [2]

Fear of foreign invasion and Catherine's diplomacy
brought about the Peace of Bergerac and the Edict
of Poitiers (Sept. 1577), but no treaty could kill the
Catholic League.

[1] Calendar of State Papers, Eliz., Foreign, 1575, No. 1072.
[2] Calendar of State Papers, Eliz., Foreign (Cipher), Dec. 16, 1576.

Cessation of war gave Henri more time to devote himself to his *mignons*, Joyeuse, d'Or, and d'Eperon, two of whom he married to the Queen's younger sisters at great expense to the crown. He had tired of Louise long since, and when she, obedient to her Confessor, reproached him with his irregular life and renewed *liaisons*, he neglected her the more, and told her that she was not so innocent as he had imagined.

She withdrew and left Henri to amuse himself in designing new ruffs for his dogs, in practising dancing steps, and quarrelling with his brother Alençon, now Duc d'Anjou, for whom Catherine was compiling a list of suitable wives, since it seemed unlikely that the English Queen would marry him after her years of dalliance.

But Anjou, ambitious for a crown, dreamed of a kingdom in the Netherlands, and Henri III, discovering his brother's scheming, had him arrested.

In sober truth the court was as Henri of Navarre described it : " We carry our poniards and wear breastplates under our tunics . . . we are all ready to cut each other's throats."

Catherine exhausted herself in travelling about the country trying to make peace between the brothers and enforce the Edict of Pacification, but the King showed himself less and less grateful for her efforts, and she felt herself being pushed aside :

" Give orders for someone to tell me how your affairs are going," she wrote urgently. . . . " I do not ask so that I may control them, but because if they go well my heart will be at ease. You are my all . . . and you do not trust me as you ought. . . . I have no wish to live any longer. I have never cared for life since your father died, excepting I might serve you and God. . . . Never has mother desired more fervently the welfare of her children ! "

Catherine de Medici was sixty, corpulent in body and racked with rheumatism, but she dared not rest. Now by litter, now on the back of a mule, she jour-

neyed through France seeking to pacify her son's
war-racked kingdom, and always she wrote letters.[1]

A wave of her old enthusiasm stirred her when
Queen Elizabeth beckoned once more. She gathered
the necessary money (though the guards went unpaid
and the King had to borrow from his courtiers)
and sped Anjou on his strange wooing. Alas! he
did not win the Virgin Queen, and returned to meet
defeat in the Netherlands when his hungry army
melted away.

Henri was touching for the King's Evil, organising
pilgrimages (in which Louise was required to walk),
and making vows in the hope of a male heir.

His curious perversion was developing noticeably,
and Catherine, in alarm for her son's health, urged his
Confessor to compel him to a meat diet under threat
of excommunication. But no child was born, and
knowing the King's desire, a court lady suggested to
shocked Louise that since she could have no children
" for reasons that were talked of in those days," she
might do well to borrow a secret means of having
them in order not to be left without authority when
the King should die, but rather to make herself the
mother of a King." [2]

The Duc d'Anjou died while Catherine was endeavouring to persuade Philip of Spain to let her son
have one of his own nieces as a bride, and age swept
on her. She had herself carried out into the green
fields beyond the city walls to rest her spirit, and
prayed that she might die while her remaining children
lived.

But for Catherine de Medici there was no respite.
The death of Anjou left Henri of Navarre as heir-
presumptive. He must be seen, reconciled with the
King once again, and persuaded to join the Catholic

---

[1] In a single collection there are over 6,000.

[2] Brantôme suggests that it might have been better for Christendom
had Louise succumbed to the temptation, " for thus France would not
have had ruin and misery . . . at all events it is a brave subject for
discussion."

faith. Margot too, her difficult daughter the unsatisfactory Queen of Navarre, needed a mother's good offices.

Months before Margot had been driven from the French court by Henri III, who had outraged and disgraced his sister by proclaiming her *amours*, real and imaginary. If it proved possible to reconcile the Queen with her husband, Henri of Navarre, Catherine might yet see a grandchild upon the throne of France. So she schemed, while King Henri III played at the fashionable cup-and-ball game in the streets of Paris. His retinue of dogs had increased so that they and their attendants added sixty horses to the baggage train when the court moved.

Lampoonists described their King as " Henri, par la grâce de sa mère, inutile Roy de France, et de Pologne imaginaire. . . ." [1]

Still hoping for an heir, Henri went to Olinville, there to bathe and purge himself, while the Queen walked with her ladies to Chartres to bring back two consecrated *chemises* for her husband and herself.

But France forgot her King's failure to provide an heir in the passion of indignation that swept the country on news of the death of Mary Stuart (1587), and watched the sailing of the Armada with fear ; it might well be that Philip intended his Spaniards to attack, not England, but France.

There was no peace, for Navarre was in the field, and the Lorraine faction demanded the enforcement of the Decrees of the Council of Trent, and the establishment of the Inquisition. Catherine de Medici started on yet another journey, though she had " a humour in her thigh," and as she travelled in her litter she wrote to the Convent of the Murate which had sheltered her in her stormy childhood, sending gifts to the community and asking the nuns to continue their prayers " for the soul of the King my

[1] Estienne's Contemporary Journal.

husband, for the Kings my sons, for the one who is
still living, and for me." She bade them pray also
that she might live to see " this Kingdom restored to
the honour of God, and all things as I found them when
I came here."

Recalled to Paris, the Queen-Mother found it in the
throes of revolution with " The Sixteen " (deputies
representing the sixteen sections of the city) looking
to the Duc de Guise for support.

With war in half a dozen provinces, Henri III
summoned Swiss troops to his aid, and forbade Henri
Duc de Guise to enter Paris.

For answer the citizens erected barricades and the
Duke rode in.

" Vive Henri ! " yelled the mob, hailing a new idol,
and the " War of the Three Henrys " began.

King Henri fled, leaving his wife with the Queen-
Mother. Louise told her beads, but Catherine ordered her litter, passed through the barricades, and
persuaded the Duke to listen to her ; she then pursued her son, and saw to it that agreement was
reached.

Tired out, she retired to Blois with her gentle
daughter-in-law in attendance. Here the Estates
assembled, and here came the Duc de Guise, arrogant
in victory, to meet a murderous death at the hands of
the King's bodyguard (Dec. 23, 1588).

" Je suis Roy de France ! I have killed the King of
Paris ! " cried Henri III.

The Pope thundered excommunication, the doctors
of the Sorbonne deposed the King, and the great
Queen-Mother, of many sons, whose motto had been
" I bring serenity and light," turned her face to the
wall and died (Jan. 5, 1589).

Paris refused her burial in the tomb she had prepared for herself beside her long-dead husband,
Henri II, and around the name of this dangerous
daughter of an unscrupulous age grew a legend so

sinister that it has endured for well-nigh four hundred years.

Perhaps the truest summary of her character was made by Tavannes : " She was female, and she loved her young." Of all her tainted brood two alone out-lived her, Margot, whose name was a scandal and a byword, and Henri III. To the King came death within the year by the dagger-stroke of Jacques Clément, a young Dominican who believed that his act was directed by God.

For the first few hours it was thought that the wound was superficial, and Henri wrote to Louise in a wavering hand :

" Ma mie, vous avez su comme j'ai été misérable-ment blessé (j'espère que ce ne sera rien). Priez pour moi ! . . ." but by the time the Queen received her letter, the King was dead.

Perhaps some day a psycho-analyst will give us a learned pathological treatise on the family of Cather-ine de Medici ; it would offer a fine field for inves-tigation. There seems no doubt that Henri III, at all events, was a degenerate of an extraordinary type.

Louise went to live quietly at Chenonceaux, which had been left to her by Catherine de Medici, though she had a difficult moment when the castle was seized by Catherine's creditors ; still, by selling her pearls she acquired sufficient money to pay the debts. " Here this Princess, who in marriage behaved to the King her husband so wisely, mildly, and chastely that the tie which bound her to him remained insoluble, though he went after others (claiming that great princes have a liberty of their own), passed her days, omitting nothing of the good and saintly work per-formed by devout women, queens, and princesses in past times.

" So, except that she wore herself praying to God for her husband's soul, her life in widowhood was much the same as in marriage."

When Paris opened her gates to yet another King Henri, Louise made her last public appearance, going in state to demand justice on the man who had murdered her husband five years before.

Dying, this Queen asked that her crown should be placed beside her on the pillow, " nor would she have it removed as long as she lingered ; after her death she was crowned with it, and so remained."

Louise was buried in the Convent of the Capucins (Paris), but over two hundred years later (1817) her body was removed to St. Denis, and is therefore one of the few not scattered to the winds in the Revolution.

" Priez Dieu pour elle ! "

HOUSE OF BOURBON

CHAPTER NINE

HENRI IV (HENRI OF NAVARRE) (1589–1610)

I

HENRI (IV) OF NAVARRE AND MARGUERITE DE VALOIS
"La Reine Margot."

II

HENRI (IV) OF NAVARRE AND MARIE DE MEDICI
"God grant it!"

HENRI IV

(distant cousin of Henri III. Nearest common ancestor St. Louis in thirteenth century).

Born at Pau .	Dec. 13, 1553
Married in Paris (1) . . .	Aug. 18, 1572
Ascended . .	Aug. 1, 1589
Crowned at Chartres . .	Feb. 27, 1591
Divorced . .	Dec. 17, 1599
Married (2) by proxy . .	Oct. 6, 1600
Married by ceremonial . .	Jan. 17, 1601
Assassinated in Paris . .	May 14, 1610

CONTEMPORARY SOVEREIGNS

ENGLAND : Elizabeth, James I.
SCOTLAND : James VI.
SPAIN : Philip II, Philip III.

POPES

Sixtus V, Urban VII, Gregory XIV, Innocent IX, Clement VIII, Leo XI, Paul V.

Descent

ANTOINE DE BOURBON
m. JEANNE D'ALBRET QUEEN OF NAVARRE
|
HENRI IV

CONSORTS

(1)
Descent

HENRI II OF FRANCE
m. CATHERINE DE MEDICI
|
MARGUERITE DE VALOIS
(" Margot ")

Born, St. Germain-en-Laye .	May 15, 1552
Married . .	Aug. 18, 1572
Marriage annulled	Dec. 17, 1599
Died, Paris .	Mar. 27, 1616
No issue.	

(2)
Descent

GIOVANNI

COSIMO — LORENZO

COSIMO
|
PIERO
|
LORENZO THE MAGNIFICENT
|
PIETRO
|
LORENZO
|
CATHERINE DE MEDICI

LORENZO
|
FRANCESCO
|
GIOVANNI
|
GIOVANNI
|
COSIMO
|
FRANCESCO
m. JEANNE OF AUSTRIA
|
MARIE DE MEDICI

Born at Florence	April 26, 1573
Married at Lyons	Jan. 17, 1601
Crowned . .	May 13, 1610
Regent . .	May 14, 1610
Died at Cologne .	July 3, 1642

Issue :

Louis XIII . .	1601–1643
Elizabeth . . (became consort of Philip IV)	1602–1644
Christine . .	1604–1663
Duc d'Orléans, 1st	1607–1611
Duc d'Orléans, 2nd	1608–1660
Henriette Marie . (became consort of Charles I)	1609–1669

HENRI IV.

[British Museum.

MARIE DE MEDICI.

[British Museum.

MARGUERITE DE VALOIS.

CHAPTER NINE

HENRI IV (HENRI OF NAVARRE) (1589–1610

I

MARGUERITE DE VALOIS, the third daughter of Henri II
and Catherine de Medici, is one of the best-known
figures of the sixteenth century, and must have been a
precocious and somewhat alarming child. Her famous
biographer Bouchot says that from babyhood the
little girl showed what the woman would be :
" Ses yeux roulaient sans cesse, éperdument, dévi-
sageant les garçons du même âge, les ailes de son nez
s'agitaient. Aussi mouvant que le mercure, elle
branlait pour le moindre objet qui l'approchait."

Obviously, the safest thing to do with a child of
this type was to marry her right speedily, and, since
closer union with Spain might benefit France, Don
Carlos seemed a suitable bridegroom. This princeling
had been born with two teeth and much vigour. He
had so maltreated his wet-nurses that, after 200
women had found the honour of suckling him too
painful, it was decided to provide him with a goat—
or else wean him. He was now lame, stunted in
growth, epileptic, and vile tempered, which was unfortunate ; but Catherine de Medici viewed the
matter from a Napoleonic standpoint. After all,
what were princesses but political merchandise ?

However, Philip II had other views for his son, so
Marguerite was left to the companionship of her
brother François Duc d'Alençon. Years later she
was to make herself unique among queens by writing
her memoirs in a peculiarly frank and self-revealing
style ; indeed, they recall in more ways than one the

immortal autobiography of Benvenuto Cellini. In
these memoirs Marguerite describes her attitude in
regard to her mother :

" She brought me up to fear her, so that not only
did I not dare to speak to her, but when she looked
at me I trembled.   When she was angered, she seemed
to give forth fire."

The girl was not a favourite with Catherine de
Medici, so was left in the background until the Duc
d'Anjou saw that her quick brains might assist him,
and persuaded the Queen to make her something of a
confidante.   For a time all went well, and Marguerite
learnt to delight in intrigue ;   then Henri d'Anjou
turned against his too clever sister and accused her of
a love affair with the Duc de Guise.

She fell ill of a *maladie pourpre*, which was probably
typhus, but having been born, apparently, without
the taint of blood that affected the lives of all her
brothers and sisters, she made a good recovery and
was soon taking a vivid interest in two proposals
for her hand, either of which might have satisfied
her ambition.[1] But once again his Most Catholic
Majesty Philip of Spain intervened.

When hints of yet another possible bridegroom
reached Marguerite, she received the suggestion with
exemplary meekness, according to her own diary
record :

" I answered that I never had a will of my own,
and that anything that pleased my mother would
please me also."   Her sole protest was made on the
ground that Henri de Bourbon, Prince of Navarre,
was a heretic.

Other chroniclers tell of tears, passionate refusals,
and wild sobs ; of a family conclave behind locked
doors ; of a devoted governess who knelt beside the
girl all night long, preaching submission.

[1] One from Sebastian, first King of Portugal, the other in the name of
Rudolph, son of the Emperor Maximilian, whose daughter Elizabeth
later married Marguerite's brother.

Catherine de Medici felt that a mixed marriage (such as that of the King's sister with a Huguenot who stood as near the throne as did the Prince of Navarre) could scarcely fail to have a good effect in a country which was divided by religious wars ; and Jeanne d'Albret, Queen of Navarre,[1] was soon to take the same attitude, judging from her letter to Queen Elizabeth :

". . . God has now looked on me with His paternal eyes, and has disentangled the troubles and disposed the hearts of those on both sides . . . to an indissoluble resolution towards the marriage of Madame Marguerite with my son. . . . I could not fail, Madame, to announce this to you, and to rejoice with you, hoping that this alliance will conduce to the peace of the realm you love, and extend its benefits to your own realm." In conclusion she prayed God to provide a husband for Elizabeth also.[1]

Jeanne wrote to Henri too, reporting that Margot seemed modest and looked beautiful and graceful— " she has a fine figure, but then she laces tightly, and as for her face, its beauty is so heightened that it annoys me." She hoped that these follies were attributable to the undeniable fact that the girl had been brought up in the " most accurst and rotten society imaginable. . . . Great as I had conceived the corruption of this court, it exceeds the idea I had formed of it. Here the men do not solicit the women ; it is the women who solicit the men. . . . I am anxious that you should take her away with you quickly, far from all that."

Having written her warning, Jeanne d'Albret died so suddenly that plausibility was given to the favour-

---

[1] Jeanne d'Albret was the daughter of brilliant Marguerite de Valois (sister of François I) who, as Duchesse d'Alençon, wrote that curious collection of tales called the Heptameron, and was another example of the Valois combination of devoutness, licentiousness, and artistic taste.

She was the Marguerite (" Daisy ") gathered by Henri d'Albret in the delicate illuminations in the " Livre d'Instruction en la Réligion Chrétienne pour les Enfants " exhibited at Burlington House in 1932.

ite cry of poison—and if the Queen of Navarre had
been poisoned, by whom could the deed have been done
except Catherine de Medici ? Had she not sent her
" dear sister " a pair of gloves ?

The negative result of a post-mortem examination
had little effect on the rumours, and few stopped to
consider that the country-bred Queen had probably
succumbed to the unhealthiness of Paris. A contemporary record mentions that the smell of the over-
crowded city could be detected nine leagues distant.

By his mother's death Henri was now King of
Navarre, and in the hot August (1572) the Huguenots
rode to Paris to attend his wedding.

Marguerite was a vision of loveliness. Her dark
hair was studded with diamond stars and the cloth-of-
gold bodice of her dress was so closely woven with
pearls that it looked like a cuirass ; her blue satin
train was carried by three princesses. But she
showed herself an unwilling bride, and declined to
make the necessary responses :

" Marguerite . . . s'obstina à ne pas dire ' oui,' et
ce fut son frère Charles IX qui, d'un mouvement
brusque, avec sa rude main de chasseur, lui fit baisser
la tête et consentir en apparence. . . . Le miracle
s'était fait et on s'était passé du pape. . . ." [1] The
dispensation had not yet been received from Rome,
a fact which proved exceedingly useful to Henri of
Navarre in a later year.

But the bond between Catholic and Huguenot, of
which Marguerite's marriage was to be the seal, broke
in an appalling tragedy.

Six nights later the young Queen of Navarre sat
forgotten among her elders till a careless movement
attracted their attention when the Queen-Mother
ordered her to bed. As Marguerite swept a curtsey,
Claude Duchesse de Lorraine detained her, protesting
that her sister must not be " sacrificed," but Catherine

[1] Michelet.

de Medici bade the girl go quickly. " Please God she
will suffer no hurt," she added in an aside to the
Duchess, " and if she remains it may make *them*
suspect." So Marguerite obeyed.

" I prayed for comfort and protection against I
knew not what," records the diary, " till the King
told me to come into bed, the which I did, and found
it surrounded by thirty or forty Huguenots whom as
yet I did not know, for it was but a few days since I
was married."

These gentlemen talked loudly of an attempt to
assassinate Admiral Coligny, and of their intention to
obtain justice on the Duc de Guise or take vengeance
themselves.

The Queen could get no rest till her husband rose
early in the morning hoping to obtain a private interview with Charles ; then she fell asleep, but only to
be awakened by a loud knocking and a shout of
" Navarre ! . . . Navarre ! "

Thinking the King sought re-admission, Marguerite
ordered the door to be opened, when a fugitive
Huguenot dashed in, pursued by four archers. The
wounded man collapsed upon the Queen's bed, and
her screams brought the Captain of the Guard.
Hastily changing her blood-stained nightdress, she
was hurried to her sister's chamber, seeing both
killed and wounded on the way and rescuing two of
her husband's household.

Navarre himself, and his cousin the Prince de Condé,
had been saved from death by the personal intervention
of Charles IX and their own hurried acceptation of
Catholicism. The Feast of St. Bartholomew had
begun.[1]

The first few years of Marguerite's married life were
passed in Paris, where Henri of Navarre remained
much against his will. Soon, poets rhapsodised over
her, one vowing that to be loved by " La Reine

[1] See Chapter Seven.

Margot " would give him happiness, though the
penalty were death, while others recited verses in her
honour or wove pretty fantasies. Venus, it seemed,
had been told by Cupid that he had found a human
woman even more beautiful than she, whereupon the
indignant goddess sent Charity to make recognisance
and learnt that her son had spoken barely half the
truth !

Poets and courtiers were not alone in expressing
extravagant admiration, for when the Polish Ambassadors came bringing the offer of a crown to Henri
d'Anjou, they looked on Henri's sister and exclaimed
that, having once seen such perfect beauty, they felt
as Turks who, reaching Mecca, burn out their eyes
over a bowl of incandescent brass.

Alone, the King of Navarre found his wife lacking
in attraction. He was a gallant young figure, and
had had a hardy upbringing from the day when, in
accordance with Gascon tradition, his grandfather
had rubbed the infant's lips with garlic and poured a
few drops of good Gascon wine down his throat.

The Béarn court was a poor one, and Jeanne d'Albret had believed in simplicity of upbringing, so her
son had run bareheaded, and sometimes barefooted,
on the hills with his foster-brothers. Now, after the
massacre of St. Bartholomew, Henri only waited an
opportunity of escaping from the toils of the Medici.
When it came, he went " without saying good-bye,"
left his Queen behind him, and abjured Catholicism so
soon as he reached the Huguenot camp in Gascony.

The " War of the Three Henrys " continued (Henri
III, Henri of Navarre, and Henri Duc de Guise), but
Margot rejoined her husband in a rare interlude of
peace to find that the place that should have been hers
was filled. Husband and wife amused themselves in
much the same manner till Béarn palled and Marguerite returned to Paris, where exaggerated tales of
her escapades had preceded her, and the King
objected to her remaining at court.

Announcing that she had erysipelas, Marguerite set off to drink the waters at Spa. She travelled in a gilded litter lined with crimson velvet accompanied by her lady-in-waiting, while six maids-of-honour followed her on horseback, and six coaches lumbered behind carrying the remainder of the household.

Fêtes were arranged in all the chief towns through which she passed. Mons offered a banquet at which the Comtesse de Lalain suckled her infant heir while seated at table, " which would have been a non-civility in anyone else, but she did it with such grace and simplicity that she received as much praise as the company had pleasure." And at Namur Don John of Austria entertained the travellers—declaring that the Queen's beauty was such as not to entrance, but to damn men.

Proceeding towards Spa, two untoward events befell the party : one of the ladies-in-waiting died (either of fever or unrequited love), and a sudden flood separated Margot and her attendants from the coaches. A chilly night without beds, clothes, and provisions so dampened the Queen's ardour for travel that she established herself at Liége and commanded the Spa waters to come to her, rather than she to them.

Six weeks later she was ready to face the perils of the homeward way. What of it if the Prince of Orange refused her a passport, and war raged in the Netherlands ? Marguerite boldly entered forbidden zones, or, rising with the dawn, galloped away, leaving her abandoned litter to be captured by the enemy.

The Duc d'Alençon met his sister in Picardy, and the pair returned to Paris, where they were surprised to find themselves honoured by a royal reception.

But the usual family quarrels began when the King refused Alençon a military command and kept him a prisoner in the Louvre till resourceful Margot smuggled in a rope and contrived to lower the Duke to safety ; unfortunately her connivance was discovered, for in burning the rope she set fire to the royal chimney!

Gascony knew her once more.

The views on morality held by this King and Queen of Navarre were at least unorthodox. She gave him no heir (by reason, it was said, of a diet of unripe fruit and vinegar), and he made no secret of his *amours*, and demanded personal service from his wife on the occasion of the birth of one of his natural children.

Presently Marguerite slipped back to the intriguing life of Paris, to the indignation of Henri III, who, after vain efforts to get rid of her, flung reticence to the winds, secured incriminating evidence from her ladies, surrounded his sister with an armed guard, and ordered the removal from Paris of " sa présence contagieuse."

Queen Margot went to her husband, who refused to receive her. If innocent, she must be avenged ; if guilty, she was no fit wife for the King of Navarre. But Catherine de Medici contrived to effect a temporary reconciliation between the pair on the illusory promise that those who had slandered her daughter should be executed.

Buoyancy of spirit soon returned, and presently Margot was writing in cheerful vein :

" Our court is so goodly and pleasant that we never could envy that of France! " whereupon the Queen-Mother took alarm and sent a warning message.

Marguerite must be circumspect and remember that she was not yet of an age when she could see and talk to those she liked without offending God, or causing scandal to the world. . . . Being the daughter of a king (and married to a prince who called himself a king), she seemed to think that she could behave without decorum . . . she ought to reject the company of those who were unworthy of consorting with a good and wise princess—and one, perhaps, who imagined herself more beautiful than she was.

Nor was Catherine at ease in regard to her daugh-

ter's treatment of her husband's many favourites, and
in this direction she must not take her mother as an
example :

"If I showed courtesy to Madame de Valentinois, it
was the King who made me," she explained frankly,
"and I always let him know that I sorely minded it.
There was never a woman yet who loved her husband
and also his mistresses!" Indeed, Marguerite must
obey Henri of Navarre, in reason, particularly now
that he was heir to the throne of France, owing to the
death of her youngest brother.

But Marguerite showed no sign of remembering the
marriage vows she had refused to utter. Henri
cared little, for his susceptible heart was fluttering in
yet a new direction.

When the Queen wearied of Gascony, she seized
upon a valuable weapon in the shape of the decree of
excommunication that had been launched by Sixtus V
against Henri on the ground of his apostasy, and,
pointing out the impossibility of living with a husband
under ban, she withdrew to the Catholic town of
Agen. Here she lived recklessly, literally at war with
Navarre, till the place was besieged, when once again
she rode for her life.

It was difficult to find another place of abode, since
various Huguenot towns refused to receive Henri's
erring consort, and Marguerite was driven into the
fortress of Usson—poverty and safety. She was here
when Jacques Clément's knife sent the last of the
Valois Kings (Henri III) to his death, and Henri of
Navarre stretched out his hand for the crown that had
been worn by three of Margot's brothers.

But Paris refused to open her gates to this excommunicated heretic who held her besieged, and
after a vain effort at compromise the Catholic League
proclaimed as King, not Henri of Navarre, but (as
"Charles X") his uncle the aged Cardinal de Bourbon,
who was even then a prisoner, and died within the
twelvemonth.

Margot remained at Usson while her husband
fought for the throne. Navarre's hard training stood
him in good stead. If his army melted away before
the forces of the League and the army of Spain
obliged him to raise the blockade of Paris; if Rome
thundered maledictions, though he signed a declaration to maintain the Catholic religion, he could still
write cheerfully to his reigning mistress before spur-
ring his horse into the ranks of the enemy at Arques.

" Are there fifty gentlemen in France ready to die
with their King ? " cried bold Henri of Navarre.

" We will all die with you, Sire ! " came a respon-
sive shout—and the day was won.

The years passed while Henri IV fought and loved.

In London and Geneva prayers were offered up for
Huguenot victories, and when Philip reinforced the
Spanish troops an English fleet anchored off Dieppe
and Englishmen marched across France to Henri's
aid.

Victory was won at Ivry (March 1590). Paris was
blockaded once again, but when the starving citizens
were eating cats, dogs, and even rats, the threatening
advance of the Duc de Mayence and the outstanding
generalship of Alexander of Parma gave the city time
to revictual.

The Estates met. One faction urged the election of
the Infanta Isabella of Spain as Queen of France,[1]
another demanded the recognition of the Duc de
Guise. Realising that the position was desperate,
Henri's Catholic supporters importuned their King
to change his faith, while the Gallican bishops promised plenary absolution.

Henri capitulated—Paris was " well worth a Mass ! "
—and the bulk of the nation declared for him.

Clad in white satin doublet, breeches, and hose, but
with a black cloak and black plumed hat, he took
" the perilous leap " and gave his soul into the keeping
of the prelates.

[1] She was niece of the last three Kings.

A general truce was declared, and Henri IV went
to his crowning, not at Rheims, which still held out
against her sovereign lord, but at Chartres, where,
most conveniently, a vial of Holy Oil had just been
found.

Royalist ladies watched the ceremony, but Marguerite, Henri's wife for twenty-two years, was not
among them. Instead, Gabrielle d'Estrées held the
first place. At eighteen, this damsel had captivated
Henri of Navarre, and since he had annulled the
marriage into which she had been forced, Gabrielle
became a keen follower of the King's fortunes, though
many whispered that he was not her exclusive interest.

Paris opened her gates (March 1594), and Henri IV
entered on foot to offer thanks at Notre-Dame while
every church in the city rang a welcoming peal.
That night he dined in public at the Louvre, eating
with " bon appétit."

Gabrielle d'Estrées arrived a few days later,
escorted by a company of archers, and was received
with the honours usually given to a queen ; her first
child was born in June of that year.

City after city now made submission to Henri,
conciliation by compensation being effected by the
King's astute minister Sully, although the Treasury
was almost empty, and the King complained that
his shirts were all torn and his doublets out-at-
elbows.

But Spain was still unvanquished and Rome required placating, so proxy penitents travelled to
Italy to do public penance in Henri's name, while he
sought worldly allies.

Of these England was the most powerful, but
Elizabeth hesitated to offer support unless the King
would return Calais, " that stronghold of indifferent
importance to France and vital security to England " ;
so the matter hung fire. Then, six months later, the
port yielded to Spanish assault, and Amiens found

herself in danger.   Henri, who had been dallying with
Gabrielle, was stirred to action.

"Mistress, I must leave you, we have another war
on our hands ! " he cried, and went to end the long
struggle with Spain (Treaty of Vervins, 1598).

King of France in fact as well as name, Henri
returned to Paris and summoned the *Parlement* to
the Louvre.   It was necessary that the realm should
be at peace within itself, and to this end he had signed
the Edict of Nantes (April 1598), which, while
recognising Catholicism as the State religion of
France, granted liberty of conscience and a restricted
right of worship to the Huguenots—yet the Edict was
still unregistered.   Henri argued the matter, speaking
"like a father to his children," and won the long-
delayed assent.   Other *Parlements* followed the lead
given by Paris, and by 1600 the Edict of Nantes was
the law of the land.[1]

The King turned to his private affairs ; Queen
Margot was in Auvergne writing her memoirs, but
Gabrielle, now Duchesse de Beaufort, was beside him
and dreaming of marriage.

Henri had desired a divorce for many years, but
the daughter of Catherine de Medici held him bound,
and was still obdurate, seeing no reason why " a
defamed baggage " like Gabrielle should wear her
crown.

All that the King could do was to solicit Rome and
legitimise Gabrielle's son César.[2]   " Puisque Dieu
n'a pas encore permis que nous ayons d'enfants en
légitime mariage . . . la reine, notre épouse depuis
dix ans séparée de nous."

Easter came (1599), King and Duchess separated
for the good of their souls and never met again.

" My love is stricken at the root," wrote Henri when

---

[1] Rouen alone resisted for ten years.

[2] Gabrielle had two other children, Alexander, afterwards Grand
Prior of France, and the Comtesse d'Elbeuf.

telling his sister of Gabrielle's sudden death. He
mourned his loss for five full weeks.

Her death brought freedom, for now Margot was
ready to join with her husband in petitioning Pope
Clement VIII for annulment of the marriage, perhaps
fearing that it would no longer be withheld.

"Dieu l'a pourvu!" came the papal announcement
after much prayer and fasting, and presently Henri
could write to his erstwhile wife :

"My sister! The delegates sent by the Holy
Father concerning the nullity of our marriage have
given sentence to our mutual contentment."

He assured her of his lasting friendship in the future,
and trusted that Heaven would bless the remainder
of their days in a manner that would add to the
national prosperity.[1]

Marguerite accepted the olive branch, and their
relationship began on a new footing. She acquiesced
in Henri IV's second marriage and accepted a seat to
view her successor's coronation. When children
were born to him, none was more enthusiastic than
this discarded wife.

"Monseigneur," she wrote on the birth of a second
son, "I have received the favour which it pleased your
Majesty to do me in causing me to be the first to
receive news of the birth of Monsieur d'Orléans.

"I can scarcely say which is the greater, my joy or my
obligation to your Majesty, and I beg you to believe
that none can outdo me in gratitude and affection.
. . . The universal joy in Paris is as great as at the
birth of a Dauphin. Songs have gone on all day, and
feux de joie will last through the night. These are,
Monseigneur, the effects of your good fortune, and of
the particular favours of God, who treats you as His
well-loved elder son. . . . I pray Him to multiply
your years, and grant to your Majesty a long and
happy life, and to me, Monseigneur, your gracious

---

[1] *Journal du Règne de Henri IV*, by Pierre de l'Estoile.

favour, as your most humble, obedient servant, sister and subject . . . ''

When plague was rampant in her household, Margot added the thoughtful endorsement : '' Faites parfumer cette lettre, and que le Roy ne le touche pas.''

She lived on, debonair and seductive to the last, and keeping a large staff of fair-haired footmen in order that their luxuriant locks might be shorn periodically to supply her with fresh wigs.

Margot was the last survivor of Catherine de Medici's infamous brood, the daughter, sister, and wife of kings, but never an acknowledged Queen of France.

Writing of Marguerite de Valois, Dreux de Radier remarks that if Henri IV had been as severe a moralist as Henry VIII of England, '' and as sensitive to the dishonour which the ill-conduct of a wife reflects on her lord,'' this Queen might well have ended her days on the scaffold.

Mézeray etched her character in less than thirty words :

'' She united voluptuousness with devotion, music and dance with piety, luxury and vanity with love of letters, Christian charity and cruel injustice, in the most curious mixture ever seen.''

A more charitable writer saw her as '' a Princess full of kindness and of good intentions for the peace of the State . . . who did no harm but only to herself.''

HENRI (IV) OF NAVARRE AND MARIE DE MEDICI

" God grant it ! "

HENRI QUATRE was forty-seven and aged beyond his years by the time he had secured the throne of France and " unmarried " himself from Marguerite de Valois.

Unfortunately, as Henri explained to his minister Sully,[1] " mariage—c'est une condition que j'appréhende fort, me souvenant toujours de combien de mauvais rencontres il me fut cause ! "—but it was essential to beget an heir.

The marriageable princesses of Europe were passed in review, for the King demanded that his new bride must have seven attributes : beauty, modesty, an even temper, intelligence, noble birth, wealth, and above all fecundity. The Infanta of Spain was ruled out as old and plain ; Lady Arabella Stuart lacked fortune ; no German princess could be considered :
" I should feel as if I had a wine barrel sleeping beside me ! "

Gradually the choice narrowed, till of the original list of fair damsels none remained save Marie de Medici. In her favour was the circumstance that Henri was indebted to her uncle, who might be persuaded to cancel the debt, did the King marry his niece ; against her, the fact that she was of the same blood as Catherine de Medici, that *fille de marchands* whose name still sounded sinister in French ears.

---

[1] Maximilien de Béthune, created Duc de Sully in 1606, was of Scottish extraction. He was seven years younger than the King, and had escaped death during the massacre of St. Bartholomew by walking boldly through Paris with a Book of Hours under his arm.

Negotiations began in Florence and Rome, although Henri's errant fancy had been caught by beautiful Henriette d'Entragues, the daughter of that Marie Touchet who had been the mistress of Charles IX.

She secured a written promise of marriage from the King contingent upon her first child being a boy, and the guarantee carried with it a gift of a thousand crowns, but, in an unusual fit of caution, Henri showed the draft to Sully, who boldly tore it up. However, the letter was rewritten.

The spring (1600) saw the marriage contract signed which bound Henri Quatre to Marie de Medici.[1] Then war delayed matters, and Henriette d'Entragues was delivered of a son ; but the child was stillborn. The King gave her the thousand crowns and despatched an unofficial messenger to enquire at Rome whether the Medici marriage could be " undone," but in October Marie went to a gorgeous ceremony in the Duomo at Florence, where the Papal Legate officiated as proxy bridegroom. Notice of the event was despatched to Paris by courier, and Sully broke the news to his master :

" Sire, we have just married you ! "

Henri IV bit his nails and scratched his head : " Ventre-Gris ! " Alack that there was no other remedy ! Sully was more content than his master, for Marie was to bring with her a dowry of 600,000 crowns, besides jewels and the cancellation of Henri's debt.

History repeated itself. Like the former daughter of the Medicis, Marie sailed for Marseilles accompanied by a band of illustrious relations, 7,000 retainers, and

[1] Marie de Medici came from a strange family. Her father had had an intrigue with the notorious Bianca Capella during the lifetime of his wife, after whose death he married Bianca. The pair died simultaneously from the effects of a poisoned tart which, it was said, Bianca had prepared for her brother-in-law. A paternal aunt was killed by her husband when he discovered her infidelity, and Pietro de Medici, an uncle, killed his wife for the same reason.

an escorting flotilla of eighteen galleys. Her own
incredibly gorgeous vessel, which showed the Medici
arms in diamonds, was hung with tapestry, cloth-of-
gold, and silver tissue.

The Knights of Malta arrived to act as escort, filled
with a determination to take first place even if they
had to fight for precedence, but a fracas was avoided
and the voyage began peacefully.

Henri was at war in Savoy when Marie landed, so
she proceeded by easy stages, receiving addresses at
the various towns through which she passed.

At Avignon the city fathers trusted that before she
came among them again she would be the mother of a
Dauphin.

" God grant it ! " answered Marie, mindful of her
uncle's farewell instruction : " Soyez enceinte ! "

Indeed, the Princess can have been in no doubt as
to her duty to France, for the King had written begging her to take good care of her health as she travelled,
" so that on your arrival we may make a goodly child
who shall be the delight of our friends and the despair
of our enemies."

In his eagerness to forward the matter, Henri
Quatre came to meet Marie at Lyons, arriving so
unexpectedly that he had to wait an hour in the
frosty December night before the gate was opened
and he could slip into the dining-hall for a secret
glimpse at his bride.

Unfortunately, the portrait of Marie which had been
forwarded to France had shown her as she had been
ten years before. Now she was nearer thirty than
twenty and distinctly Austro-Flemish in appearance,
figure, and weight.

" It is so cold to-night that I hope you will lend me
half your bed," said the King, hiding his disappointment as he bent to kiss her.

Contemporary chroniclers differ as to Marie's reply.
One heard her answer that she had come only to
please and obey his Majesty's will. Another reports

that the Princess was taken with such fright that she
went cold as ice and had to be warmed up with hot
cloths.   Perhaps the latter story is nearer to the truth,
for Henri was grizzled of hair and beard, with a long
hooked nose and so projecting a chin that one of his
mistresses had declared " there was no room for love
to perch upon his lips."   He could still eat fourteen
quails at a sitting.

The Papal Legate and three Cardinals confirmed
the marriage in due course, after which Henri departed for Paris (and Henriette d'Entragues), leaving
Marie de Medici to follow at her convenience.   He
rejoined his bride, however, in time to escort her to
Fontainebleau.   Her state entry into Paris was
delayed, for reasons of economy and until she had
justified her position as Queen of France—which she
hastened to do at the earliest possible moment.

Elaborate preparations were made for the birth of
Marie's first child, her room being equipped with a
double set of hangings which let down tent-fashion,
forming a large outer pavilion some twenty yards in
circumference, with a smaller tent concealing the lying-
in couch.

Seats and stools were arranged in the outer pavilion
for the King, the Princes of the Blood, and those
ladies who had been selected for the honour of being
present at the birth, while little César Vendôme,
son of the dead favourite Gabrielle d'Estrées, ran
in and out, all eagerness to know exactly what was
happening :

" If it depends upon you, *please* make a boy and I
will give you all I have ! " he said coaxingly to the
midwife.

Two monks knelt before a reliquary in perpetual
prayer and five doctors waited outside, but it was
upon the *sage-femme* who received the child that all
eyes rested.

She covered it up so quickly that none saw its sex,
and said that it was weakly.   On Henri's order to

treat the infant in the ordinary way, she took a gulp of
wine and then blew a little between the baby's lips.

" Midwife, is it a son ? " asked the impatient King,
then turned to kiss the fainting Queen :

" Ma mie—God has given us what we asked ! "

He kissed the Princes of the Blood too, and pushed
the hangings aside so that all those waiting in the
ante-chamber came crowding in, to the indignation of
the midwife.

" Tais-toi, sage-femme ! " said Henri, ignoring her
remonstrance, " ne te fâche pas, cet enfant est à tout
le monde ! "

He hung over the baby, not content until the tiny
fingers had been clasped around the hilt of his sword :
" May you be able to use it, my son, in defence of
crown and people ! "   But at last he was persuaded to
withdraw and the baby was washed in wine and oil of
red roses.

It was fifty years and more since a son had been
born to a reigning sovereign, and over eighty since
the birth of a dauphin ; France became delirious with
joy, and a deputation harangued the month-old
infant when he entered Paris in October.

The whole country was cognisant of the details of
his toilet and showed interest in the Prince's succession
of wet-nurses. The first had failed to supply him
with sufficient nourishment, " although she tried to
remedy the defect by overeating herself " ; the second
was scarcely clean; and the third " never suckled the
child without his going into a temper."

Long before the Dauphin was weaned (when two
years old), Marie de Medici had added to the nursery
group, which included the children of Gabrielle
d'Estrées and of Henriette d'Entragues, who had given
the King a son within twenty days of the Dauphin's
birth.

Fourteen months later Henri IV wrote to Madame
de Montglat, the children's governess : " My wife
was brought to bed yesterday according to God's

will. . . .   She is more vexed than I, who do my best to console her. . . ."

But the generous King ordered official rejoicings " even though, so far as we can judge, the birth of a daughter is not so advantageous as the birth of a son."[1]

Thirteen months later there was a similar act of misjudgment on the part of the Queen, to the disappointment of the Dauphin Louis, who had arranged to have his cannon fired in honour of the birth of a brother : " But as it's only a girl, I shan't trouble ! "

In the succeeding years Marie was more successful, and Henri welcomed two more sons, one who died in childhood and Gaston. The Queen's last child was another daughter.[2]

Marie de Medici had given France six children in nine years. Henriette, now Marquise de Verneuil, and others had also added to the King's large establishment.

The Dauphin called his half-brothers and sisters " féfé " and " sœusœu," recognising them as his father's children :

" But I am a dog of another breed ! "[3]

The court was not a happy one, for Marie de Medici was lacking in several of the attributes Henri had desired in a wife. Then, too, she had brought with her from Italy certain dangerous attendants, among them her foster-sister, Leonora Galigaï, and Concino Concini who ultimately married Leonora. Henri IV hated both, and sometimes vowed that he would send the Italians back to Florence, including Marie with all her possessions—except, of course, her dowry.

" She gives me neither amusement nor content," he complained to Sully, who was often called upon to

[1] Elizabeth, who was to marry Philip IV of Spain.
[2] Henriette Marie, who was to marry Charles I of England.
[3] At thirteen Louis gravely explained to César that " the greatest honour and advantage you have in this world is that of being my brother."

play the part of peacemaker between the hot-tempered pair. And the list of the King's favourites lengthened ; those with good memories could name fifty now, " besides others of small importance."

Still Madame de Verneuil had not lost her hold, and she planned for the day when " the Florentine banker's fat daughter " should be discarded, dreaming that her own son might be proclaimed heir to the throne in place of the Dauphin Louis ; all her children had been legitimised.

Plotting recklessly, and helped by her brother the Comte d'Auvergne, Henriette intrigued with Spain. The conspiracy was discovered, but the King revoked the sentences passed upon the chief culprits, although for a time the Marquise was exiled from court. When she returned she was forced to yield the pledge of marriage which had been given to her by the King in the days of his first infatuation.

A younger, fresher beauty than Henriette's was soon to catch the monarch's errant fancy. When Charlotte de Montmorency came to court, the King had eyes for no other charmer. He first saw the beautiful fifteen-year-old girl when she was taking part in a ballet arranged by Marie de Medici : she leapt from a rock with a bow and arrow in her hand straight into the King's heart.

Years before, Henri had cut a Gordian knot and freed Gabrielle d'Estrées from a loveless marriage. Now he decreed that Charlotte's engagement to the Maréchal de Bassompierre should be broken off in order that she might marry the Prince de Condé, who, so Henri believed, would prove a complaisant bride-groom.

The King's orders were obeyed, Bassompierre was offered consolation in another direction, and Charlotte duly went through a marriage ceremony with Condé according to plan—after which the Prince absconded from Paris, carrying his wife with him !

The youthful spirit of Henri of Navarre awoke in the

ageing King of France. Charlotte must be recovered,
even though the attempt brought on war with Spain,
for which there was a pretext in connection with a
dispute concerning the succession of a German
princeling.

Disdainful Philip refused to give up the fugitives
who took refuge in the Low Countries, Henri's views
on the succession question strengthened, and he and
Sully talked of the formation of a Christian Republic
—after the humbling of Austria and Spain.

Preparations for war were begun, and men poured
into camp. A Council of Regency was established,
and after nearly ten years as a consort Marie de
Medici was crowned Queen of France.

Sully was incapacitated by an old wound, and the
King, anxious for a last conference with his minister
before leaving Paris, set out to visit him.

The royal carriage was blocked in the narrow Rue
de la Ferronnerie, and Ravaillac, a victim of religious
mania, leapt upon the wheel and struck at Henri with
a stolen knife. This was the twentieth attempt upon
his life.

Marie de Medici heard the hoarse cry of the infuriated populace and came out from her chamber as
the courtiers carried in the dead body of the King.

NOTE.—For the continuation of the story of Queen Marie as
Regent, see Louis XIII.

CHAPTER TEN

LOUIS XIII (1610–1643)

ANNE OF AUSTRIA

" Perfide et ingrate ! "   (LOUIS XIII.)

LOUIS XIII
(son of Henri IV)

Born at Fontaine-bleau	Sept. 27, 1601
Ascended	May 14, 1610
Legal majority	Oct. 2, 1614
Married at Bor-deaux	Nov. 24, 1615
Died at St. Germain	May 14, 1643

CONTEMPORARY SOVEREIGNS

ENGLAND : James I and Charles I.
SPAIN : Philip III and IV.

POPES

Paul V, Gregory XV, Urban VIII, and Innocent X.

Descent

HENRI OF NAVARRE
m. MARIE DE MEDICI
|
LOUIS XIII

CONSORT
Descent

PHILIP III OF SPAIN
m. MARGARET OF AUSTRIA
|
ANNE OF AUSTRIA

Born in Spain	Sept. 22, 1601
Married at Bor-deaux	Nov. 24, 1615
Became Regent	May 15, 1643
Died in Paris	Jan. 20, 1666

Issue :
Dauphin Louis, 1638
Philippe, Duc d'Anjou, 1640

ANNE OF AUSTRIA.

LOUIS XIII.

149]

CHAPTER TEN

LOUIS XIII (1610–1643)

(The Regency of Marie de Medici and the story of Anne of Austria.)

THE assassination of Henri IV gave the crown to Louis XIII when he was nine years old.

On the day succeeding his father's death the child was escorted to the *Parlement* of Paris, where he announced " de sa petite voix " that he gave his mother authority to rule in his name. A week's experience taught this small monarch that there was little joy in reigning. Lessons seemed longer and drearier than ever ; nor could Louis prevail upon his tutor to shorten them in exchange for the promise of a bishopric " some day."

" I *wish* I was not King and that my father were still alive ! " he said mournfully.

For the second time a daughter of the Medici was Regent [1] of France and free to reverse the policy of the preceding reign. Sully found himself powerless to restrain her actions or extravagance, for behind the official Council stood secret advisers, and chief among these was Concini, now the Marquis d'Ancre.

Indignant Princes of the Blood watched the adventurer's phenomenal rise, powerless to check it ; they saw him appointed Governor of Amiens and presented with the bâton of a Marshal of France, although he had never been in battle.

Exterior affairs were scarcely more satisfactory, for Spanish propaganda cast doubt upon the validity of Henri IV's divorce and the legitimacy of Louis XIII.

[1] Catherine de Medici was Regent in 1560 and again later.

To silence Spain, the Queen-Regent reopened negotiations for the double marriage of Louis and his sister Elizabeth, with two of Philip III's children, the Infanta Anna and her brother, although the project had been rejected by Henri of Navarre some years before.

The ambassadors settled details while Marie organised splendid espousal celebrations, despite an empty Treasury. " L'année de la magnificence " was perhaps the happiest of her Regency.

Louis XIII's official majority was declared a week after his thirteenth birthday, for reasons of State.

" Madame," said the youthful King, turning to his mother during the ceremony, " I desire and intend that you shall continue to hold authority. After me, you shall be chief in my Council."

Enough for him was the surety that Marie de Medici could mete out no more condign punishment. Some years before, when she had swept him a deep curtsey at a public reception too soon after a strictly private interview, this King had been most inconveniently explicit :

" Madame . . . I should prefer less reverence and fewer whippings ! "

Paris welcomed her King, who made a torchlight entry after holding his *Lit de Justice* at Rheims. The court established itself at Fontainebleau, where hunting parties, ballets, and high play became the order of the day.

Louis devoted himself to falconry with de Luynes, a Provençal who had been made Master of the Aviary, while a daring *Parlement* began a covert attack on Concini (who had accumulated seven million livres during his residence at court) and the rebellious princes gathered their armies.

The Franco-Spanish treaty was signed, and Marie de Medici at length carried her children south, surrounded by a brilliant retinue.

Madame Elizabeth contracted smallpox on the

journey, but, ultimately, both bridal parties arrived
at their respective destinations.

Louis and his mother waited at Bordeaux. Philip
III and his court established themselves in a convent
at Burgos. Proxy marriages took place in both cities,
the Duke of Guise espousing Madame Elizabeth in the
name of Don Philip, Prince of the Asturias,[1] and the
Duke of Usseda acting for Louis on the French side.

Once more magnificent pavilions had been erected on
the banks of the Bidassoa between France and Spain,
and the royal bodyguard added to the splendour of
the scene. Here, a century before, Éléonore, bride of
Francis I, had been exchanged for a King's ransom.

The two little Princesses met, curtsied, and kissed.
Then Anne [2] entered France and yet another Elizabeth
passed for ever into Spain.[3]

Louis and Anne met at Bordeaux. On her betrothal, the Infanta, when asked by the French
Ambassador what message he was to carry to her
fiancé, had responded :

" Assure his Majesty that I am impatient to be with
him ! "

A dismayed governess, who thought the sentiment
hardly modest, had tried to amend the message, but
" I was always told to tell the truth ! " said Anne.
Now she looked eagerly at the King, who was her
junior by five days, and found him shy, sulky, and
unresponsive.

She went to the evening wedding ceremony resplendent in cloth-of-silver, after which the pair were
escorted to the episcopal palace by torchlight.

The winter was spent in Tours, and while Marie de
Medici strove to control the rising tide of public
discontent, Louis and Anne discovered that they had
little in common.

---

[1] Later Philip IV.
[2] Two days before Anne had renounced her rights of succession to the
Spanish throne.
[3] Elizabeth, daughter of Catherine de Medici, had married Philip II.

He flew his falcons, carved shrines, and played his guitar. She wrote : " Tell my father that nothing but my beloved Spain can solace me ! "

Before long the two were quarrelling " like froward children," and members of Anne's entourage were complaining that she forgot " with incredible facility " whatever excellent counsel they offered.

On the return to Paris, Marie de Medici moved her court to the Luxembourg, while the King and Queen established themselves at the Louvre. Anne danced her way through pageants and ballets, chattered unwisely to the Spanish Ambassador, and learnt to know the members of her circle.

Among these was one Jean Armand DuPlessis de Richelieu,[1] Bishop of Luçon, who had been appointed almoner to the young Queen.

Six years before, wearying of " the most filthy diocese in the world," Richelieu had come to Paris seeking his fortune. A friend secured him an inexpensive lodging suited to his purse, but after six months' unavailing effort to find employment, Richelieu was driven back to Luçon, having acquired the knowledge that " poverty is a poor accompaniment for noble birth, and a good heart is the only weapon against misfortune."

But Richelieu had met Concini, and when ambition sent him to Paris once more, and chance gave him the opportunity of delivering a speech before the King and Queen-Mother, Concini acquiesced when Marie de Medici selected the Bishop for the service of her daughter-in-law.

Richelieu acquitted himself well in his new post, and presently found himself in the possession of a salary of 6,000 livres, " granted in consideration of the good and praiseworthy service which he has rendered, and continues to render, every day." [1]

[1] This was not the first time a DuPlessis had been of use to the crown. Richelieu's father had arrested Jacques Clément after the assassination of Henri III.

A few months later a political upheaval advanced him a further step. Alarmed by the rise of a League of Princes formed by Condé, Guise, Vendôme, and Mayenne, Marie de Medici had arrested Condé, whereupon Condé's mother had aroused Paris by rushing through the streets crying that the Queen-Mother's favourite intended to murder her son. The palace of the Marquis d'Ancre was sacked, and panic-stricken Marie turned to Richelieu. At thirty-two he found himself a Minister of State; foreign affairs and war were both within his sphere.

In an attempt to conciliate Europe, which had been rendered uneasy by the Spanish marriages, he despatched envoys abroad. At home he raised an army in the King's name, and proclaimed the rebel leaders who were imputing the prodigal extravagance of the Regency to d'Ancre's maladministration.

But Louis was no longer a child, and while de Luynes was snaring birds by his master's side he talked of scandals and plots. Evidence was easily secured, and presently the Gentlemen-of-the-Guard awaited d'Ancre's arrival. When the Marquis entered the Louvre, he was stabbed on the ground that he had offered resistance.[1]

The news spread fast, and ministers crowded to offer their congratulations to Louis " le Juste " upon this happy deliverance. A few hours later the Marquise d'Ancre was imprisoned in the Bastille charged with the practice of sorcery.[2]

When the mob obtained possession of d'Ancre's body, the corpse was dragged through the streets and hanged head downwards on a gibbet.

The Queen-Mother found herself powerless to save the woman who had been her foster-sister and confidante, for Louis issued a dignified message re-

[1] That night d'Ancre's little son was required to dance in a court ballet, and Anne gave him a consolatory gift of sugar plums.
[2] She was condemned as a witch and put to death.

questing his mother's withdrawal from Paris as he now intended to control affairs of State.

Her children Gaston, Christine, and Henriette were to remain with the King. Anne and Louis bowed their farewells from a window in the Louvre as Marie drove away to find a refuge at Blois; with her went the Bishop of Luçon.

Louis's spurt of energy evaporated, and soon it became evident that de Luynes had usurped the authority d'Ancre had held. He was created a duke and married Marie de Rohan. Louis appointed the new duchess chief of Anne's household—Anne refused to accept her, and King and Queen were not on speaking terms for six weeks—such occurrences were frequent.

The temporary peace brought about by the downfall of d'Ancre and the banishment of the Queen-Mother was not of long duration, for, aided by the Duc d'Épernon, and a ladder, Marie escaped from Blois one dark night, although her window was a hundred and twenty feet from the ground.

She joined a rebel group at Angoulême and waged spasmodic war upon the King until Richelieu effected a reconciliation.

"How you have grown, my son!" exclaimed the Queen-Mother, tactfully ignoring recent unpleasantnesses.

"I have grown for your service, Madame," replied Louis with a courtly bow.

Deprived of political power, Marie turned her attention in other directions. She obtained a Cardinal's hat for Richelieu and summoned Peter Paul Rubens to adorn the Luxembourg with a pictorial record of her life. One canvas was to show Juno watching over the birth of this precious infant; a second, Minerva and the Graces superintending her education; a third, Henri IV receiving her (flattering) portrait at the hands of Love; and a fourth, Prudence

and Generosity attending her in her Regency. Yet
another portrayed the Triumph of Virtue—Marie
returning from Blois.[1]

Meanwhile Anne moped in the Louvre because a
foolish romp had caused her to lose her hope of a
child ; Louis led an army against the Huguenots, and
Richelieu, surveying the dangerous state of Europe,
sought allies for France.

"Petite Madame"—Henriette-Marie—was offered
to Charles of England, and the betrothal was celebrated amid an outburst of popular enthusiasm.

Among those who came to Paris during the negotiations was the Duke of Buckingham, magnificently
adorned with the crown jewels of England and escorted
by a retinue of 700 retainers.

To the indignation of Louis XIII (he had once
ordered the withdrawal of a councillor who had
ventured to kiss a rose dropped by the Queen), the
Duke made no secret of his admiration for Anne, who
was dangerously condescending during the brief eight
days Buckingham spent at the French court.

According to arrangement, both the Queen-Mother
and Anne were to escort Henrietta to the coast, but
Marie de Medici fell ill at Amiens, and Anne walked
with Buckingham in the moonlight on the banks of
the Somme.

A startled cry summoned the attendants, who
should never have lost sight of their mistress, and a
fluttering Queen explained that the cause of her alarm
had been discovering herself alone with Monsieur
l'Ambassadeur. Many-tongued rumour swiftly
spread a report that Buckingham had attempted to
kiss this "fairest and most beautiful of sovereigns,"
and scandal raged when, after the cavalcade had
started next day, the Duke rode back on pretext of a

[1] The twenty-four paintings were executed within three years, since
the artist employed his pupils to work with him upon them. So
successful was the series that an order to portray the history of Henri
IV was given in 1628. This was left unfinished.

forgotten message to Marie de Medici, and so saw
Anne once more.

Louis was no complaisant husband. If the Queen
had done no wrong, she had been careless of her
dignity. Her household must be reorganised so that
she should be well guarded in the future.

Anne saw Richelieu's hand in the compulsory dismissal of certain of her attendants, and rejected all
his efforts at conciliation.

After a dreary two months spent at Fontainebleau,
she was brought back to Paris, but still so straitly
kept that courtiers flocked rather to Marie de Medici
at the Luxembourg. The Spanish Ambassador (Marquis de Mirabel) advised Anne to make a deliberate
effort to attract the King, but Louis was morose,
having been freshly offended by a report that Buckingham was wearing the Queen's portrait, and Anne
preferred the pleasanter task of designing new
flower-beds at St. Germain. Here Gaston, the Duc
d'Orléans, followed to kiss her beautiful hands when
the Queen called him " mon frère," and sympathised
with his refusal to marry Mademoiselle de Montpensier, who had been selected by his elders.

A group of malcontents gathered around the restless
heir-presumptive, among them César Vendôme and
his brother the Grand Prior of France, the Comte de
Soissons (who hoped to marry Mademoiselle de Montpensier himself), and the Comte de Chalais. They
schemed wildly, planning the assassination of Richelieu, the abdication of the King, the accession of
Gaston, the freeing of Anne from her irksome bonds,
and a re-marriage with her husband's brother when he
had seized the crown.

Such rash plotting could not be long concealed
from Richelieu's *agents d'espionage*, and presently one
secured an unsigned paper in which mention was made
of the projected marriage between Gaston and Anne,
as approved by the Queen herself and Philip of Spain.

Richelieu struck swiftly, and the chief conspirators

found themselves under arrest when merciless interro-
gations resulted in contradictory evidence. The
Vendômes[1] and Soissons were sent to the Bastille;
Gaston bought immunity by matrimony; Chalais[2]
went to the foot of the scaffold, and Anne, terrified
that she was to be divorced and returned to Spain so
that Richelieu could marry the King to one of his
nieces, was summoned for examination before a
Council. For a while she faced her accusers boldly :
" I should not have gained much ! " said Anne when
taxed with a willingness to marry Gaston. But she
emerged from the ordeal in tears and dire disgrace.

" She wished for my death and coveted another
husband in my lifetime ! " said Louis bitterly.

Entrée to the Queen's salon was restricted. She
was forbidden to receive except in the King's presence,
nor might she grant any private interview without
permission from the Cardinal. Madame de Chévreuse,[3] who had become her confidante, was banished
from court.

While Louis and Richelieu waged war, now against
the Huguenots and now with Spain and Italy,
Marie de Medici kept royal state in Paris and Anne
lived in seclusion, avoiding surveillance whenever
possible.

She had founded the Convent of the Val-de-Grâce,
and under cover of visiting the nuns contrived to give
secret audience to the Spanish Ambassador, and carry
on a clandestine correspondence with Madame de
Chévreuse and various other exiled favourites, most
of whom wrote rashly indiscreet letters.

When plotting was at its height, Louis fell ill, and
d'Orléans, seeing the crown almost within his grasp,

---

[1] The Grand Prior died in prison three years later.
[2] The Comte was master of the King's wardrobe. It was said that he
had undertaken to poison Louis's shirts and scratch his master's neck
with a poisoned pin when called upon to adjust his ruff.
[3] Formerly the Duchesse de Luynes. She had married secondly
Charles de Lorraine, Duc de Chévreuse, son of that Henri de Guise who
had been killed at Blois by order of Henri III.

sent messages to his mother urging her to have
Richelieu arrested so soon as the King died.

Realising his danger the Cardinal made preparations
for flight, but the bursting of an abscess relieved
Louis, and he struggled through convalescence and
stormy interviews with the Queen-Mother, who claimed
that he had promised the dismissal of his minister.
The weary King took refuge in flight, leaving his
mother in the belief that Richelieu's downfall was
imminent. But the Cardinal followed Louis to Versailles, and presently Paris was laughing over the
" Day of Dupes," for Richelieu continued in authority
and Marie de Medici found herself under ward at
Compiègne, whence she was presently allowed to
escape to Flanders.

Anne was scarcely happier than the Queen-Mother,
for some of her unfortunate correspondence had been
discovered, and once more her household was sifted
of suspects.

Louis avoided her in private, and any necessary
communications were made through Richelieu, who
had been created a duke. Mademoiselle de Haute-
fort, one of Anne's maids-of-honour for whom the King
had developed a platonic affection, strove to reconcile
the pair, but without success, for Louis saw his wife
as dangerously " Spanish at heart," and would place
no faith in her :

" La reine est fausse ; elle est perfide et ingrate ! "

A rising in Lorraine on behalf of the Duc d'Orléans [1]
sent Louis to do battle once more. He took Anne
with him to lessen the chances of intrigue at a time
when Spain was threatening invasion, for Richelieu's
intelligence men sent word that French State secrets
were known in Philip's court.

When the rebellion was put down, and King and
Queen returned to Paris, Louis sought consolation at

---

[1] Gaston had lost his first wife on the birth of a child, " La Grande
Mademoiselle," and had married the daughter of the Duke of Lorraine
without the King's consent.

the hands of another of Anne's attendant maidens,
Louise Angélique Motier de la Fayette, till she retired
to a convent ; Anne shrouded the girl in her novice's
veil.

The lonely King returned to his music and the
carving of little shrines, while, in the intervals of
endeavouring to arrange a peace with Spain, Richelieu
harangued him on the danger to the State occasioned
by his lack of an heir when the next in succession was
Gaston Duc d'Orléans.

Louis might have listened less unwillingly, though
King and Queen had drifted far apart, but as he
hesitated, one of Anne's trusted messengers was
arrested and a further supply of incriminating letters
reached Richelieu's hands. Once more Anne had to
face an indignant Council and hear herself accused of
treasonable correspondence with Philip and the
Infante Ferdinand, with the Spanish minister, and
Madame de Chévreuse, and with the Queens Marie de
Medici and Henriette-Marie.

No one believed Anne when she vowed that the
indiscreet papers were forged, and swore that she had
never exchanged treasonable correspondence with any
foreign power. Nor was it considered a factor in her
favour when a search at the Val-de-Grâce revealed no
evidence against her. Arrested Abbess and interrogated nuns betrayed nothing, but Anne herself broke
down. Yes, she had written to her brothers by *des
voies secrètes*, but only innocent enquiries after their
healths !

Richelieu showed no mercy, and an unwilling,
frightened Anne wrote a confession :

" We, Anne, by the Grace of God Queen of France
and Navarre, avow and admit that we have several
times written to Monsieur le Cardinal Infante, our
brother . . . that we have sometimes testified our
discontent and resentment at our domestic position
. . . and we acknowledge to have received letters . . .
offensive to the King. . . .

12

" We promise never again to be guilty of like faults ;
and for the future we engage to live with the King
(our very honoured Lord and husband), as becomes a
person who holds no other interest but the welfare of
his royal person and realm. . . ."

Louis received the confession, weighed the evidence,
and undertook to " obliterate from his mind all past
events " and make a new beginning. But he was
running no more risks. For the future every letter
Anne sent abroad was to be read and examined by a
trusted person appointed by the King, and if the
Queen again failed in obedience to her husband's
wishes, the pardon he now gave her was to be revoked.

" I promise the King to serve faithfully and religi-
ously in all that he is pleased to command me," wrote
Anne.[1]

And now there came a gleam of hope for future
happiness. The arm of St. Isidore, one of Spain's
most sacred relics, was sent to France for the Queen's
benefit. Anne and her ladies carried it in procession
to Notre-Dame, and in every church throughout the
land people knelt in prayer. Hope was high, and
flamed yet higher when word reached the court that
the Virgin Mary had made a miraculous appearance
in a distant church, bringing promise that the nation's
petition would be granted, and on a dark evening
Louis went to the Louvre and was received by Anne
and her maidens.

An eager nation flocked to its churches once more,
when Louis XIII dedicated himself and his realm to
the Mother of God in thanksgiving for Anne's seem-
ingly miraculous pregnancy. It was twenty-three
years since the gorgeous wedding ceremony in Bordeaux.

Amid tremendous public excitement Louis " Dieudonné " was born, and only in the group surrounding
the Duc d'Orléans was there dismay and incredulity ;

---

[1] Bibl. Nat., Sup. MSS., Fr. 4068.

they whispered of illegitimacy and launched innuendoes against Anne and the Cardinal. Had Richelieu
added to his other achievements by giving France an
heir ?

Two years later Louis welcomed his second son,
" le petit Monsieur," but Anne's motherhood, although it gave her importance, did nothing to restore
the King's faith. When war broke out once more,
the Queen was left at St. Germain under watchful
eyes, forbidden to visit Paris during Louis's absence,
or to withdraw her children from the care of their
gouvernante at Vincennes.

A new conspiracy, with the ostensible object of
securing the " rights " of the Duc d'Orléans, again
turned suspicion on Anne, but she had learnt caution
and refused to be directly involved.

Sovereign and minister returned to Paris to take
what precautions they might for the welfare of the
realm, for both saw death approaching fast. Neither
trusted the Queen, the Queen-Mother, nor Monsieur
the King's brother ; and the heir to the throne was
but five years old.

The death of Marie de Medici (July 3, 1642) simpli-
fied the matter by one degree.

War had driven her from the Low Countries to seek
a temporary refuge in England, but her unpopularity
as the Catholic mother of Henriette-Marie obliged an
unwilling Parliament to vote her £10,000 as an induce-
ment to leave the country. The fleet escorted her to
Dunkirk, where she was met by· a stern command
from Richelieu forbidding her to return to France.
Pride made an appeal to Florence impossible, and
Spain would allow no permit of residence in the
Netherlands.

With half the countries of Europe closed against
her, the unfortunate Queen found a last refuge in the
Free City of Cologne. Reports of her dire poverty
were circulated assiduously, causing Louis XIII dis-
quietude concerning his behaviour to his mother :

" Monsieur le Cardinal," he warned Richelieu,
" vous m'en répondrez devant Dieu ! "—but a death-
bed will proved that this Queen of many tribulations
still possessed a certain amount of property. As a
personal remembrance she left her betrothal ring to
Anne, who several years later had her mother-in-law's
remains brought from Cologne for reburial in the
royal tombs at St. Denis.[1]

The Cardinal Duc de Richelieu outlived his patro-
ness and enemy by five months, long enough to draw
up an edict which diverted the crown from d'Orléans
should Louis's sons fail.

" I pray to God to condemn me if I have had any
other aim than the welfare of God and the State ! "
was his last sentence.

Mazarin, who had been in Richelieu's confidence for
some time, took up the burden and explained affairs
of State to Anne while the failing King faced the
problems of the future.

If the Regency was Anne's by right of precedent,
she must be surrounded with restrictions, for " the
office of Regent is weighty and the Queen needs
guidance."

Gaston, too, was a public danger. He must be
appointed Lieutenant-General. " We trust and rely
upon his honour that he may pay implicit obedience
to our will," wrote Louis XIII.

Both Anne and Gaston were required to take oath
that they would adhere to the articles of the King's
Edict, and before sending it to be registered in
Parlement, Louis added the words : " Ce que dessus
est ma très expresse et dernière volonté que je veux
exécutée. . . ."

The assembled court heard Anne declared Regent.
She could not restrain her tears, and afterwards
sent a message to the King assuring him that she

[1] The world owes Marie de Medici not only the Luxembourg and its
Rubens (now in the Louvre), but the beautiful boulevard long known
as the Cours-la-Reine.

had always been " his Majesty's faithful and devoted consort."

" Dans l'état où je suis, je dois lui pardonner, mais je ne suis pas obligé de la croire ! " commented Louis, and with fast-failing strength hastened on a last State ceremony—the public baptism of his two little sons. An hour later he asked the elder child if he knew his own name.

" Je suis Louis Quatorze," answered the four-year-old heir gravely.

" Pas encore, mon fils, pas encore ! " said the dying King. He lived till May 14 (1643), the anniversary of Henri IV's death thirty-three years before.

NOTE.—For Anne of Austria as Regent, see Louis XIV.

CHAPTER ELEVEN
LOUIS XIV (1643–1715)

I

Louis XIV and Marie-Thérèse.

"Presto! Presto! Qu'el Rey m'espera!"

II

Louis XIV and Madame de Maintenon.

"Qu'en pense votre Solidité?"   (Louis XIV.)

LOUIS XIV
(son of Louis XIII)

Born at St. Germain . .	Sept. 5, 1638
Ascended . .	May 14, 1643
Legal majority .	Sept. 7, 1651
Crowned . .	June 7, 1654
Married (1) .	June 9, 1660
Married (2) .	1683–4 (?)
Died at Versailles	Sept. 1, 1715

CONTEMPORARY SOVEREIGNS

ENGLAND : Charles I, Charles II, James II, William and Mary, Anne, George I.

SPAIN : Philip IV, Charles II, Philip V.

POPES

Innocent X, Alexander VII, Clement IX, Clement X, Innocent XI, Alexander VIII, Innocent XII, Clement XI.

Descent

LOUIS XIII
m. ANNE OF AUSTRIA
|
LOUIS XIV

CONSORTS
(1)
Descent

PHILIP IV OF SPAIN
m. ELIZABETH OF FRANCE
|
MARIE-THÉRÈSE

Born at Madrid .	Sept. 10, 1638
Married at St. Jean-de-Luz .	June 9, 1660
Died at Versailles	July 30, 1683

Issue :

Louis " le Grand Dauphin "	1661–1711
Anne-Elizabeth	*b.* and *d.* 1662
Marie-Anne .	*b.* and *d.* 1664
Marie-Thérèse .	1667–72
Philippe . .	1668–71
Louis-François	*b.* and *d.* 1672

(2)
Descent

THÉODORE AGRIPPA D'AUBIGNÉ
|
CONSTANT D'AUBIGNÉ
m. JEANNE DE CARDILLAC
|
FRANÇOISE D'AUBIGNÉ
(Madame de Maintenon)

Born at Niort en Poitou . .	Nov. 28, 1635
Married (1), to Paul Scarron .	1651
Married (2) .	1683–4 (?)
Died at St. Cyr .	April 15, 1719

No issue.

LOUIS XIV.

CHAPTER ELEVEN

LOUIS XIV (1643–1715)

(The Regency of Anne of Austria and the story of Marie-Thérèse.)

I

THE death of Louis XIII brought freedom to his consort Anne of Austria. She carried her two little sons to Paris, where the people acclaimed Louis Dieudonné, and the beautiful Queen-Mother in her mourning robes, while *Parlement* annulled the edicts by which the late King had tried to restrict Anne's authority. Thanks be to Heaven, France had a Regent under whom the country might hope for peace !

Those who had been exiled by Louis XIII were allowed to return, the dismissed were reinstated, and Anne showed herself bountiful, giving " in beautiful liberality " till all Paris resounded with the cry : " The Queen is so good ! "

One of the Regent's first acts was to confirm Mazarin in his office of first Minister, although many people murmured against him as a foreign interloper. He was of Sicilian extraction, a year younger than herself, and one of the handsomest men at court. As a youth Mazarin had studied under the Jesuits in Rome ; Richelieu had procured him a Cardinal's hat, but he was only in minor orders, having decided that diplomacy was a more attractive career than the Church.

As Queen of France, Anne had lived a dull and circumscribed life ; as Queen-Regent, her days were full and she was happy. Ballets, theatrical entertainments, and pageantry kept the court gay, but she still found time for sober living according to the

Memoirs of Madame de Motteville, wherein the routine of the Queen's days is described.

Immediately upon awakening, Anne " made her prayer," and then announced her readiness to receive the officers of State, after which the King and his brother " petit Monsieur " were summoned. Another prayer, breakfast in bed, " bouillon, a cutlet, sausages, and boiled bread, of which she ate a little of all and dined on no less, and then the King handed her her *chemise*, and she kissed him, after which she put on a few more garments and heard Mass (very devoutly) before finishing her toilet."

Dinner was served in the Queen's Cabinet, and then, after " devoting an hour to God," Anne was ready to receive again, or else pay visits ; she would often go to the Val-de-Grâce.

The Council saw her in the evening, and Cardinal Mazarin usually remained behind for a private interview. An hour in her oratory, supper, laughter with her women, and bed in the small hours ended Anne's day. Such a life might have continued indefinitely, but unfortunately France was not at peace, and suddenly an amazed court heard that *Parlement* had assembled in antagonistic mood.

A stern message reduced the malcontents to order, but only temporarily, for one day *Parlement* arrived in a body at the Palais-Royal [1] and demanded to see Anne. However, it withdrew abashed when the Captain of the Guard brought a message from the Queen to the effect that she " did not think it right that *Parlement* should seek her without permission— and she had just taken medicine and could not receive it."

A month later Anne decided to forgive the *faux-pas*, so the judicial body was ordered to attend her before she withdrew to Rueil for the summer. She was even gracious enough to concede " points of no great weight."

---

[1] Built by Richelieu ; name changed from Palais-Cardinal.

But the Regent's holiday was interrupted by the arrival of Queen Henrietta Maria of England, who came as a fugitive, and Anne hastened back to Paris to welcome this sister-in-law whom the English had dared to accuse of treason.

" A bas les Anglais ! " cried the crowds, hailing the daughter of Henri of Navarre, and France, despite poverty engendered by perpetual wars, made haste to provide her with an income.

" Messieurs, I have come here to talk to you of my affairs ; my Chancellor will tell you all my will," said seven-year-old Louis XIV, holding his *Lit de Justice* with his mother beside him, and a respectful *Parlement* registered nineteen decrees without protest, though beneath the surface there were murmurings at Mazarin's rule.

The little King had passed out of the hands of women. He was translating the Commentaries of Cæsar, and his tutors read him to sleep with the history of France. Childish games were laid aside, he was learning to ride, to dance, and often went bathing in the Seine with his mother and her ladies, accompanied by his tutor. As the whole party, including the tutor, wore long grey linen shifts—so long that they trailed upon the ground—" modesty was in no wise wounded."

But an interminable war raged ; maimed and stricken men followed the court, and discontented murmurings grew more insistent despite the passage of a royal ordinance forbidding people to talk of State affairs. Nor was the nation pleased with the connection between Mazarin and the Queen. Innuendoes were heard, and scandalous leaflets circulated from hand to hand ; then a group of the Cardinal's nieces arrived at court and Paris saw his power increasing. But the King was stricken with smallpox and everything else was forgotten.

Louis XIV recovered and the long tussle between

Crown and *Parlement* began in earnest.   A deputation
of merchants lodged a protest against a new tax and
were warned by the President of the Palais de Justice
that if they were not obedient to the King's will he
would have a gallows erected and hang the leaders ;
they retorted that such a gallows would be useful for
hanging those judges from whom no justice could be
obtained.   On the same day Mazarin was interviewed
by the Masters of Petitions, who refused to have their
number increased, since they had bought office.

Immediately afterwards Anne found herself followed
by a sullen crowd, which murmured that she had lost
that beautiful quality of liberality which had endeared
her to all.   And Louis, going to *Parlement* to give
royal countenance to his Chancellor (who was to
deliver an oration on the duties of obedience and submission in subjects), heard few cries of *Vive le Roi!*

The Queen-Regent reprimanded the body for un-
dutiful behaviour, and bade it go away—nor was it to
reassemble.

Parlement protested its fidelity—went away—and
reassembled.   Anne summoned the recalcitrant body,
intending to let it know her views " without equivoca-
tion," but it declined to attend on her, and when a
second peremptory message was despatched, it was
found that, " being weary of waiting," the *Parlement*
had departed ;   the court was amazed at this dis-
respect to royalty.

A third message resulted in the appearance of a
thin *Parlement* which was told to attend to the King's
business within eight days, and Anne carried off her
children to visit certain shrines leaving Mazarin to
play the part of peacemaker.   He was not successful,
and resistance stiffened.   Anne returned to hear all
Paris humming :

> " Un vent de Fronde
> S'est levé ce matin,
> Je crois qu'il gronde
> Contre le Mazarin ! . . ."

Once more *Parlement* was summoned and came on foot to the Palais-Royal, where dukes, peers, and marshals of France were assembled in the presence of the King and a gravely stern Queen-Regent. A royal order annulling the decrees of *Parlement* was promulgated, and that body was reminded that its sole duty was to administer justice, and that internal discord was heartening France's enemies abroad.

The court was anything but happy. Mazarin was obliged to pawn the crown jewels to supply the royal kitchen, while Anne and Louis XIV wept in one another's arms, she protesting that her son was being made into a mere cardboard king. Conditions at the Louvre were no better, for Queen Henrietta Maria's servants were threatening to desert in a body for lack of wages, and the Prince of Wales had sailed to make a desperate throw in Scotland.

Supported by Mazarin, Anne gathered her courage and went to *Parlement* once more, but her attempts at conciliation were received in silence, and in defiance of her commands the Chamber of St. Louis was constituted a permanent body to reform abuses. The court saw this as an attack on royal authority, and the nation also was rendered anxious. By what right did these lawyers usurp the functions of the Estates-General ? Why, too, it asked itself, was the Cardinal established in a building adjoining the Palais-Royal, and what truth was there in this rumour of a secret connecting door ? [1]

Two printers were condemned for publishing a scurrilous pamphlet, but when the mob was told that these men were to suffer death for writing verses antagonistic to Mazarin, they were rescued from the gallows platform.

News of the victory of Lens (Aug. 20, 1648) helped Paris to forget her troubles. France was

---

[1] Marriage would have been possible between Anne of Austria and Cardinal Mazarin, for he was in minor orders only ; but there is no irrefutable evidence on the matter.

saved from invasion and Spain would be forced to make peace !

In the hour of triumph Mazarin and Anne struck at *Parlement* by arresting its leaders, among them Broussel, an old army officer who had denounced the new taxes.

Barricades were flung up in an hour. Mazarin was roughly handled, other dignitaries had to run for their lives, and *Parlement*, having warned its President that he would be cut to pieces if Broussel were injured, hastened to confront the unintimidated Queen. But while Mazarin waited booted and spurred for flight, a royal carriage fetched Broussel back to Paris.

Te Deums were sung and order restored ; then two wagons loaded with gunpowder lumbered past the Porte St. Antoine, wild rumours flew through the city, and the citizens surged to the palace, where, finding themselves confronted by two stolid sentries, anger gave place to laughter.

A fortnight later Anne carried the King to Rueil, starting secretly at six in the morning. There she received a deputation which demanded that the King should return to Paris within twenty-four hours, answering that it was the season for change of air, and also that the Palais-Royal needed ventilating from the infection of the smallpox.

A week later it was discovered that the Queen-Mother had contrived to carry off " petit Monsieur " while the city slept, and panic overwhelmed the people, who felt sure that Anne was meditating the infliction of some drastic punishment. Those who could streamed through the gates, carrying their valuables ; those forced to remain laid in provisions.

While Mazarin signed the Treaty of Westphalia (Oct. 24, 1648) which ended the Thirty Years' War, men worked for peace at home, and at last a formula was accepted, although one that in the eyes of the court seemed the assassination of royal authority.

Anne returned, bringing her children, but the

" persecution " by *Parlement* continued and defama-
tory placards began to appear in the streets. So in
the small hours of a dark January morning (1649) she
put the King and his brother into a carriage and
removed them to St. Germain-en-Laye, leaving a
message explaining that she had been driven away by
violence, but would never cease to love Paris.

An explanation was issued under Louis XIV's
signature. He, it seemed, had left the capital on the
advice of his very honoured mother, in order that he
should no longer be exposed to the pernicious designs
of the officers of " our Court of *Parlement*."

" To arms ! " sounded the cry once more.

Condé's [1] army approached Paris, loyalists followed
the Queen to urge the dismissal of Mazarin, and the
Cardinal's enemies hastened to join the new party,
who called themselves the Frondeurs.[2]

A herald appeared with a message from Rueil.
Louis was ready to pardon the city, but on condition
that *Parlement* withdrew to Montargis and that those
recalcitrants who had become Frondeurs returned to
their allegiance.

While the deadlock continued and food became
scarce in Paris, since Anne had forbidden the surrounding villages to supply necessities, terrible news
arrived from England, and Henrietta Maria, though
ill with grief over the execution of King Charles, sent
a warning message : The Queen-Regent must not
irritate her subjects unless she had power to quell
them . . . " the populace is a wild beast, and
untameable. . . ."

Anne thought that Charles's tragic death should
make all kings tremble, but maintained her attitude.

By March repeated conferences had had their effect
and the Declaration of Rueil promised tranquillity,

---

[1] The Duc d'Enghien had become Prince of Condé on the death of his
father, Dec. 1646.
[2] The name had been taken from the frondes (slings) of the Paris
gamins.

though when Paris discovered that Mazarin's signature was affixed to the treaty, the Frondeurs threatened to burn it.

All had hoped that the royal family would return for Holy Week, but the Queen-Mother was in no forgiving mood, and it was August before the chastened Parisians were permitted to prepare a welcome.

"Vive le Roi! . . . Vive la Reine-Régente!" cried the people, and even Mazarin was cheered as he drove by in a royal carriage.

But *Parlement* showed itself still restive, lampoons were circulated, and the Prince de Condé and the Duc de Longueville were seen as the focus of enmity. Both were arrested, then, having appointed the Duc d'Orléans as Lieutenant-General of the Kingdom, Anne, the King, and Mazarin went with the army to besiege and reduce rebellious cities. On return they found *Parlement* and capital yet more out of hand, " vomiting insults " against the Cardinal and demanding the release of the Princes.

Travel-weary as she was, the Queen-Regent summoned the members (receiving them in her nightcap as an invalid should), but despite her intervention a decree was registered ordering Mazarin to leave the country within fourteen days, together with all his relations.

Discretion carried Mazarin as far as Havre, and Paris stirred angrily in the belief that the Queen was preparing for flight and would take her children with her.

Heralds ran through the streets crying that the King was sleeping, but the mob would not be quieted. So, taking her stand by her son's bed, Anne stood while the citizens surged through till morning dawned—and through the long hours the young King lay, breathing gently with fast-closed eyes, and Anne whispered an occasional request for silence !

For a month and more the suspicious people kept watch over the palace, and no woman of the Queen's height was allowed to pass through the city gates until she had unmasked.

Louis XIV celebrated his early majority (Sept. 7, 1651) in a lull brought about by the release of the Princes and the withdrawal of Mazarin from France.

Looking very small in his gold-embroidered coat, the King rode to the ceremony on a curvetting horse, while Anne drove in a royal coach with eleven-year-old Monsieur beside her.

So enthusiastic were the shouts of *Vive le Roi* that they were said to have " reached Heaven."

" Messieurs," said Louis, " I have come to my *Parlement* to tell you that . . . I intend to take the government on myself, and I hope, by the goodness of God, to exercise it with piety and justice."

Anne too had her part to play : " Monsieur, this is the ninth year that by the last will of the late King, my very honoured lord, I have taken care of your education, and the government of your State. . . . Now that the law of the Kingdom calls you to . . . this monarchy. I return to you, with great satisfaction, the power which was given to me. . . ."

Louis stepped from the *Lit de Justice* to kiss his mother, " and all did him homage."

But if Anne's Regency was at an end, there was no peace in France. Civil war raged again, Mazarin returned leading an army, though *Parlement* offered a reward of 50,000 crowns to whosoever would kill him,[1] the King's forces under Turenne clashed with those led by Condé, the guns of the Bastille opened fire on the royalists, and Anne prayed for the souls of the departing at the Val-de-Grâce.

Knowledge that Spain was helping the Princes, and the burning of the Hôtel de Ville while the Assembly was in session, brought reaction. Mazarin withdrew once more and the restoration of order became the main pre-occupation ; little opposition

---

[1] The amount to be raised by the sale of his library.

was offered when Anne required the Cardinal's return in order that he might deal with England and Spain.   France turned to the crowning of her King.

Louis XIV was growing up.   While watchful Europe reviewed its list of eligible princesses, he was caught by the bright eyes of Mazarin's niece, Marie Mancini, one of an impecunious brood of ten.

Anne thought the Infanta Marie-Thérèse of Spain the only bride worthy of her son, but had little hope of securing her, since she stood near her father's throne. Henrietta of England had been suggested, but Louis objected, saying that he did not like the little bones of the Holy Innocents, and though the Queen of Portugal sent her daughter's portrait, and hinted at a rich reward for Mazarin if he would bring about the match she desired, Mazarin turned to Savoy.

It was arranged that the two courts should meet at Lyons, and here the Duchess (a daughter of Henri IV) brought her unwilling daughter, for Princess Margaret had a presentiment that the journey would be fruitless.

The French court reached Lyons five days before that of Savoy (by another road a messenger was travelling fast from Spain), and Mazarin met the Duchess two leagues from the city.   Monsieur, the King's brother, waited at one league; the King and the Queen-Mother at half a league, as etiquette decreed.

Margaret was scrutinised.   She was very small and somewhat swarthy in appearance.   Anne decided that she had few attributes except birth and virtue, but Louis showed no disappointment, though Marie Mancini whispered :

"Are you not *ashamed* that they want to give you such an ugly wife ? "

But Philip of Spain had decided " to quit all craft," and his messenger arrived to crave an eleventh-hour interview with Mazarin.   He had travelled in disguise, not having had time to obtain a safe conduct.

MADAME DE MAINTENON.

MARIE-THÉRÈSE OF AUSTRIA.

176]

So it was that Cardinal Mazarin could bow before Anne, saying :

" Madame, I bring you Peace—and the Infanta ! "

Savoy withdrew, Margaret dignified and urbane, her mother furious, although she had been presented with a document guaranteeing Louis's marriage with her daughter if his Majesty did not find himself compelled to marry the Infanta of Spain " for the welfare of Christianity and my Kingdom."

The court returned to Paris while the Cardinal departed to meet Don Louis de Haro and embark upon a lengthy series of conferences on the Isle de Faisans. These preliminaries accomplished, France sent the Duc de Gramont to make a formal demand for the Infanta's hand, and his arrival created a sensation, for he rode into Madrid at full gallop followed by forty cavaliers.

While the ministers wrestled with each other in a series of twenty-four conferences, de Gramont reported on Marie-Thérèse as being the image of her aunt *la reine Anne*.

The Treaty of the Pyrenees was signed at last (Nov. 7, 1659) and Anne, writing to the Infanta, could subscribe herself " Good Mother and Aunt of your Majesty." She was writing to Mazarin too, letters that were to be published two hundred years later in the hope of throwing light on the mysterious connection that had existed between the two : " If I could show you my heart as plainly as I write on this paper, I am certain you would be content—or you must be the most ungrateful of men ! " [1]

Summer came before the courts of France and Spain arrived at their respective frontiers, and Louis XIV had a farewell interview with Marie Mancini en route : " You weep—and yet you are master ! " she said tauntingly.

[1] Published by M. Chéruel in the *Journal de l'Instruction Publique*, Oct. 1851.

Anne established her retinue at St. Jean-de-Luz.
The King of Spain was at San Sebastian. Marie-
Thérèse sent tender messages to her aunt, but Louis,
more precipitate, wrote to Marie-Thérèse as if she were
already betrothed to him ; the worthy bishop, to
whom the missive was entrusted for delivery, held it
back for propriety's sake, although he asked the
Infanta to give him a message for the King.

" What I say to the Queen, my Aunt, is intended for
the King," she answered with decorum.

Philip IV and his daughter now advanced to
Fontarabia and the marriage was celebrated by
proxy, Don Louis taking the place of the bridegroom, who waited across the river.

A few members of the French court had obtained
permission to be present and noted that the Infanta
said "yes" very modestly. They found her beautiful,
" or she would have been, had she been taller, but her
clothes are horrible ! "

On the following day Anne arrived at the neutral
ground of the Isle, accompanied by Monsieur, now
Duc d'Orléans, and entered the Conference Hall,
which had a gallery stretching into either country.
Two thrones had been erected in a central chamber,
one of which was technically in France and the other
in Spain, and here brother and sister met after a
separation of nearly forty-five years. Philip " bent
his head over Anne's hair."

The Infanta sank on her knees before the Queen-
Mother, and the Duc d'Orléans saluted his sister-in-
law from the correct distance of three feet ; no one
sat down, although the interview lasted for an hour
and a half. Even so etiquette was outraged for a
moment when Louis XIV (theoretically incognito)
looked through an open door to exchange a long
glance with blushing Marie-Thérèse.

He was shocked by the ugliness of her head-dress
and the " guard-infanta," a huge, semi-circular mon-
strosity with many hoops, but left " hoping it would

not be difficult to love her." She thought him " very gallant and most handsome " : Anne and Philip were highly elated.

" As things are we shall soon have grandchildren ! " said the King of Spain.

Next day Philip and Louis met officially and Marie-Thérèse passed into her mother's country. Everyone was tired, and Anne sent the young Queen into her own chamber to be unlaced from her tight-fitting, cherry-coloured robe, whereupon the modest Spanish maiden requested that all men should be excluded from the house.

Seeing her weariness, Louis suggested that she should sup in bed, but Marie-Thérèse refused, " so he took her by the hand and led her to Anne, who received her *en chemise.*" After supper the Infanta wrote a last message to her father, which she submitted for the King's inspection before despatching.

Early on the following morning all attended Mass, after which Marie-Thérèse was attired in French fashion for the first time and her attendants discovered that she had never before worn a *camisole.*

The final marriage ceremony occupied some hours. This concluded, the young Queen was escorted to the King's house and required to dine in public. Scarcely was the meal ended before the King desired to go to bed—and Marie-Thérèse wept.

" It is too soon ! " she sobbed. Comforted, and told that the King was waiting, she " sat herself upon a hassock and let herself be undressed without making any difficulty, saying : ' Presto ! Presto !—the King expects me ' . . . and so they went to bed with the blessing of the Queen their mother."

The journey back to the capital was a triumphal progress, and Louis insisted that his wife should always share his lodging, " even if it were only in a village."

An inquisitive courtier asked Marie-Thérèse if she

had never fallen in love before ; but she answered
with wide-eyed amazement : " How could I ?   There
were no Kings in Spain except my father."

Benedictions were showered upon the young couple
as they entered Paris, she in a golden carriage drawn
by six pale grey Danish horses, and *le Roi Soleil*
riding beside her on a magnificent Spanish bay.
Homage was offered while the pair sat on a throne
which had been erected at the Porte St. Antoine, and
when a white dove alighted on the Queen's head, the
populace was delighted, accepting the incident as an
augury of peace.

Racine composed his first verses in honour of the
auspicious entry and Queen Henrietta Maria viewed
the procession from a balcony.   Not far from her was
a Madame Scarron [1] (not yet known to fame) who
thought that Marie-Thérèse should be well satisfied
with such a husband.

Even *Parlement* was pleased and offered its thanks
to the Cardinal for the peace just concluded, of which
the royal bride was the visible sign.   He had his part
in the wedding entry ;   forty footmen ran before his
carriage and seventy-two gaily caparisoned baggage
mules followed it.

Fêtes and amusements suitable to a youthful court
became the order of the day until Mazarin's death in
the spring (1661) gave the supreme power into Louis's
hands.

The Cardinal had once told him that he might be
the most glorious King in history, since God had given
him the necessary qualities ;   it was for Louis to
employ them.   Now was his chance, and when
ministers came asking to whom reports were to be
rendered in the future, Louis XIV answered :
" A moi, messieurs."

Business of State now claimed *Le Grand Monarque*
for eight hours a day, and when he emerged from his

_____
[1] Later Madame de Maintenon.

cabinet Louis wanted amusement; this Marie-Thérèse, shy, gentle, devout and loving, could not give. Henrietta of England (now Duchesse d'Orléans) supplied the lack, and when she failed, her maids of honour, Louise de la Vallière and Mademoiselle La Motte-Houdancourt.

Marie-Thérèse's first child, *Le Grand Dauphin*, was born sixteen months after her wedding. Two daughters followed in the succeeding years, but both died when a month old, and Marie-Thérèse carried her grief to Anne, who lay so ill that she said there was not an inch of her body without pain.

" My troubles will be nothing, if God preserves to me my Mother! " said Marie-Thérèse. " If I lose her —what have I ? "

Hemlock was applied, but Anne became worse and cancer in an advanced form was discovered.

" God wills to punish me this way for having had too much vanity, and for loving the beauty of my body too well! " said the dying Queen.

Louis XIV lay on a mattress at the foot of his mother's bed, and Monsieur prayed beside her :

" Madame, you have loved me so much here below ! Love me still when you are in Heaven ! "

Marie-Thérèse was desolate indeed ; four months before Anne's death a courier had brought word of the death of her father, Philip IV of Spain (Sept. 1665). Since the articles of marriage had been so drawn that in the event of Spain's non-payment of Marie-Thérèse's almost impossibly large dowry her renunciation of succession rights would be void, Louis XIV now claimed Spanish territory in Flanders, and took the Queen with him to receive the keys from the various burgomasters. Louise de la Vallière was expecting her third child and could not follow the camp ; Madame de Montespan came in her stead.

" When I am thirty," Louis had once promised Marie-Thérèse, " I will stop playing the gallant."

Now she could only weep and pray between the births
of her short-lived children ; sometimes, driving out
with the King's two favourites, Marie-Thérèse would
catch a murmured recognition of " *les trois reines.*"

Once only was her position fully recognised. This
was when Louis appointed her Regent before starting
on his campaign into Flanders, saying : " C'est a peu
près le seul événement de sa vie ! "

As the years passed and the King's illegitimate
families increased, the Queen retired more and
more into the background, though she experienced a
flicker of happiness when, through the influence of
Madame de Maintenon (governess to Madame de
Montespan's children), Louis showed her slight attentions. " She so loves the King that if he speaks
kindly to her she is happy all the day ! " said a
watchful courtier.

But Marie-Thérèse's hold on life was slight, and she
made no struggle in her last illness.

" Voilà le premier chagrin qu'elle m'ait jamais
donné ! " said Louis XIV, turning from her death-bed.

A funeral oration was delivered by the Abbé
Bossuet at St. Denis, and a phrase used by him
remained long in the minds of the people—it was to
the effect that the whiteness of the Queen's skin was a
visible sign of the inward purity of her heart !

II

LOUIS XIV AND MADAME DE MAINTENON

"Qu'en pense votre Solidité?" (*Louis XIV.*)

" THE Queen is not to be pitied. She died like a saint,
and your Majesty now has a friend in Heaven who
will demand of God the pardon and the grace you
require. Reflect on this, Monseigneur, and be as
good a Christian as you are great a prince ! " So
wrote Madame de Maintenon to Louis XIV on the
death of Marie-Thérèse, and the *Grand Monarque*
turned towards the sympathiser.

Françoise d'Aubigné was born in a prison. At
sixteen years of age, her mother (a daughter of the
Governor) had been seduced by Constant d'Aubigné ;
she brought freedom to her husband as a wedding gift,
although he had been charged with the murder of his
wife and her lover, and had been imprisoned for debt
and counterfeiting.

Having no income on which to support a wife and
family, Monsieur d'Aubigné returned to find a temporary shelter in the *Conciergerie* about the time of the
birth of his daughter Françoise. Then a Huguenot
aunt took the unwanted child, also her two brothers,
while d'Aubigné tried to live by his wits and his wife
looked for work.

When Françoise was ten or eleven years old, her
father obtained a post in the West Indies, but after an
unsatisfactory year abroad the family returned as
penniless as before.

The same aunt came to the rescue, but someone
discovered that Françoise d'Aubigné, who had been

baptised into the Catholic faith, was being brought
up as a Huguenot, and she was removed from her
heretical surroundings by royal decree.

In her new home Françoise was sent out daily to
learn her lessons in the open air while guarding a flock
of turkeys ; the little girl was equipped with a velvet
mask to shield her complexion from the sun's rays.

Religious instruction was provided, but Françoise
refused to profit by it and had to be sent to a convent,
whence, still refusing conversion, she was returned to
her mother, who could not afford to keep her. A
second convent opened its doors to the obstinate
child, and here she embraced the Catholic religion ;
but the problem of her future was still acute, for no
one wanted this girl of seventeen. Then Paul Scarron,
playwright and satirist, offered a solution, and Françoise d'Aubigné chose marriage with him, rather than
the veil, although he was a " crippled, paralysed,
condensation of human misery." She was to be his
companion, hostess, secretary, and nurse (but not his
wife other than in name), and went to her wedding
in a borrowed gown. Scarron used to say that she
brought him " a pair of large eyes, a beautiful figure,
and four *louis d'or*."

The milieu into which the girl was now thrown
developed her intelligence, and soon Paul Scarron
found a delight in educating her. Their brilliant
circle widened ; now came Madame de Sévigné and
the Comte de Gramont, now Mademoiselle de Haute-
fort, the Queen's maid-of-honour ; and now the
famous beauty, Ninon de l'Enclos, who found Madame
Scarron " virtuous by conviction as well as by tempera-
ment :

" I tried to cure her, it was impossible ! . . . but
there—' Elle fut trop gauche pour l'amour ! ' "

Eight years passed swiftly, and when Scarron died,
his widow, now a cultured woman of twenty-five,
was destitute once more. Creditors seized everything, and Madame Scarron took refuge in the con-

vent that had sheltered her in her unhappy childhood. Here, owing to the efforts of friends who contrived to obtain a continuance of Scarron's pension, she lived happily and quietly, going only occasionally into the brilliant world to which her marriage had given her the *entrée*.

She watched the State procession of Louis XIV and his bride and heard the current court gossip—of the King's waning regard for his too devoted wife and of new beauties who found favour in royal eyes—La Vallière, Mademoiselle La Motte-Houdancourt, and now Athénée de Montespan, celebrated as the most beautiful woman in France.

Presently a woman of discretion was needed at court, and who could be better than Madame Scarron, now living in a backwater on her frugal pension? But to the amazement of the few in the secret the widow refused the offer which was made to her, nor would she yield to persuasion until made to realise that the request came from the King.

Le Grand Monarque must be obeyed. So Madame Scarron awaited the birth of Madame de Montespan's child and carried it off hidden in her cloak.

Other babies followed the first, and these too were given into her charge. When the King's secret leaked out, Madame Scarron found herself of sudden importance, and this was enhanced when Louis legitimised his children by royal edict. Now she took second place only to the *gouvernante* of the Dauphin.

The position was difficult, and more than once Madame Scarron tried to resign, despite her love for the little Duc du Maine ; but the Church had seen her value, and a hint that she had been placed at court to save the King's soul silenced her protests.

Marie-Angélique de Fontanges, one of the Duchesse d'Orléans's maids-of-honour, was now the reigning favourite, and Madame de Montespan left the court ;

but Madame Scarron had become Madame de Maintenon and Lady-of-the-Bedchamber to the Dauphine.
An amazed court discovered that the King had spent
three hours in her society ; men might whisper of
" Madame de Maintenant," but Louis XIV had found
a woman to whom he could give his confidence.

The Queen died, and he turned not to the bright
eyes of a new favourite, but to this woman who was
three years his senior, and had been the governess of
his illegitimate children.

There was no State marriage, merely a brief
ceremony at midnight in the presence of five people,
and Madame la Marquise de Maintenon took her place
by the King's side ; she was wife, if not Queen.

" Do not forget me before God," she wrote to her
Confessor.   Alas ! the good abbé was so impressed by
his penitent's exalted rank that he became too lenient
and had to be replaced by " a saint " who showed
himself uninfluenced by worldly honours.

Louis's gift to his bride was a château to which
could be transferred a group of little maidens who
were now housed in a barn where Madame de
Maintenon went daily to teach them their cate-
chism.

Le Grand Monarque had reached the culminating
point of his reign.   Statues of him were in course
of erection all over France, and an Academy of
Inscriptions was founded to compose devices for his
medals.   It was well that in the troubled years to
follow Madame de Maintenon could sit in her niche
across the room, busy with spinning wheel or tapestry,
while Louis worked with his ministers.

" La Religion prétendue réformée " had raised its
head once more, despite the efforts of the clergy and a
royal edict which had decreed the conversion of all
children reaching the age of seven years.

There were risings in various districts necessitating
the despatch of a regiment of dragoons, after which
tales of miraculous conversions reached the court,

" sometimes of whole towns by mutual consent."
This was something to thank God for, as Madame de
Maintenon felt, for she had been anxious as to the
effect of the dragoons ; indeed, she had ventured to
warn the King that conversion was better brought
about by persuasion than by severity. Louis's reply
shocked her :

" Madame, I fear that the indulgence you wish
shown to the Huguenots comes from a remaining
affection for your old religion ! " This when the
Bishop of Chartres had told her that God had placed
the King's salvation and the welfare of the Church in
her hands !

Madame de Maintenon could only pray that the
King's efforts would cover him with glory in the eyes
of God and men.

Louis XIV signed the Revocation of the Edict of
Nantes (Oct. 17, 1685), and followed it up by obliging
Victor Amadeus of Savoy to expel the Vaudois from
their valleys on the ground that Protestant neighbours
were undesirable.

A few days after the Edict was issued, Bossuet
delivered a sermon that met with wide approval :
" Heresy has fallen at a stroke . . . the deluded
flocks are returning ! Let our hearts overflow with
gratitude to our Most Christian King. . . . Let us
raise our acclamations to the skies ! "

But a wave of emigration swept the country and
with the fleeing Huguenots went both trade and
knowledge. Europe was aroused and France wit-
nessed the formation of the League of Augsburg.

While William of Orange invaded England and
Louis XIV welcomed fugitive James II and Mary of
Modena, Madame de Maintenon was occupied in con-
verting and marrying her relatives, also in carrying
forward the dearest dream of her heart in founding
St. Cyr, a convent to which might come poor, but
well-born, maidens, there to live in happiness and
safety till grown to womanhood, when, provided with

a dowry by the King, and a husband selected by herself, they could enter the world.

" Never Queen of France has undertaken such a work ! " exclaimed Louis, amazed at the grandeur of the conception, but he was fascinated. If she drew up a curriculum in which devotion had greater place than learning—" for too much reading is pernicious to our sex "—he added ribbons and laces to the uniform that had been designed for the demoiselles.

Private theatricals were to be permitted at St. Cyr, so Racine was commanded to produce a moral play without love interest, the result being *Esther*. King and court attended, and the excited debutantes prayed before they took the boards. The affair was a *succès fou*, with untoward results in the way of clandestine love affairs that had to be nipped in the bud, and Madame de Maintenon was driven to tighten the regulations and make the uniform less becoming.

St. Cyr was ready to accommodate Madame de Maintenon when Louis marched into Flanders (1691) to do battle with England, Holland, and the Germanic States.

" Mesdames, I leave you what is dearest to me on earth," said *Le Grand Monarque* to the good nuns.

Mons fell after a siege of fifteen days (sieges were Louis's *forte*), and Madame met the victorious King at Compiègne.

> " Grand Dieu, sauvez le Roi,
> Grand Dieu, vengez le Roi,
> Vive le Roi ! "

So sang the demoiselles, and Louis, greatly pleased, accorded to St. Cyr the honour of training eleven-year-old Marie-Adélaïde of Savoy, the wife of his grandson the Duc de Bourgogne, who was to be allowed to visit her once a fortnight. But the charming child so fascinated the King that she was soon fetched to court to become the centre of its pageantry.

" God give me strength to support the pleasures of
this life," prayed la Marquise. Sometimes on the
migrations of the royal group from palace to palace
(all made in full court dress without regard to the
weather) she would be so ill at starting that those
around her would not have been surprised to see her
arrive dead, but always Madame de Maintenon was
in her place when the King had need of her, ready to
answer his frequent appeals :

" Qu'en pense votre Solidité ? . . . Qu'en pense
la Raison ? "

She followed him, as did the whole court, on his
exhausting military campaigns,[1] till the Peace of
Ryswick (Sept. 1697) gave her relief.

If by this treaty Louis recognised William as King
of England and yielded his conquests in Spain and the
Netherlands, discreet propaganda presented the affair
in a satisfactory aspect. " The King gives peace to
Europe on the conditions he chooses to impose,"
wrote Dangeau in his *Journal*, and Louis turned to the
organising of a review at Compiègne where his courtesy to Madame de Maintenon was so noticeable as to
amaze more than one ambassador. But she was not
as happy as of yore, for the King was showing slack-
ness in fasting on saints' days and the new generation
growing up around her offended her sense of propriety :

" I find the women of to-day insupportable," she
wrote. " Their clothes are as foolish and immodest
as they themselves are coarse and lazy."

A new war cloud loomed when Charles II of Spain
died, having willed his throne to the Dauphin's second
son, the Duc d'Anjou, in the hope of saving his country
from partition. The Emperor Leopold and Louis XIV
were rival claimants, each having married one of
Philip IV's daughters.

[1] Louis XIV took an artist with him to paint his victories for pos-
terity.

A Council assembled in Madame de Maintenon's rooms, and after much discussion Louis decided to accept the crown for his grandson, despite a former treaty to which he had been a party.

"Messieurs, here is Philip V, King of Spain," he announced to the ambassadors. "The crown is his by right of birth,[1] by decree of the late sovereign, and by the unanimous wish of the nation."

"Il n'y a plus de Pyrénées!" exclaimed the Spanish minister in a famous phrase.

France confronted the Grand Alliance and the War of the Spanish Succession began with battles on land and sea while *le Roi Soleil* bent over the death-bed of James II and, in defiance of treaty obligations, gave recognition to his son as James III of England.

The English captured Gibraltar, Marlborough marched towards Blenheim, and the French people clamoured for bread.

Madame de Maintenon found no rest except at St. Cyr. Louis, now seventy years old, would often lock himself in her room and shed tears which he could not control; but even there he was not safe, for ministers frequently appeared bringing bad news, when Madame de Maintenon would retire into a corner to pray until she was required : " Sometimes I hear that all is going wrong; then my heart beats and I cannot sleep. . . . From six o'clock in the morning there is no breathing space ! "

Occasionally even the King noted Madame de Maintenon's exhaustion and would summon her women to put her to bed : " But all the time they are undressing me I know that the King is waiting with impatience ! "

At other times she would sit for hours, momentarily expecting a summons, and only the consolations of her Confessor gave her courage to endure. " Remember," he would tell her, " God will give you credit

---

[1] Marie-Thérèse's dowry had never been paid, nor was her renunciation of her right of succession ratified by the Cortes.

for all the time you spend doing nothing, awaiting the King." [1]

Blenheim was followed by Oudenarde and Malplaquet, and France became a huge hospital. St. Cyr was crowded with the daughters of officers killed in the war : " I hate the English as a nation," decided Madame de Maintenon. " I should not have believed myself capable of such wickedness, but it is true."

In a dark hour the Duchesse de Bourgogne gave birth to her second son,[2] and to add to the nation's misery a virulent epidemic of smallpox swept the country ; it attacked members of the court, and the Dauphin died.

France could struggle no longer : " There are occasions when it is necessary to know how to lose," wrote Louis XIV to his grandson on the Spanish throne, and the Congress of Utrecht began its deliberations (Jan. 12, 1712).

Madame de Maintenon found it still more difficult to answer to the King's demands, for the beloved Duchesse de Bourgogne died in her arms a week after the Duke's death. Their two children were baptised in haste, both being christened Louis by the King's orders, since the elder was evidently dying, and the court rang with the cry of poison, pointing at the Duc d'Orléans as the culprit, since he had studied chemistry.

Philip V was dangerously near the crown. Not till he issued a proclamation renouncing his rights of succession to the throne of France, and the Duc d'Orléans and the Duc de Berry made a similar pronouncement concerning Spain, did Europe cease to tremble.

The Cortes ratified Philip's decree and England sent a tactless request for a similar ceremony by the Estates-General, by which Louis felt himself insulted :

[1] Lavallée, *Lettres Historiques*, Vol. II, p. 454.
[2] The future Louis XV.

" The Estates in France have nothing to do with the question of the succession to the crown," he answered briefly : " L'Etat c'est moi ! " [1]

The Peace of Utrecht was signed at last (April 11, 1713), under which France made peace with England and Holland, ceded Nova Scotia, Newfoundland, and Hudson's Bay, and recognised the Protestant succession, while indignant Spain saw perfidious Albion established as a Mediterranean power.

Louis XIV had grown old. Preparing for the end, he elevated Madame de Montespan's sons (the Duc du Maine and the Comte de Toulouse) to the rank of Princes of the Blood, and nominated a Council of Regency for his great-grandson. Madame de Maintenon too was very frail :

" I do not know what God intends, leaving me, old as I am, at a court and tied to a prince who will never remain in one place," she complained, and feared that she would live to be a hundred.

" Madame, it would be to my great happiness," responded Louis.

The end was coming fast and the loyal wife, unacknowledged Queen of France (who was so much more queenly than many who had worn the crown), helped the King sort and burn his papers.

For thirty years her daily prayer had been the same : " Lord, grant me to gladden the King, to console him, to encourage him, to sadden him also when it must be for Thy glory. Cause me to hide from him nothing that he ought to know through me, and which no one else has the courage to tell him."

" I have always heard that it was difficult to die, but I do not find it so very terrible," Louis said thoughtfully, and summoned the child to whom the crown must descend.

" Relieve your people of excessive taxation as soon

[1] Voltaire's words, perhaps—but Louis's thought.

as you can.   Do that which I have had the misfortune
not to be able to do myself. . . . J'ai trop aimé la
guerre. . . .   Do not imitate me in this ! "

The little Dauphin was carried away, but Madame de
Maintenon remained, sitting almost invisible behind
the curtains of the bed, till the King lost conscious-
ness and her task was at an end.

" You may leave ; you can do no more," said her
Confessor.

" I want nothing but God and my children ! "
sobbed Madame la Marquise as she reached St. Cyr.
At last she could rest and pray undisturbed.

Of Louis she once said : " He loved me more than
anyone else, but at the same time he loved me only so
far as he was capable of loving, for men, when not
moved by passion, have little tenderness in their
friendship. . . .   Had it not been for my religion, I
do not think I could have remained at court."

For her the end came peacefully while the sorrowing
nuns knelt weeping at her door.

" In a few hours I shall have learnt many things,"
said Madame de Maintenon as she slipped into her
long sleep.

CHAPTER TWELVE
(LOUIS XV) 1715-1774

LOUIS XV AND MARIE LECZINSKA.

" C'est une sotte chose d'être reine ! "

LOUIS XV
(great-grandson of Louis XIV)

Born at Versailles	Feb. 15, 1710
Ascended . .	Sept. 1, 1715
Crowned at Rheims . .	Oct. 25, 1722
Attained legal majority	1723
Married at Fontainebleau .	1725
Died at Versailles	May 10, 1774

CONTEMPORARY SOVEREIGNS

ENGLAND : George I, II, and III.
SPAIN : Philip V, Ferdinand (VI) " the Wise," and Carlos III.

POPES

Clement XI, Innocent XIII, Benedict XIII, Clement XII, Benedict XIV, Clement XIII, and Clement XIV.

Descent

LOUIS XIV
|
LOUIS " LE GRAND DAUPHIN "
|
LOUIS DUC DE BOURGOGNE
m. MARIE-ADÉLAÏDE OF SAVOY
|
LOUIS XV

CONSORT
Descent

Stanislas, King of Poland and Duc de Lorraine
m. Catherine Opalinska
|
MARIE LECZINSKA

Born at Breslau .	June 23, 1703
Married . .	Sept. 5, 1725
Died at Versailles	June 24, 1768

Issue :

Louise-Elizabeth .	1727–59
Anne-Henriette .	1727–52
Marie-Louise .	1728–33
Louis le Dauphin .	1729–65
Duc d'Anjou .	1730–33
Marie-Adélaïde .	1732–1800
Victoire-Louise .	1733–99
Sophie-Philippine .	1734–82
Thérèse-Félicité .	1736–44
Louise-Marie .	1737–87

NOTE.—Marie-Adélaïde and Victoire-Louise lived through the French Revolution and into the Napoleonic era.

MARIE LECZINSKA.

LOUIS XV.

CHAPTER TWELVE

LOUIS XV (1715–1774)

At the birth of Louis, son of the Duc de Bourgogne, three lives stood between him and the throne of France ; two years later his elder brother, his father, and his grandfather had been swept away and this frail child was heir-presumptive.

" The Dauphin lives ! . . . The Dauphin still lives ! " said the people morning after morning, beset with fear that the child might die as suddenly as his parents. But his governess, Madame de Ventadour, watched the boy night and day, and guarded his food from all possibility of poison as carefully as she kept the little Prince from the attentions of the doctors, who would have bled him, as they had bled his elder brother, to death. Louis XV succeeded when he was five years old.

When the Governor of Paris carried the child King from his carriage and placed him among the cushions on the enormous *Lit de Justice* immediately after his accession, Madame de Ventadour knelt beside her charge and spoke in his name :

" Messieurs, the King has bidden you to assemble in order to make his wishes known ; his Chancellor will explain them."

Madame de Ventadour retained her post till Louis was seven years old, when she explained that he must pass into the hands of a governor, and he wept bitterly, despite her exhortations to be *sage*.

" It is impossible for me to be *sage, Maman*, if they take me away from you," sobbed the forlorn little

King who had lost both his parents in babyhood, but
his tears were of no avail.

The court assembled at the Tuileries to see him
disrobed and witness the excellent physical state in
which the child was transferred; he was then
dressed in entirely new clothes and presented to his
masculine attendants.

The Regent Philippe d'Orléans ruled the kingdom
while his great-nephew, the delicate, black-eyed, fair-
haired sovereign, learnt his lessons under the superin-
tendance of Cardinal Fleury; all France marvelled
at the child's cleverness when it was announced that
he could write, having mastered the art of calligraphy
in three hours.

When ten years old Louis XV began to attend the
meetings of the Regency Council, but speech was not
expected from him. A twelvemonth later, however,
he was called upon to approve a marriage that was
being arranged for him with the Infanta Anna-Maria-
Victoria, aged three years.

As a *quid pro quo* the Regent sent his two daughters
into Spain to marry the Prince of the Asturias and
Don Carlos.

Anna-Maria-Victoria arrived and proved to be a fair,
plump, pink-and-white baby. She drove through
Paris nursing her doll and sitting on Madame de
Ventadour's knee, and next morning Louis presented
his fiancée with a magnificent *poupée* valued at
20,000 livres. This so delighted the Infanta that
she volunteered to kiss all the ministers who came
to pay their first official visits to " the Queen of
France."

She was not old enough to appreciate the ensuing
fêtes through which Louis XV passed " avec un bien
mauvais visage," but the fireworks excited her, and she
kept plucking at the King's sleeve asking :

" Monsieur ! Monsieur ! Is it not beautiful ? "

" Oui," he answered morosely.

"Il m'a parlé!" cried Anna-Maria-Victoria. "Il m'a parlé!"

The child was installed in the State apartments at Versailles and remained there for three years, except for occasional sojourns at the Louvre. The Regent died and Louis XV attained his official majority, but all that befell the "Queen" was an attack of measles, which gave her an opportunity of showing that she intended to be an obedient wife, for she refused to be bled until a file of Guards brought an order from her "husband."

But history was to repeat itself. Two hundred and thirty years before another King of France had returned his bride [1] to her indignant father; now Louis XV was to rid himself of this incubus in the same simple fashion.

Anna-Maria-Victoria [2] was told that "papa wanted her" and sent off on her long journey to the frontier, for Louis was fifteen, France needed an heir to the throne, and the little Infanta was not yet seven years old.

Spain vowed that there was not enough blood in France to avenge the insult, and Philip V, crying that this was an "affront inouï," despatched the two French Princesses who had been accepted in exchange for Anna-Maria-Victoria in such haste that they had to await their escort at Bayonne; this though one of them had been Queen of Spain for six months.

The nation's first hope that Louis XV would develop into a great King had already vanished, for he would not devote more than an hour a day to State affairs, but at least he must marry. A list was compiled showing "L'État-général des Princesses de l'Europe qui ne sont pas mariées avec leurs noms, maison, âges et religion." [3]

Catholics, Calvinists, Lutherans, and members of

---

[1] Margaret of Austria.
[2] She was later to become Queen of Portugal.
[3] Archives Nationales, Monuments Historiques, Ff. 139–40.

the Greek Church found a place on the comprehensive record, as did all princesses ranging in age from twelve to twenty-five years, so it was possible to reduce it considerably. Forty-four princesses were set aside as too old, twenty-nine as too young, and ten as too poor, while the granddaughters of George I, if suitable in age, were considered dangerous in regard to religion. Three names now remained—the two young sisters of Monsieur le Duc de Bourbon, and Marie Leczinska, the twenty-two-year-old daughter of Stanislas, the deposed King of Poland, now subsisting in a small town in French Alsace on the uncertain bounty of divers courts.

The power behind the throne in France was a Madame de Prie, mistress of the Duc de Bourbon, and she, scanning the reduced list, decided upon the Polish demoiselle whose name had been added as an afterthought, together with a brief official memorandum : " There is nothing detrimental known concerning this family."

Surely so poor a princess would feel gratitude to the woman who selected her to be Queen of France ?

The King accepted the arrangement with equanimity although his grandfather, the King of Sardinia, entered a protest against the mésalliance and no Frenchman could pronounce Leczinska—" Quel nom terrible pour une reine de France ! "

Marie Leczinska had had unusual experiences for a princess, inasmuch as she had been lost on two occasions when her father had fled from his kingdom. The first time she was mislaid by two attendants, who each thought the other had the child, and was found lying peacefully in her cradle in the yard of an inn by the regiment of cavalry sent back to rescue her. On the second occasion a peasant woman hid her from possible enemies by bestowing her in an oven.

Now, according to the deputies sent to report upon her by Madame de Prie, Marie spent her days sitting between her mother and her grandmother absorbed in works of charity. She knew no cosmetics but fresh water in summer and snow in winter, and was a combination of all the virtues, if somewhat broad in figure.

> " On dit qu'elle est hideuse,
> Mais cela ne fait rien !
> Car elle est vertueuse
> Et très fille de bien ! "

So sang Paris, but presently a rumour spread that the Demoiselle Leczinska had webbed fingers and was both scrofulous and epileptic, so a medical commission started in haste for Wissembourg.

" We have had the honour to see her Royal Highness," wrote officialdom, " and have examined her figure, her arms, the colour of her face and her eyes. We now declare that she is well made and has no defect in hands or arms, all movements being free. She has healthy teeth, bright eyes (but at the same time gentle), and though her sedentary life and the long hours passed in church have given her some stiffness of the loins, this is dissipated by heat or friction and does not occur in summer ; her complexion is bright and natural, showing well-established health."

Madame de Prie was reassured and ordered some chemises as a gift for this Cinderella princess of her selection.

Meanwhile King Stanislas had received, and accepted, the offer for his daughter's hand. The problem of Marie's future had been his chief cause of anxiety since he had lost his throne ; indeed, he had once approached a mere count, hoping to secure a husband for his daughter, and trusting that the proffered honour would spur the young man to secure a dukedom, but the affair had fallen through, and now the father's natural excitement caused incoherence.

" On your knees to offer thanks to God ! " he cried, bursting into the little room where his mother, wife, and daughter sat busy with their needles,

" What ? are you again King of Poland ? " asked
Princess Marie as she obeyed the parental behest.

" Heaven has vouchsafed us a greater boon,"
answered Stanislas. " You are Queen of France ! "
His attitude was much that of the French pamphleteer
who wrote :

> " Notre roi vous épouse, et cent fois la journée
>   Vous devez bénir l'heure de votre destinée,
>   Contemplez la bassesse où vous avez été
>   Et du prince qui m'aime admirez la bonté,
>   Qui, de l'état obscur de simple demoiselle,
>   Sur le trône des lys par mon choix vous appelle ! . . ."

To Cardinal de Rohan, Bishop of Strasbourg, fell the
duty of presenting Louis's formal proposal to Marie
Leczinska, and her reply (as recorded) leaves no
doubt of her attitude, and the manner of her upbringing :

" I am penetrated with gratitude, Monseigneur, for
the honour done me by the King of France. My will
belongs to my parents, and their consent will be
mine."

After a proxy wedding, during which Marie fainted
once, " though only for form's sake," the bride started
on her journey to Fontainebleau through a sea of
mud, with thirty horses to drag her carriage out of the
ruts. Starving peasantry besought the Queen for
alms as she passed and towns offered loyal addresses.

" I am travelling in fairyland," Marie wrote to her
beloved father, " and these people say the prettiest
things in the world. Yesterday they told me that I
had all the virtues of an angel, to-day that the very
sight of me makes everyone happy. . . . To break
the spell I put my hand up to my head, and then,
dearest Papa, I find I am only she whom you love,
your Maruchna ! "

A mud-bespattered court met the traveller outside
Fontainebleau, where the marriage was celebrated
with magnificence and the Grand Almoner of France
delivered an oration describing Marie Leczinska as " a

virtuous and prudent woman made by God after His own heart."

Voltaire and Molière vied with each other in organising court festivities, and Queen Marie insisted on giving away all the jewels in her *corbeille*, saying : " It is the first time I have ever been able to make presents ! "

Louis XV showed himself delighted with this bride, who was seven years his senior, and amid such happiness as was now Marie's none but a very level-headed princess would have paid attention to the *bon conseil* Stanislas had written.

" Hearken, my daughter . . . Forget thy people and thy father's house. . . . Beware of flattery and prosperity, in which there lies the more danger in that it is practically unknown to you. . . ."[1]

There was joy at court when the Queen gave birth to twin princesses, but some murmuring when a third princess arrived within the year.

Louis was showing signs of boredom, but he escorted Marie on a first visit to Paris (Fontainebleau and Versailles had been her residences for three years) in order that she might pray at Notre-Dame for the gift of a Dauphin, who duly arrived, closely followed by a brother.

" Un second fils est une grande assurance pour la tranquillité du royaume," said Barbier.

Marie Leczinska was more fortunate than most Queens, for marriage had not separated her from her own people. Stanislas, his mother, and his wife were provided with accommodation at the Château Chambon (arriving the day following their daughter's wedding), and the exiled King watched Marie's fast-increasing family with fond approval.

The Queen would have been happier if she had been able to keep her children under her own roof, but after the birth of her eighth little daughter, Cardinal

[1] Archives des Affaires Étrangères.

Fleury decided that so many princesses cumbered the palace, besides being an expense to the nation, so all were ordered away to the Abbey of Fontévrault. One child was reprieved; the others, even to the baby of twelve months, were carried off.

Marie seems to have acquiesced, and was overcome by the King's kindness when he had the children's portraits painted for her a few years later.

" The two eldest are really beautiful, but I have never seen anything so agreeable as the little one," she commented.

Marie Leczinska who gave the nation ten children in as many years was unfortunate enough to provide France with one surviving son. With the new-born " Madame Dernière " in her arms Marie protested that she would go through it all again to give France another Duc d'Anjou; but she was thirty-five, and Louis had wearied of her charms.

Three sisters had stirred the dormant strain of gallantry in Louis XV, and now round the skirts of one clung a stalwart boy known to the court as *le demi-Louis*.

Marie had lost the near support of her father, for Stanislas was striving to recapture his throne, and had taken the field wearing a cockade which had been pinned upon his breast by his daughter; if he failed in regard to Poland, he secured Lorraine by diplomacy, so providing a rich dower for the erstwhile dowerless Queen of France.

Another war (Austrian Succession, 1740–8) obliged Louis to take up arms in person. Marie begged to be allowed to follow his fortunes, but met with refusal on the ground of expense, though a *petite maîtresse* drove off next day, and half the Queen's ladies-in-waiting applied for leave of absence in order that they might find a place in the train of the reigning *belle dame*.

" The King is fighting and the Queen is praying," said the approving people.

Marie Leczinska made her toilet, went to Mass, indulged in " serious reading," practised various musical instruments, paid an occasional visit to St. Cyr, and strove to live up to her favourite maxim, which was never to reflect more on the faults of those around her than on their virtues.

News of the King's progress reached Versailles at intervals. It was known that Madame de la Tour-nelle had been created Duchesse de Châteauroux ; that Courtrai was taken, and Menin and Ypres were being besieged. Then in the height of summer (Aug. 1744) Louis reached Metz and fell dangerously ill.

Queen and Dauphin started for the front. Messen-gers turned the Prince back before he reached Verdun, but Marie was more fortunate ; she arrived at Metz to find that though the King's life was in danger, the Bishop of Soissons would not administer the sacra-ments so long as the Duchesse de Châteauroux remained by the royal bedside.

When the Church triumphed, Marie took the place vacated by the Duchess and volunteered full forgive-ness for the King's misdeeds. When the patient showed signs of recovery she decked herself in a rose-coloured gown and announced herself as the happiest of women.

A courier carried the good news to Paris and a thankful people gave him a suffocating welcome. They kissed the messenger, likewise his horse, and even his boots as they tore him from the saddle.

The King followed, with the Queen two months later, to be hailed as Louis *le Bien-Aimé*. But he was already regretting his enforced repentance, and very soon the unyielding Bishop of Soissons was retired to his diocese and the Duchesse de Châteauroux returned to court ; when she died almost immediately, a startled King saw it as a direct act of divine judg-ment.

A feverish contest now ensued among the ladies of the court, for all knew that the Queen could never fill the place left vacant by the dead favourite ; but her successor was to be taken from another sphere.

Five years before the King's eldest daughter had been sent to Spain as a peace-offering for the insulting return of the Infanta Anna-Maria-Victoria, and now in the hope of removing any remaining bitterness France decided to accept the discarded Infanta's half-sister, Maria-Raphaella, as a bride for the Dauphin. At the ensuing wedding ball Louis's attention was caught by Antoinette Poisson, once the daughter of a butcher, now wife of a minor official, soon to be the Marquise de Pompadour by the King's favour.

But the war of the Austrian Succession had not been brought to its conclusion, and Louis XV went to battle once more, taking the Dauphin with him to Fontenoy, where the Duke of Cumberland commanded the allied Anglo-Hanoverian Dutch and Austrian troops, and the Maréchal de Saxe had himself carried along the front in a litter, since dropsy prevented any other means of locomotion.

When the signal for battle was given, an English officer of the Guards stepped forward to meet a Grenadier :

" Gentlemen of the French Guards, fire ! " cried the courteous English soldier.

" Mais non, milord," replied the other with a bow. " *We never fire first.*" Whereupon each saluted the other and returned to his own side, a hundred guns opened fire, and so began the Battle of Fontenoy (May 11, 1745). Never since the Black Prince confronted the French at Poitiers, four hundred years before, had King and Dauphin taken the field together.

A drum-head served as a table when the Dauphin wrote to Marie Leczinska : " My dear Mama, I congratulate you most heartily on the victory just gained by the King. He is well, thank God, and so am I who had the honour to accompany him. I will write

to you again this evening or to-morrow, and I finish
by assuring you of my love and respect. I beg you
to embrace my wife and sisters."

Louis wrote also, and to Madame de Pompadour
as well as to his wife, signing his letters with his
favourite motto : " Discreet and faithful."

The court welcomed the victorious warriors, and
Madame de Pompadour employed Voltaire to write
an opera in which she could play a leading part ; but
the people murmured because the cessation of war
had brought no decrease of taxation, and when the
King next went from Versailles to Compiègne he had
a new road made, so that he could avoid the capital.
Paris dubbed it " Le Chemin de la Révolte."

The wife to whom the Dauphin had sent his love
after the battle of Fontenoy died in childbed, and now
the King was planning a second marriage for his
unconscious son. Marie-Josephe of Saxony was
suggested as a suitable bride by her uncle, the Maréchal
de Saxe, who undertook to forward the matter.

"Madame," he wrote to her mother with bluff
soldierly directness, " yesterday the Most Christian
King sent for me that he might request your Majesty
for the hand of the Princess Marie-Josephe for Monseigneur le Dauphin. I flatter myself that this
proposal will not displease either the Princess or your
Majesty, for in truth the crown of France is a fine
morsel, and the Prince who will wear it some day is
fine also. . . . Nor need the Princess fear boredom
while waiting, for the kingly father-in-law is charming."

Marie-Josephe arrived in trepidation, for her father
was that Augustus who had driven Stanislas Leczinski
from his Polish throne, but Queen Marie welcomed the
anxious girl and saw to it that she had some rest after
the first lengthy court ceremony, when, stiff in jewels
and cloth-of-gold (her skirt alone was sixty pounds in
weight), she had to stand for nearly nine hours.

15

The nuptial benediction and the ceremonial putting to bed followed four days later.

"The Dauphin covered his face, but the Princess was not at all confused," said Maréchal de Saxe, who had official place beside Marie-Josephe's pillow. Indeed, she talked to him all the time, with charming ease, and he thought the blessing of the marriage bed and the youthfulness of the Princess surrounded by praying priests "all very touching and thought-provoking." [1]

The Treaty of Aix-la-Chapelle (Oct. 30, 1748) and the subsequent proclamation of peace (Feb. 1749)

[1] Marie-Josephe came with no illusions as to her own importance. When her husband fell ill, she nursed him with devotion and would not spare herself when the doctors warned her of danger. "If the Dauphin lives, what else matters? France can always get another Dauphine should I die." Of her seven children three were to become Kings of France and one Queen of Sardinia.

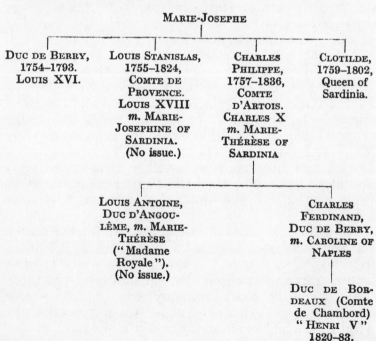

MARIE-JOSEPHE

| DUC DE BERRY, 1754–1793. LOUIS XVI. | LOUIS STANISLAS, 1755–1824, COMTE DE PROVENCE. LOUIS XVIII m. MARIE-JOSEPHINE OF SARDINIA. (No issue.) | CHARLES PHILIPPE, 1757–1836, COMTE D'ARTOIS. CHARLES X m. MARIE-THÉRÈSE OF SARDINIA | CLOTILDE, 1759–1802, Queen of Sardinia. |

LOUIS ANTOINE, DUC D'ANGOULÊME, m. MARIE-THÉRÈSE ("Madame Royale"). (No issue.)

CHARLES FERDINAND, DUC DE BERRY, m. CAROLINE OF NAPLES

DUC DE BORDEAUX (Comte de Chambord) "HENRI V" 1820–83.

took place before the birth of the first grandchild, but the impoverished people cried to Marie-Josephe for bread when she drove to her churching at Notre-Dame. Louis XV was no longer the adored of his people and Madame de Pompadour's white hands served the Queen in the intervals of dispensing patronage.

Louis had sent notice of the new appointment in writing, and Marie gave him a brief answer: " Sire, I have a King in Heaven who gives me strength to endure my troubles, and a King upon earth whom I shall always obey." Long since she had decided, " C'est une sotte chose d'être reine ! "

Peace was hardly more enduring abroad than at court. In France armies were soon to march in every direction, while English and French clashed alike in India and in Canada, where Wolfe met Montcalm on the Plains of Abraham, till, exhausted by ten years of intermittent war, the world watched the signing of the Peace of Paris (Feb. 10, 1763) and the Treaty of Hubertsburg (Feb. 13, 1763). By the one France relinquished her vast Canadian territories; by the other, if continental affairs were settled, she was left isolated, as was the King a year later by the death of Madame de Pompadour.

He had tired of her, but was still in her toils, for she had saved him trouble, and now he drifted like a rudderless vessel, though he watched the passing of her funeral cortège without visible emotion :

" Madame la Marquise has bad weather for her last journey," was his brief comment as her coffin was carried out into a storm.

Within a month Marie Leczinska was shocked to think " that she who is now no more is as completely forgotten as if she had never existed."

A greater tragedy was the death of the Dauphin, and, shaken by the loss of her son, Marie aged suddenly when Stanislas, now eighty-nine, fell asleep in dangerous proximity to a fire and the dressing-gown which was her last gift to him proved inflammable; help came too late to save the King.

There was no one left to love Marie Leczinska. Who but her father had counted even her tears as " jewels of infinite value " ? So she died gladly two years later.

Louis XV paid his Queen a last visit as she lay dead ; perhaps he remembered the bride who had come to him in a fervour of gratitude, for he kissed her brow.

In the stars it was written that Marie Leczinska was to be the last Queen of France to die while still upon the throne.

Soon Paris had a new song:

> " Quelle merveille !
> Une fille de rien—
> Une fille de rien,
> Quelle merveille !
> Donne au Roi de l'amour
> Est à la Cour ! "

It was true. Within three months of the Queen's death Madame de Pompadour's successor was in residence. Her liveries were magnificent, and on Sundays she was to be seen at Mass in the chapel reserved for royalty.

The new beauty was Jeanne Bécu, aged twenty-five, the illegitimate daughter of a monk (so it was whispered) and a woman who had been cook in the house of a famous *demi-mondaine*. Jeanne's childhood had been passed in the seclusion of " a refuge for girls in danger of going astray." Immediately she emerged her troubles began. No sooner did the mother secure a situation for her daughter than Jeanne's cornflower-blue eyes, rose-leaf complexion, and golden curls were her undoing, and irate parents dismissed her.

At last the girl caught the attention of Comte Jean du Barry and found her destiny. His training pre-

pared her for Versailles, the King saw her, and in a
bound this daughter of joy reached the highest rank
of her profession.

"She makes me forget that I am sixty," said Louis
XV, and turned a deaf ear to suggestions that he
should marry again, though the sister of Marie-
Antoinette (who was then being considered as a
possible bride for his grandson) was suggested as being
eminently suitable.   His only concession to propriety
was to arrange for the marriage of "Mademoiselle
l'Ange" to a brother, produced for the purpose by the
resourceful Comte Jean, since the King's mistress
must have a husband.

Madame de Pompadour had reigned for over thirty
years ; Madame du Barry was to rule the King for
six.

When Louis was stricken with smallpox she shared
the duty of nursing him with his frightened daughters,
withdrawing only when it was necessary for the King
to make his last confession.   After thirty years of
neglect it occupied him seventeen minutes.

Crowds thronged the park outside the palace and
crowds struggled for the right of entry to the death
chamber, wherein six doctors, five surgeons, and three
apothecaries felt the King's pulse and examined his
tongue individually and hourly.

"Messieurs," announced the Grand Almoner to the
waiting crowd, "his Majesty desires me to tell you
that he asks God to pardon him for his offences
against Heaven and the scandal he has caused his
people."

"I governed and administered badly because I had
little talent and was ill-advised," said the dying King,
summarising his career.

Two days later his dead body was carried away from
Versailles without ceremony.

"Voilà le plaisir des dames ! " shouted a ribald
group as Louis *le Bien-Aimé* passed in his coffin.

CHAPTER THIRTEEN
LOUIS XVI (1774–1793)

LOUIS XVI AND MARIE-ANTOINETTE

" They have deprived me of all except my heart ! "
(MARIE-ANTOINETTE.)

LOUIS XVI
(grandson of Louis XV)

Born at Versailles . Aug. 23, 1754
Married at Versailles May 16, 1770
Ascended . . May 10, 1774
Guillotined . . Jan. 21, 1793

CONTEMPORARY SOVEREIGNS
ENGLAND : George III.
SPAIN : Carlos III and IV.

POPES
Clement XIV and Pius VI.

Descent
LOUIS XV
|
LOUIS " LE DAUPHIN "
m. MARIE-JOSEPHE OF SAXONY
|
LOUIS XVI

CONSORT
Descent
Empress Maria-Theresa of Austria
m. Francis of Lorraine
|
MARIE-ANTOINETTE

Born at Vienna . Nov. 2, 1755
Married . . May 16, 1770
Guillotined . Oct. 16, 1793

Issue :
   Marie - Thérèse
   Charlotte (" Mme
   Royale ") . 1778–1851
   Louis Joseph Xavier
   (first Dauphin) . 1781–89
   Louis Charles (Duc
   de Normandie,
   and second
   Dauphin) . . 1785–95 (?)
   Sophie Hélène Bea-
   trice . . 1786–7

LOUIS XVI, MARIE-ANTOINETTE, AND THEIR CHILDREN.

CHAPTER THIRTEEN

LOUIS XVI (1774–1793)

" WE are too young to reign ! " cried Louis XVI when
a rush of hurrying feet down the wide corridors of
Versailles told him that Louis XV was dead and that
loyal courtiers were hastening to offer suitable
congratulations. The new sovereigns were discovered
kneeling hand in hand, overcome by a sense of their
own ignorance. In three months' time Louis would
be twenty years old ; Marie-Antoinette was eighteen.

It was four years since Austria's need of an ally
had sent the child to wed the heir-apparent to the
throne of France.

In the intervals of conducting military campaigns
and consolidating her claims to the Austrian crown,
the Empress Maria-Theresa had sixteen children.
Marie-Antoinette was the ninth, and suitability in age
decided her fate. Portraits were exchanged, and the
busy mother engaged two French actors in order that
the future Queen of France might learn to speak the
language of the country which was to be hers. Unfortunately, one of these men happened to be notorious, so scandalised France made representations to
the Empress, the actors were dismissed, and Maria-
Theresa sent an urgent request that Mercy-Argenteau,
Austrian Minister at the French Court, and Choiseul,
the King's Minister, would bend their decorous minds
to the engaging of a Confessor, and also of a skilled
hairdresser of unblemished reputation : there must be
no further mistakes in connection with the entourage
of the young archduchess.

Between the arrival of the Abbé de Vermond and the coiffeur, and the proxy wedding when Marie-Antoinette knelt to make her marriage vows beside her mother, she learnt to wear French garments and turn graceful French phrases. Perhaps her new position went to the head of this light-hearted duchess, for when she wrote a duty letter to her future grandfather-in-law the Empress was constrained to add a postscript : " She has the best will in the world, but she is so young ! Pray forgive my daughter if she is sometimes a little giddy and careless."

Marie-Antoinette renounced her rights of succession to the Austrian throne and paid farewell visits to the tombs of her ancestors, while Maria-Theresa drew up a paper of instructions for the Dauphine's guidance. She was to begin each day well, to pray often and read much—but nothing without asking her Confessor's permission—and every month she must memorise a new Rule of Conduct.

As she valued her happiness, she should refrain from listening to gossip. Above all, Marie-Antoinette must remember that a wife's first duty was to obey her husband and minister to his pleasure ; she must ever show herself willing, gentle, and amusing.

" Be so good that the French people will say I have sent them an angel ! " besought the anxious Empress as her little daughter started on the great adventure.

Deeds of exchange were executed at the frontier, and in a pavilion built for the purpose on an island in the Rhine, the Dauphine was handed to three French commissioners, who immediately resigned their charge to her ladies in order that she might be divested of every article of attire, and reclad in genuinely French garments ; not even a garter of foreign origin must be worn by the Dauphine of France. A smiling lady-in-waiting and the chief tirewomen accepted the relinquished apparel as their lawful perquisites.

Sixty travelling carriages awaited the new Princess and her train at Strasbourg, where oxen were roasted whole in the streets, fountains spouted wine, and bells rang as the people shouted their welcome to the charming bride.

" From to-day, I understand nothing but French ! " said Marie-Antoinette, and was ready with another gracious speech when Choiseul met her a few leagues from Compiègne, for had he not been one of the instruments employed to bring about this fine marriage ?

" I shall never forget, Monsieur, that it is to you I owe my happiness," said Marie-Antoinette.

All the royal family awaited her arrival in the shade of the forest, and, if the Dauphin hung aloof, his grandfather was delighted with the graceful child who knelt asking his blessing, and Versailles rained flowers upon her when she went to her official wedding. Even the Dauphin, although he had departed on a hunting expedition two days after his marriage, soon began to fall under Marie-Antoinette's charm.

" My dear husband is very much altered and all for the better," she wrote to her mother in unconscious revelation.   The Dauphine's letters were oddly childish, and often she would describe a donkey ride as lengthily as some important event ; already Comtesse de Noailles, her principal lady-in-waiting, had been christened " Madame Étiquette."

The court to which the young Princess had come would have presented difficulties to one older and wiser than Marie-Antoinette.   Three of her aunts by marriage, Mesdames Adélaïde, Victoire, and Sophie, watched her every action, a fourth, Louise, a Carmelite nun, was often at St. Cyr, while within two years of Marie-Antoinette's own marriage the Dauphin's brothers, the Comte de Provence and the Comte d'Artois, brought home sister-brides, princesses of Savoy and great-great-grand-daughters of Princess Henrietta Anne, Duchesse d'Orléans.

The Comtesse de Provence could be dismissed in a sentence, according to current opinion, since the only good thing about her was a pair of fine eyes, but the

Comtesse d'Artois,[1] though very small, had "a fine complexion and a tolerably pleasing face, though one not remarkable for anything except the length of her nose."

The Dauphin's sisters were also of the court circle, but these two were younger than Marie-Antoinette. More important was Madame du Barry, whose function, it appeared, was " to amuse the King."

" Then I declare myself her rival ! " exclaimed the Dauphine, but found herself no match for the woman whose origin was so very different from her own.

With sophistication came knowledge, and presently ever-watchful Mercy-Argenteau was compelled to invoke the authority of the Empress Maria-Theresa, for Marie-Antoinette persisted in ignoring the King's favourite, and the King's annoyance was obvious.

"Madame du Barry is stupid and impertinent," argued the Dauphine, "and it is shocking to see her influence over his Majesty."

" . . . The Antoinette of twelve or thirteen years of age knew how to receive her company very prettily, and say something polite and gracious to everyone," wrote the Empress urgently. " Is the Dauphine to fail with a simple private person ? " One little sentence was all that was required of her, and that, not to oblige the lady, but to please the King !

Marie-Antoinette responded that one little sentence would never content the du Barry, but pressure continued, so one day, when the Comtesse curtsied low, the Dauphine spoke :

" There are a great many people at Versailles to-day ! " If not in the most tactful vein, the speech delighted Louis XV, the du Barry, and the Dauphin (though the censorious aunts were dismayed), and Marie-Antoinette claimed her reward.

---

[1] The Municipality of Paris announced that it would provide free marriages for a hundred poor girls in honour of the Comte's wedding. One presented herself *toute seule*, and, being asked for her bridegroom, answered : " Mais, je croyais que la ville fournissait tout ! "

In the three years since her marriage she had been
to Paris but once, and that incognito to enjoy a
masquerade ball. Now she pleaded to be allowed to
enter in State, and royal assent was given.

" Mon Dieu ! Quelle foule ! " cried the young
Dauphine as she stood at a window in the Tuileries.

" Madame, with all due respect to Monseigneur le
Dauphin, two hundred thousand lovers are before
you," came the ready answer, and Marie-Antoinette
drove back to Versailles to describe the stupendous
scene to the King.

" Your Majesty must be greatly beloved in Paris,
for all were so very kind to us," she told him. Truly,
the lessons in the making of pretty speeches had not
been forgotten.

But such days were rare. For the most part life at
court was boring, with its endless etiquette and strict
rules from the moment when a slipper bath was rolled
into Marie-Antoinette's apartment and she was put
into it, carefully buttoned into a " long gown of
English flannel." Following the bath came breakfast, and the Valet of the Wardrobe with a large book
containing patterns of all her gowns.[1] The Dauphine
would make a selection by sticking pins into the
pattern of the dress she desired, and the *femme de
chambre* then returned the book to the valet, who
carried it to the wardrobe, where the tirewomen
placed the necessary garments in a basket and summoned the Porter of the Wardrobe to carry the *prête du
jour* to the Dauphine's apartment, as at night he
would carry another covered basket containing her
nightgown and nightcap.

After a preliminary dressing, Marie-Antoinette
visited the aunts, and then put herself into the hands
of her hairdresser, who plied his art under the eyes of

[1] When Queen, Marie-Antoinette had " 12 full dresses, 12 undresses,
and 12 rich hooped petticoats every winter and summer, with as many
more for spring, though these were required to serve her for the succeeding winter before being discarded." (MADAME CAMPAN.)

those honoured by the *entrée*.   Then came Mass and
dinner in public with the Dauphin, when both would
eat fast to get the meal over, so that he could escape
to his hunting, but Marie-Antoinette would be required
to visit the aunts again as a prelude to a walk or drive.

There were letters to answer, for the Empress wrote
frequently and required a monthly record of her
daughter's readings and occupations ; lectures delivered by Mercy-Argenteau, who was as eager as his
predecessor, Kaunitz, that the Dauphine should
remember her duty towards Austria ; and a vest she
was making for the King : " It is dull work," complained Marie-Antoinette, " *mais avec l'aide du bon
Dieu*, it will be finished one day ! "   A few hours at
the card table ended the long day, and the Dauphine
was ready for bed at 11 p.m.

This was the routine for the first four years Marie-
Antoinette spent at the French court.   Then came
the accession of Louis XVI.

" I will promise to make as few mistakes as
possible," murmured the young Queen, stirred to
emotion.

It was said that the new King loved goodness,
justice, peace, and economy, and when he renounced
the accession grant in favour of the poor, and Marie-
Antoinette followed his example by declining the
customary tribute, heaven on earth was anticipated.

" Vive le Roi ! Vive la Reine ! " cried the people,
watching their sovereigns walking in the Bois de
Boulogne or eating strawberries and cream at La
Muette, and acclamations of delight were loud when
Marie-Antoinette sprang from her horse, on meeting
the King, to fling herself into his arms, " whereupon
he gave her two sound kisses ! "

But even before the coronation there was some
decrease of popularity, for corn was scarce and many
people disapproved of certain changes in the Ministry.

It was not customary for Queens of France to share

coronation honours, so though Marie-Antoinette went to Rheims, her place was in a tribune with the ladies of the court ; but first she stood in the street " like an ordinary person " to watch the King's state entry.

The ceremony began at 6 a.m., when the ecclesiastics in full canonicals, and the peers in gold and purple, marched to the house where the King waited.

The Chanter struck the door with his bâton and the Grand Chamberlain asked the customary questions :

" What do you require ? " came the answer.

" We ask for our King."

" The King sleeps ! "

The Chanter struck again, and even a third time, only to receive the same answer : " The King sleeps ! " But then came a cry from the Lords Spiritual : " We demand Louis XVI, whom God has given us for King ! " and instantly the door was opened.

Wrapped in a crimson robe and with a plumed cap agleam with diamonds, Louis lay on a State bed awaiting his subjects. The bishops advanced, and having offered a short prayer escorted his Majesty through a covered gallery into the cathedral, arriving simultaneously with the Grand Prior of the Abbey of St. Remi, who had come mounted on a white horse and escorted by four knights known as the hostages of the Holy Ampulla, each of whom had sworn to risk his life, if need be, in defence of the phial of sacred oil which was carried by the Grand Prior. With the delivery of the phial to the Archbishop began the actual ceremony of the coronation (June 11, 1775).

Louis XVI took the oaths, received the sword of Charlemagne, prostrated himself before the High Altar, and knelt to receive the Seven Anointings. . . . " May he humble the proud . . . May he be a lesson for the rich . . . May he be charitable towards the poor . . . May he be a peacemaker among nations ! " prayed the Archbishop, and Louis seated himself upon

the throne.   Then came a symbolic freeing of birds,
and the great doors were flung open to admit a rush of
people.

"Vive le Roi !   Vive le Roi ! . . ."

That evening King and Queen walked through the
streets without guards and Marie-Antoinette smiled
upon those who were too timid to approach the King
they revered.

"It is evident that when the poor people are so
good to us we should do all we can for their happiness,"
she wrote to her mother.   " I shall never forget this
day ! "

A youthful court gathered around this " petite
reine de vingt ans," who looked surprised if anyone
over the age of thirty ventured to appear at her
parties, and if the etiquette of the toilet could not be
abridged (and she was compelled to stand shivering
while her garments were passed from hand to hand,
according to the rank of those in attendance), Marie-
Antoinette broke her bonds in other directions.

There were theatre parties, balls, races to attend,
sleighing excursions, and masquerades in Paris, when
often the pleasure-loving Comte d'Artois would attend
her, rather than the bored King, who cared only for
hunting.   And there was a new interest, too, in the
pulling of political strings.

The Duc de Choiseul had been dismissed under the
du Barry *régime*, and now Marie-Antoinette strove to
influence the King in favour of the ex-Minister.   If
she failed in this, she saw to it that Madame du Barry
had no longer an *entrée* at court : " The creature has
been put into a convent, and everything that bears
her shameful name is banished ! " she wrote, in
triumph.[1]

---

[1] Fourteen years later Madame du Barry was to offer all her possessions to the stricken royal family.   Later still the ci-devant courtesan
suffered death on the guillotine, charged with having assisted the
émigrés.

France slipped towards bankruptcy while the King kept his careful hunting records and changed his ministers. The people cried for cheaper bread, the Comtesse d'Artois gave birth to a child, and the *poissardes* (those women of the fish markets who claimed special privileges) came swarming to Versailles. They followed the Queen back to her own apartments after the event, crying that she was failing in her duty towards France, in that she had given the nation no heir.

" It is not my fault ! Indeed, it is not my fault ! " Marie-Antoinette protested to the mother who had lectured her more than once on the subject.

Seeking fresh interests, the Queen gave full reign to her passion for jewels, and appeared at a fancy-dress ball in the character of Gabrielle d'Estrées so gorgeously arrayed that an outcry arose. People protested that " the Austrian " was ruining France by her evil example, nor was judgment kindlier when Marie-Antoinette spent long nights at the faro table, though she would carry round a collecting box and demand tribute *pour les pauvres*, and a curé waited at the door to carry off the booty. When her brother the Emperor Joseph visited the Château, he decided that the French court was little better than a gambling hell.

His visit had one good effect, for he gave Louis XVI some useful advice, and shortly after Joseph's departure the King could write to him : " J'espère que l'année prochaine ne se passera pas sans vous avoir donné un neveu, ou une nièce."

The intervening months were critical for France. News of an insurrection in America had reached her some time before,[1] and interest had been heightened by the arrival of a trio of Americans, chief among whom was Benjamin Franklin, in sober brown suit

---

[1] The Declaration of Independence, which proclaimed the birth of the United States of America (July 4, 1776), was received with enthusiasm in Europe, where it was believed that the young Republic would " soon cut England's coxcomb."

16

and unpowdered hair. He was mobbed by admiring women, who presented him with a laurel wreath, and Maximilien Robespierre, a rising young lawyer, dedicated one of his speeches to this hero from the New World. But even Franklin [1] could not extract a declaration of future action from the King, though he created immense enthusiasm among fire-eating young Frenchmen, who hastened to volunteer for oversea service.

The nineteen-year-old Marquis de Lafayette fitted out a frigate and slipped off under the noses of two British cruisers, and Jean Axel, Comte de Fersen (who had lost his heart to Marie-Antoinette at first sight of "this prettiest and sweetest of princesses"), joined Rochambeau's expedition while the court buzzed with excitement.

Lord Stormont, the watchful English Ambassador, sent off frequent confidential reports :

" The open manner in which everybody now talks of the probability of a rupture with Great Britain is remarked by the most careless observer, and certainly deserves mention. After all that we have seen of the duplicity of the courts of France and Spain, there is nothing insidious that may not be justly expected from them. . . . Jan. 1778."

" . . . As I cannot alter the falsehood and perfidy of this court, my principal object must be to disclose it more and more, and to this part of my duty I direct my constant attention. . . ."

" Paris is in such a ferment as I never remember to have seen. . . . I am surrounded by spies."

" . . . A man of some eminence in this country, but totally devoid of principle, is planning to give

[1] " Ça ira," a phrase attributed to Franklin and used by him in connection with the advancement of liberty in America, was to be taken as the *motif* for one of the most famous songs of the French Revolution.

England a foul blow by firing all her docks. . . .
Feb. 1778." [1]

At a court ball Lord Stormont had watched the
Comte de Provence deliver a whispered message to the
Queen, and her obvious excitement had led him to
the unwelcome conclusion that France had determined
to lend open aid to the " rebels." His prescience was
justified, and with England and France on the verge
of war, the ambassador was ordered to withdraw
" without taking leave."

But to Marie-Antoinette the year held an event of
yet greater importance in the birth of her first child.

As the date approached, prayers were offered up
throughout France, and when the Princes of the
Blood and State officials took up their allotted
positions in the Queen's ante-chamber, all Versailles
flocked to the palace, determined to avail itself of the
right of public entry.

" La reine va s'accoucher ! " came the long-awaited
announcement, and a mighty rush broke resistance
and would have thrown the tall screens on to the
Queen's bed, if they had not been securely tied.

The heat was intense, citizens fought for footholds
on the chairs and tables, and *gamins* climbed on to the
mantelpiece to obtain a better view. The Princesse
de Lamballe had to be passed over the heads of the
crowd when she fainted, and the Queen lay perilously
near death till the King burst open one of the windows
which had been hermetically sealed to keep out
draughts.

Alas ! after all the prayers the child was only a
girl.

" Poor little one," said Marie-Antoinette tenderly,
" no one wanted you, but you shall be more truly mine.
A prince would have belonged to the State."

When the Queen went to Paris for her churching,
although a hundred maidens were portioned and

[1] F. O. Papers, Record of 1778, No. 306.

married at Notre-Dame, and generous distribution of
bread and sausages was ordered, there were few
shouts of " Vive la reine ! "　She had kept the country
waiting eight years, and still there was no Dauphin.

In her joy over the baby, Marie-Antoinette forgot
her chagrin.　" I do believe I love her more every
day," she wrote to the Empress Maria-Theresa when
the child showed signs of recognising her mother.
" She has been able to say ' *papa* ' for two days now.
. . . Her teeth are not yet through, but one can feel
them."

Madame Royale's birth was followed by that of a
second child within three years, and the King was the
first to tell the Queen of its sex :

" Monsieur le Dauphin is waiting and demands an
audience ! "

But the nation was restive, and on the day of the
Prince's christening ribald verses were nailed to the
church door connecting the Queen's name with that
of the Comte d'Artois.　Men spoke of her as a Jezebel,
and complained that " the Austrian " was sacrificing
France, and good French money, for the benefit of the
land of her birth.

" What have I done to these people ? " asked the
bewildered Queen, and returned to find solace at
Petit Trianon.

Yorktown had capitulated four days after the birth
of the Dauphin, and now France heard the news.[1]
While Marie-Antoinette led the simple life, statesmen
framed the American Constitution, the Peace of
Versailles was signed (Sept. 3, 1783), and England
recognised the independence of the United States.

Mirabeau thundered on the Rights of Man, and
young warriors returned aglow with a passion for
Liberty and Equality, already forgetful of a warning
addressed to them before they left Boston :

" Do not let your hopes be inflamed by our triumphs

[1] Thirty-one days after the event.

on virgin soil. You will carry our sentiments with you, but, if you try to plant them in a country that has been corrupt for centuries, you will encounter obstacles more formidable than ours. Our liberty has been won with blood ; you will have to shed it in torrents before Liberty can take root in the old world."

Regardless of the trend of public opinion, a royal edict was registered announcing that henceforward only those who could show four generations of nobility would be eligible for commissioned rank in the army. And still expenditure increased while men demanded bread.

The Queen's second son was born and created Duc de Normandie.[1] She passed to her churching through silent streets, for it was believed on all sides that she had a dangerous ascendancy over the King.

Marie-Antoinette herself had few illusions in this direction. " I have not much influence," she had written to her brother, the Emperor of Austria, " but I allow people to think that I count for more than I do, or I should have even less power than I have."

Among those who watched the Queen's procession to Notre-Dame were the Grand Almoner, Cardinal de Rohan, and the royal jeweller, Boehmer. Both were disturbed when they saw her Majesty pass, for each had looked to see her adorned with a certain diamond necklace.

A few days later a cryptic sentence from Boehmer caught the Queen's attention. Enquiries led to the unravelling of a complicated story of intrigue, in which forged letters and a woman of the town had been introduced to delude the Grand Almoner into a belief that the Queen, who had spurned his covert admiration, would accept through his agency, and without the King's knowledge, a necklace of fabulous value. Furious that anyone should have believed that she would have engaged in a discreditable transaction, and

[1] Later the " Child of the Temple," and titularly Louis XVII.

employed a man she detested to assist her, Marie-Antoinette insisted upon drastic action, the King acquiesced, and the Cardinal was arrested as he went to Mass. *Parlement* acquitted him, and the people, seeing de Rohan found innocent, cried that the Queen must be guilty, so registering yet another mark against " the Austrian," whom they had begun to hate.

Gone were the days when " two hundred thousand lovers " cheered Marie-Antoinette. Now if she walked among them in her muslins, or took part in private theatricals at Petit Trianon, they murmured of her lack of royal dignity, and when she passed regal in velvet fur and jewels, they saw her as a spendthrift.

Every unpopular change in the Ministry was alleged as due to the manœuvring of the nation's evil genius.

" Cease interfering, and leave our good King to govern his country ! " cried an infuriated woman, pulling Marie-Antoinette by the arm, and horrified courtiers who ventured to Paris brought back tales of the burning of the Queen's effigy.

" It is because the English have been corrupting our people with their gold," said the Queen, and then forgot the insults offered to her as she mourned the death of her youngest daughter. Nor was she free from anxiety concerning the Dauphin, who was showing increased delicacy ; his figure was no longer straight : one hip was higher than the other, and the spine seemed crooked.

In the hope that change of air would benefit the child, St. Cloud was purchased at an enormous price. There was dancing on the lawns around the château, and the public could watch the Queen as she sat at needlework or played with her *chou d'amour*, the little Duc de Normandie, who was " as rosy and plump as a peasant's child."

The deficit was increasing, and the country seething with unrest, when the King summoned the Assembly

of Notables and a party led by Lafayette demanded
the convocation of the Estates-General. Foreigners
watched the trend of events from Paris and reported
signs of acute anxiety among those who gathered in
crowds to discuss public affairs.

Ministers fell, *Parlement* defied the King and was
sentenced to exile, while a *Lit de Justice* enforced
registration of royal decrees.

Necker returned to power, and a new era began
with the founding of the Jacobin Club[1] and the
summoning of the Estates-General after an interval
of a hundred and seventy-five years—" A fatal
step ! " cried Marie-Antoinette—and an avalanche of
broadsides descended on the court in response to a
request that " all instructed people should submit
schemes likely to be of assistance in the organising of
the future Assembly."

The deputies arrived and walked in procession with
the King, Queen, and the Princes of the Blood Royal,
and sittings began in the Salle des Menus-Plaisirs,
where after a chilly opening the dignified beauty of
Marie-Antoinette won her a burst of applause. But
the temper of the gathering was dangerous, and it was
evident that a clash was imminent. It came when
the members arrived for another meeting and found
the great hall closed to them. Seeking shelter from a
pitiless downpour of rain in the Jeu de Paume, they
took oath to give a constitution to their country.

The Archbishop of Paris, who had been summoned
to advise the King, was roughly handled by the
crowd, although he was under escort. Talleyrand,
Bishop of Autun, arrived secretly at midnight, and
was refused an audience despite the efforts of the
Comte d'Artois.

A royal session opened, and the Tiers-État heard
that though the King " willed liberal things," no

[1] The name was derived from the street in which the club met ; a
year later 150 societies were affiliated to the parent body.

decree was to become law without his sanction, and on the morrow the body might meet again, each order in a separate chamber.

Louis XVI withdrew, followed by the nobles and the majority of the clergy, but the remainder sat on, although Dreux-Brézé brought the King's commands for immediate dispersal.

" We are here by the will of the people," said Mirabeau, " and only force can expel us."

The body sat on, confirming former resolutions and passing others more violent. In succeeding sessions they were joined by a group of clergy and a small band of nobles, led in by the Duc d'Orléans ; victory was won.

The Dauphin died while the King's prerogatives were disappearing before his eyes, but no time was left to grieve, for the National Assembly was framing a constitution. Necker fell, and Camille Desmoulins harangued the Paris mob.

" Aux armes ! Aux armes, citoyens ! " The frenzied people invaded the Hôtel des Invalides, equipped themselves with weapons, wrecked the Bastille (July 14, 1789), and carried the Governor's head on a pike to the Palais-Royal : " Vive la Liberté ! Vive la Nation ! "

" Execration of the nobility is now universal among the lower orders," wrote the English Ambassador, reporting on the July happenings. . . . " Thus, my lord, the greatest revolution that we know anything of has been effected, and if the magnitude of the event be considered with the loss of very few lives. . . . From this moment we may see France as a free country, the King a very limited monarch, and the nobility reduced to the level of the rest of the nation. . . . It is said that an army of 50,000 citizens will go to Versailles to bring the King forcibly to Paris. . . . Everyone is wearing the red-and-white cockade in honour of the Duc d'Orléans.

" In the present distracted state of Paris it is much to be wished that his Majesty's subjects should refrain from visiting this country as much as possible. . . . There is a necessity for the most cautious behaviour. . . ." [1]

Alarmist rumours were being circulated, and the King and Queen urged all who could to seek safer surroundings : among those who left secretly was the Comte d'Artois, who had received anonymous information that a reward would be offered for his head.

Louis XVI recognised the accomplished fact of the union of the three orders in the Assemblée Nationale, and agreed to the reappointment of Necker [2] for the third time. With Lafayette riding before him, he went to Paris (where a hundred and fifty thousand men were in arms) to assure the citizens of his good intentions and his determination to restore tranquillity. When he accepted a red cockade at the hands of the mayor, a shout of " Vive le Roi ! " momentarily drowned those other cries of " Vive la Nation ! . . . Vive Necker ! . . . Vivent les Gardes Françaises ! "

Marie-Antoinette remained at Versailles burning papers, packing her jewels, and counting the anxious hours till the King returned. In the event of his detention, she had determined to give the royal children into the care of the Assembly.

" Messieurs . . . I come to place in your hands the wife and family of your sovereign. . . . Messieurs ! Do not let those united by heaven be thrust asunder on earth ! " She recited sentences from her appeal as she waited.

But Louis came back, and for a space life became normal once more, although more than one suggested

---

[1] F.O. Records, 27, Vols. 32–3.

[2] This Genevan banker, who had made a fortune in France by buying up English securities, first took office after the fall of Turgot in the early years of the reign.

that Rambouillet would be a safer abode for the royal family than Versailles.

Lafayette had produced a Declaration of the Rights of Man modelled on the Jefferson Declaration of Independence, which the King vetoed ; the Assembly argued in stormy session ; Mirabeau thundered against the court denouncing the Queen's evil influence; and in Paris the scarcity of bread was having increasing effect. Then the Flanders Regiment arrived at Versailles, and the Gardes du Corps revived an old custom by offering entertainment to the new arrivals.

When the King, Queen, and Dauphin appeared during the banquet and the band played " O Richard, O mon Roi, tout l'Univers t'abandonne! " the emotionally stirred soldiers tore off their national cockades and mounted black ones supplied by the Gardes.[1] Exaggerated accounts of this incident and the expenses incurred by the entertainers reached Paris, where it became dangerous to be seen without a tricolour. Disturbance increased, and when a girl of the people snatched a drum from a soldier and ran beating it and crying, " BREAD ! BREAD ! BREAD ! " a rabble of women poured out from the Faubourg St. Antoine, to be augmented by hordes from St. Marceau. Armed with whatever weapons they could snatch, these five thousand women toiled through the dust to Versailles, and with them went 20,000 of the Milice Bourgeoise ; it was said that they had threatened death to Lafayette if he refused to lead them.[2]

Word of the march of the women reached Louis, who hastened back from a shooting excursion in the Forest of Meudon alarmed for the Queen and his children, who were at Trianon, and by nightfall all the royal family had assembled at the palace, but no one could sleep for the shouting of the mob.

In the small hours the people broke in, overpowered

[1] F.O. Records, 27, Vol. 33.
[2] Summarised from Lord Fitzgerald's Despatches to the Secretary of State under dates in October 1789, Record Office.

THE DAUPHIN (LOUIS XVII).

the guards at the door of the Queen's chamber, and wrecked her furniture on finding that she had escaped.

" To Paris ! To Paris ! " The menacing cry grew loud, and Louis went on to the balcony.

" Vive le Roi ! " yelled the throng below.   " Vivent les Gardes du Corps ! "   Then, in a mighty roar, came a demand for the Queen, and Marie-Antoinette stepped out, leading Madame Royale and the Duc de Normandie, Dauphin since his brother's death.

" Pas d'enfants ! " came the shout, and the mother sent the children back and stepped forward alone, expecting death.

One man raised his musket to shoot her, but another struck it up, and the ball passed over her head. Lafayette took the Queen's hand and kissed it.

" To Paris ! . . . To Paris ! " The cry had become insistent.

When a start was made, the mob surged round the royal carriage displaying the heads of the guards who had been killed at the Queen's door. It took over seven hours to accomplish the eleven miles, and when the haven of the Tuileries was reached, it was found that no preparations had been made, so the exhausted children were put to sleep on camp-beds.

" Mon Dieu !   Will it be yesterday over again ? " exclaimed the four-year-old Dauphin on awakening. . . .   " Papa, why are the people so angry ? "

The puzzled King took the child upon his knee and tried to explain : " I wished to make France happier. . . . I needed money to pay expenses occasioned by the war. . . . *Parlement* opposed it, saying that my people alone had right of assent. . . . I assembled the principal inhabitants of every town at Versailles. . . . They asked concessions of me which I could not make out of respect to myself or justice to you. . . ."

The people outside were still shouting, so King and Queen made repeated appearances at the windows, and when Louis XVI could find no words, Marie-

Antoinette spoke for him. Very gradually the cry of
" Vive la Nation " gave place to that of " Vive le Roi,"
with an occasional shout of " Vive la Reine," and all
tried to make themselves believe that the danger was
over. When the Queen led the Dauphin on to the
balcony, cheers greeted them, and women scrambled
for the flowers she dropped upon them.

Next day the foreign ministers were accorded an
audience, though the vicinity of the palace was not
quiet and the rooms were still disordered. They
found the King " much dejected," and tears ran
down the Queen's cheeks as she talked.

" In a short time," reported Lord Fitzgerald, " we
may be better able to judge how matters will turn out.
At present it is impossible to say, for the blind and
headless will of the populace directs all, and all
submit with fear and trembling to their government,
as the dangerous maxims that all men are equal, and
that numbers can overcome a few, are in the mouths
of every vagabond. . . . Nothing is now left to the
superior classes but the well-proportioned exercise of
that reason and education which may, in time, give
them again superiority over the multitude. . . .
The King's sanction has been obtained to the Articles
of the Constitution, and the *Droits de l'homme*, which
I enclose. . . . Birth, fortune, and favour are to lose
all things, and every man from the meanest station in
life is to rise to the highest honour in the State, if he
has sufficient merit to convey himself. . . . Such, my
lord, is the total subversion of all things in this
country, and so general is the disturbance that I can
conceive nothing but a bloody civil war can ever
restore matters to any degree of order. . . ."

The year drew to a miserable close. Spies inside the
palace and guards without watched the royal family's
every movement ; all knew that they were prisoners.

King, Queen, and children would spend the morning
together and attend Mass, then Madame Elisabeth

encouraged the Dauphin and his sister to play battle-
dore and shuttlecock while the Queen went to her
tapestry frame, where swiftly moving fingers betrayed her pent-up nervous energy.

"What have I done to the people?" she would ask
the Princesse de Lamballe. "Once they loved me!"

After the one-o'clock dinner the pitiful court would
walk in the gardens for an hour, keeping close to the
palace walls, while street-sellers drove a thriving trade
in tricoloured cockades.

Madame Royale made her first communion at St.
Germain-l'Auxerrois, the bells of which had rung in
St. Bartholomew's day, and sometimes the Dauphin
would dig in his little garden or pick a bunch of
flowers for "Mama-Queen," forgetful of the shouts of
"Vive la Nation!"

In the spring Louis made a short speech in the
National Assembly that won applause. When he
returned, followed by a group of deputies, Marie-
Antoinette presented the Dauphin : "I will teach him
to respect the liberties of the people and to uphold the
laws of which, I trust, he may one day be the stay and
shield," she promised.

The child was received with such enthusiasm that it
was hardly necessary for him to whisper, "Was that
right, Mama?" after he had uttered the word or two
required from him. He had been taught that he must
please.

By early summer (1790) spies were less in evidence,
and the royal family was allowed a brief holiday at St.
Cloud.

The anniversary of the fall of the Bastille was
celebrated on the Champ de Mars, where an altar had
been erected at which Talleyrand officiated.[1] Lafay-

[1] Talleyrand was one of the first to accept the Civil Constitution of
the Clergy, whereby the State enforced its authority over the Church to
the detriment of its allegiance to the Pope. He was excommunicated
in 1791, and his chaplain described him as deserving infamy in this
world and damnation in the next ; but 1802 saw him released from the
ban and restored to secular life.

ette attended, representing the people, and heard Louis XVI take oath as a constitutional King.

With the New Year (1791) came a deputation from the Paris guards bringing a box of dominoes for the Dauphin. They had been cut from the débris of the Bastille, and the child who had learnt to read as a *belle étrenne* for his mother could spell out the words engraved upon the lid : " Stones from those walls which imprisoned innocent victims of arbitrary power, converted into a toy for the Dauphin as a mark of the people's love, and to teach him their power. . . ."

Partly as a *ballon d'essai*, the King's two aunts now left for Rome. Jacobins tried to prevent their departure, a mob seized their baggage, and they were threatened with• imprisonment in Burgundy, but Rome was reached at last. The Princesses' escape angered Paris, which was already indignant because the Comte d'Artois gave no sign of returning, and the *émigrés* were known to be urging foreign intervention, so once more crowds surrounded the Tuileries and also the Luxembourg, where they forced the Comte de Provence to swear that he would remain in France. Loyalists rushed to defend an imagined attack on the royal family, and a regrettable incident occurred when one dropped his dagger (most men carried concealed weapons), for the guards insisted on searching everyone and secured a fine haul.

The all-pervading sense of danger increased, and with it the plotting that centred around the Queen, yet no man knew whom he might trust.

Mercy-Argenteau, the Comte de Fersen, and an anxious band were laying plans to rescue the King, and some believed that Lafayette would join them, but Marie-Antoinette was convinced that he was dangerous ; to her mind, even Mirabeau seemed safer.

The long strain had told upon Louis, and an illness produced a wave of the old loyalty. When he recovered, Te Deums were sung, Paris was illuminated, and the people cheered the King and Queen when they drove down the Champs Élysées. Then the pendulum swung back again and the Assembly passed a decree forbidding " le premier fonctionnaire publique " to absent himself above twenty leagues from the place where the Legislature sat while it was in session. If, at any other time, this " fonctionnaire " should leave the kingdom and not return when required by proclamation, it was to be accepted that he had abdicated the crown.

Equality and fraternity were now being experienced in all quarters; *les poissardes* even invaded ministerial drawing-rooms and embraced the Corps Diplomatique. But all such happenings were forgotten in the universal mourning on the death of Mirabeau. " A remarkable instance of how vice may be overshadowed by a sense of public utility," commented Lord Gower when twenty-eight thousand people followed the demagogue to his grave. Mirabeau's death was a blow even to the royal family, for those who were planning the rescue had made payment and hopes had risen; but Fersen would not despair. The Queen secreted her jewels, and the King worked on the lock of a secret door. Day after day he wrote the same monosyllable in his diary—" Rien." [1]

In the Assembly Robespierre urged the total annihilation of the monarchy; in the streets the market women set upon and flogged some hundreds of nuns because they had attended Mass celebrated by a priest who had refused to take the civil oath,[2] and an effort was made to force the King to attend a Constitutional Mass. When the royal family attempted to go to St. Cloud for Holy Week the National Guard opposed with a hand of steel.

[1] The King's diary record was equally laconic on July 14, when the Bastille fell.

[2] Those priests who refused to accept the Civil Constitution of the Clergy were persecuted. It was said that the Pope intended to consider France as separate from the Catholic Church unless the Constitution was withdrawn.

" Do you still assert that we are free, Monsieur de Lafayette ? " asked Marie-Antoinette.

Six weeks later Fersen completed his plans. On an agreed night he disguised himself, drove a hackney coach to the place of rendezvous, and received the royal children from the Queen's hands. Inside the palace the day's routine had been followed, and Marie-Antoinette had withdrawn at her usual hour. The King had held his *coucher*, attended by Lafayette, and had gone to bed at half-past eleven, when his valet, having drawn the bolts, retired to undress before returning to the King's chamber. In those few minutes Louis slipped out of bed and reached the Queen's apartment. Madame Elisabeth too had been warned. Comte de Fersen found her as he walked up and down in the anxious hour after the arrival of the children and their governess. Next came the King in a brown coat and simple round hat, and at last the Queen.

The long drive began while Paris slept. Once outside the walls the party changed into a berline. " Quicker ! Quicker ! " cried Fersen, and the postillions spurred on the horses.

At 3 a.m. the berline drew up at Bondy, where fresh horses awaited the travellers and three trusted members of the King's late bodyguard took over Fersen's charge. At 6 a.m. Meaux was passed. Surely now they were safe ?

More posthouses, fresh horses, and on, still on. . . . But the horses tired, the King walked up a hill, and the royal children wanted air. . . .

The night had passed peacefully in Paris and the flight of the royal family was not discovered until the *valet de chambre* drew the curtains of the King's bed at 7 a.m., when the news spread like wildfire.

Within an hour drummers were beating a call to arms and the people rushed to the Tuileries while church bells clanged an alarm and guns fired distress signals.

Yells of "traitor" assailed Lafayette, but he took control, and when the panic-stricken deputies came scurrying into the Assembly, they learnt that couriers were already on the road.

The King had been stopped at Varennes, barely twenty leagues from Metz and safety. Drouet, a post-master's son, being suspicious, had made a cross-country ride and pulled a wagon across the road, so blocking an archway, just fifteen minutes before the berline came lumbering down the narrow way.

The beat of drums continued from commune to commune, and messengers carried on the news till every hamlet and village knew of the King's flight and the King's capture. Madame Campan, the Queen's Lady-in-Waiting, heard the throb of a drum in the valley of the Mont d'Or, where people flocked out to be told how the King and Queen had fled "in order to ruin France," but had been stopped, and were now well guarded by a hundred thousand men. Some few disbelieved, so details were added and the crowd was told how Marie-Antoinette, "with her usual haughti-ness," had lifted up her veil and turned on the good citizens who were upbraiding Louis for having attempted flight, saying :

"Well—since you recognise your sovereign, respect him !"

Doubts vanished. There was no longer a King in France ![1]

On the day that the royal family were carried back to Paris, the Assembly suspended Louis's functions. Once more the Tuileries became a prison, and even as she slept Marie-Antoinette was under guard. There was a rumour that "the Austrian" was to be separ-

---

[1] All who had helped in the capture were rewarded. Drouet received £12,000 and was elected to the Convention in the following year ; even the wine-drinkers at the inn, and the postillions who had delayed the King's horses, shared in the distribution, while Varennes received a flag from "a grateful country."

ated from her husband and children and sent to the
convent of the Val-de-Grâce, but nothing happened,
though all were interrogated as to their motives in
trying to escape.   No one was allowed access to the
palace without a pass from Lafayette, but, despite
the strict surveillance, Marie-Antoinette contrived to
send out brief notes to those who had planned the
flight.

"I am alive. . . . Do not write, for that would
betray us, and above all do not come back," she wrote
to the Comte de Fersen, and to Esterhazy : "I have
no friend to whom I can tell my sorrows, and yet I
ought to be thankful that they are safe and far away!"

"June 26, Sunday," wrote Louis in his diary.
"Rien.   Mass.   Conference with the Commissioners
of the Assembly.
"Monday, 27th.   Idem.
"Tuesday, 28th.   Idem.   Took whey."

France was not as tranquil as her King, and the
wildest tales found credence.   When a hundred
aristocrats chartered an English fishing-boat to carry
them to Jersey, the whole countryside from Brest to
Rochefort was aroused in the belief that 6,000 English
had landed on French soil with evil intent,[1] and the
Assembly sat long hours passing decrees against the
émigrés ; indignation was heightened by the fact that
the Comte de Provence had escaped across the border,
regardless of the promise to remain that had been
extracted from him some months before.   Danton
voiced the desire for a republic.
   A petition demanding the repudiation and trial of
the King was placed on an *Autel de la Patrie* on the
Champ de Mars, from the steps of which leading
Jacobins launched violent denunciations.

---

[1] Public Records, F.O., 27, Vol. 36.

Louis continued his entries :

" July 14.   Was to have taken medicine.
" 17.   Affair of the Champ de Mars.
" 21.   Medicine at six ; and the end of my whey."

Six weeks later the Constitution (upon which a commission had been working for some time) was ready for presentation to the King.   It was almost as difficult to decide how this should be done as to draft the measure, for acceptation during confinement might be repudiated later ; yet if Louis were allowed his liberty, prior to signing the document, no one knew what action he might take.

An unhappy deputation faced the King and found themselves graciously received : his Majesty would examine the paper as soon as possible.

Restrictions were relaxed, some of the guards were withdrawn, a degree of privacy was permitted, and once again foreign ministers found it possible to attend at court.

King and Queen were quick to seize their chance and bid for popularity.   Money was sent out for distribution to the poor, and a general amnesty was declared. Both smiled gallantly as they set forth in the State coach for the King to take the prescribed oath. Tissue of absurdities though the Constitution might be in the Queen's eyes, she realised that Louis must accept it.

Public rejoicings followed with the ringing of bells, illuminations, dancing in the streets, and shouts of " Vive le Roi ! "   Even the Queen was cheered when she appeared at the opera, though a free fight soon developed in the pit and cries of " No master ! No Queen ! " silenced those who tried to cry " Vive la Reine ! "

A new Assembly met.   This was composed mainly of country attorneys, and Royalists described it as " a horde of wretches, madmen, and fools."   It passed yet

wilder decrees against the *émigrés* than had done its
predecessor, for the Princes still refused to obey the
King's commands to return.

A declaration by Austria and Prussia that the state
of affairs in France was a matter for European intervention occasioned a new outburst of vituperation
against Marie-Antoinette, who was accused of treasonable correspondence with her brother. War fever
flared, and every man denounced his neighbour as a
spy. Printed libels were circulated about the Queen
and cried under the windows of the palace ; the royal
family lived in daily fear of poison, and the Comte de
Fersen stole back in disguise to urge another attempt
at escape.

"Not again," said Louis XVI, "I suffered too
much the first time." Beyond the Rhine the Princes
strove yet harder to form a European alliance and
begin a counter-revolution, foreign nations began to
mobilise, the Committee of Public Safety came into
being, and Louis declared war against Austria (April
20, 1792).

In May the Girondins secured the adoption by the
Assembly of a drastic decree against refractory
priests, and a month later an extreme measure was
passed providing for the formation of a camp of
20,000 men (many of them from revolutionary
centres) under the walls of Paris. The King vetoed
both. Three ministers were dismissed, and, fearing a
coup d'état in the face of the enemy, Paris rose once
more.

" Vive la Nation ! " yelled the people, raiding shops
for weapons and rushing to the Tuileries.

The King awaited the onslaught as the crowd burst
in, brandishing pikes, knives, and hatchets.

" Fear nothing, Sire ! " said one of the half-dozen
guards who ranged themselves near him.

" Feel here if there is any sign of fear," answered
Louis, placing the man's hand over his heart.[1]

[1] Gower and Sutherland, Public Records, F.O., 27, Vol. 39.

The King must wear a red cap with the tricolour, so swore the mob, and Louis accepted the head-dress.

The King must drink to the health of the nation. A man passed a half-filled cup, from which he had already drunk. The King drank.

Marie-Antoinette was in the Council Chamber behind the great table with her children near her, and the Princesse de Lamballe beside her chair, when Santerre, a brewer of the Faubourg St. Antoine, marshalled his followers through.

" Let the people see their Queen," he ordered, and they came in an unending stream.

" A bas l'Autrichienne! . . . Vive la Nation! "

Someone flung a red cap and bade the Queen put it on the Dauphin's head. She obeyed.

A girl pushed forward carrying a toy guillotine bought at the street corner, and to it was attached a doll labelled " Marie-Antoinette."

" Why do you hate me so ? " asked the Queen. She endured till the end, and then broke into sobs.

" I shall not escape them another time," said Louis ; " there is little difference in being assassinated two months earlier or later."

All dreaded the coming anniversary of July 14, even the foreign diplomatists who considered assembling together for greater security, and while Louis XVI studied the life of Charles I of England, Marie-Antoinette padded a waistcoat, hoping that it would turn aside a dagger stroke.

" I love the nation! " said the little Dauphin nightly, mindful of instructions. " Is that right, Mama-Queen ? "

The fourteenth passed, while in the Assembly deputies came to blows when discussing the question of the King's deposition, and the Duke of Brunswick published a Declaration warning France that the Allies held Paris responsible for the safety of the royal family. On August 10 (1792) the tocsin rang out at midnight and street fighting began. Early next morning Louis went to review the Gardes and returned white and shaken, having been subjected to open insult. A few nobles followed him, but the mob yelled outside and the " Terror " had begun.

" Come," said the King, " there is nothing more to be done here."

He walked first, the Queen followed with the Dauphin clinging to her hand until he was pushed off his feet, when a soldier picked him up and carried him ; Madame Royale clung to Madame Elisabeth.

All reached the Assembly, where the stormy debate continued while the forlorn group listened. The night was spent in the cells of an adjoining monastery while the mob wrecked its fury on the palace.

Three days later (Aug. 13) " the family of Capet " was driven to the Temple, as being the only building the Municipality considered safe.

" Ça ira ! Ça ira ! " sang the people. " Vive la Nation ! . . . À bas la monarchie ! . . . " The prisoners heard the proclamation of the Republic five weeks later (Sept. 21, 1792), and heard, too, frenzied shouts of delight when the spiked head of the Princesse de Lamballe was waved aloft beneath their windows.

Friends plotted a rescue and the allied armies advanced, while inside the Temple life settled into routine : lessons for the children (but the multiplication table was forbidden, since it might be utilised as a cipher), writing (till pens, ink, and paper were removed), reading, piquet, mending—tapestry work was not allowed, since patterns might hide secret messages.

The King's trial began in December.

Louis was allowed three advocates. The man upon whom his first choice fell declined to take the case, on the ground that he had not practised for eight years. More courageous was seventy-year-old Monsieur de Malesherbes,[1] who wrote, offering his services :

" I have been twice called to be counsel for him who

---

[1] He was guillotined in 1794.

was my master in times when that duty was coveted
by everyone.   I owe him the same service now that it is
a duty which many people deem dangerous."

The opening speech showed that the case was pre-
judged : " Citizens of the Tribunes . . . Louis Capet
is at the bar. . . .   You are about to give a great
lesson to Kings . . . a great and useful example to
Nations . . ." but the King's advocates advanced a
bold defence.   Louis was described as having been
the friend of his people and a king who had granted
both liberty and reform, and the deputies were
reminded that history would judge the judgment which
was then to be given, and that its judgment would be
that of the Ages.

The King rose to declare that his conscience was
clear and his defenders had spoken the truth.   Tumult
broke out as he left the hall ; one deputy cried that
they did not want to judge, but to kill the King ;
another mounted the tribune to demand that the
proceedings should be annulled.

Louis XVI made two appearances before the Convention, and voting began in January, at 8 p.m. on
the 16th, by roll-call, as desired by Marat.

" He must be condemned to death, and at once,"
thundered Robespierre ; " you have not to pronounce
sentence for or against a man, but to adopt a measure
of public safety. . . ."

For twenty-six hours, all through the night and
following day, the people in the galleries cheered or
hissed the voters.

" Death ! . . .   Death ! . . .   Death ! " and then
someone to urge that if death must come to the
King, it should be delayed.

" Death, and never did word weigh so heavily upon
my heart," said Carnot.

" Death. . . ."

" Death. . . ."

" Death. . . ."

Now came Philippe Egalité, once Duc d'Orléans,

and even the tribunes were silenced when he who was the King's cousin recorded his vote—"Death!" Horror was painted on the countenance of every individual.[1]

Three hundred and sixty-one [2] members out of a total of seven hundred and nineteen voted for the death penalty unconditionally, but twenty-six had voted for death with reservations, and these were added, so bringing the total to three hundred and eighty-seven.

To Monsieur de Malesherbes fell the duty of breaking the news to the King, and the official condemnation followed. Louis Capet had been found guilty of conspiring against the State, and was to be executed within twenty-four hours.

The King saw his family that night while a guard watched, then gave himself into the hands of the Abbé Edgeworth, his Irish-born confessor. He had written his will on Christmas Day: "I leave my soul to God. . . . May He receive it in His mercy. . . . I beseech my wife to forgive me for all those evils which she has suffered for me. . . . I recommend my son (should he have the misfortune to be a king) to forget all hatred and resentment. . . ."

Edgeworth followed his King to the guillotine.

"I die innocent . . ." began Louis XVI, but Santerre gave a signal, drums sounded, and the executioner stepped forward to bind the King's hands.

"Fils de St. Louis, montez au Ciel!" cried the Abbé.

"Vive la République!" yelled the mob around the Temple, and in the morning Marie-Antoinette asked her gaolers for mourning garments.

[1] From an account written by an eye-witness.
[2] Thiers.

Nine months later she was called upon to appear before judges to whom the public prosecutor had guaranteed a death sentence.[1] She heard herself accused of conspiracy, intrigue, and treachery ; of having plundered France for the benefit of Austria ; of licentiousness and incest.

Standing still and silent at the bar, she heard her death decreed and a hoarse shout of triumph from the knitting women in the tribunes.

On October 16 (1793) the Queen drove to the guillotine, sitting on a rough plank in a muddy cart, to meet death within sight of the Tuileries, where once " two hundred thousand lovers " had welcomed her.

" Pardon, monsieur ! " said Marie-Antoinette, finding that she had stepped upon the executioner's foot. A moment later he held her head aloft.

" Vive la République ! . . . Vive la Liberté ! " yelled the people.

[1] *Marie-Antoinette,* by the Marquis de Ségur.

HOUSE OF BOURBON-ORLÉANS

CHAPTER FOURTEEN

LOUIS-PHILIPPE, KING OF THE FRENCH
(1830–1848)

Louis-Philippe and Marie-Amélie

"La Santa."

LOUIS-PHILIPPE

(Fifth Cousin to Louis XVI, XVIII, and Charles X)

Born at Paris	.	Oct. 6, 1773
Married at Palermo	. .	Nov. 29, 1809
Accepted the crown	. .	Aug. 7, 1830
Deposed	. .	Feb. 23, 1848
Died at Claremont	. .	Aug. 26, 1850

CONTEMPORARY SOVEREIGNS

ENGLAND: William IV, Victoria.
SPAIN: Ferdinand VII and Isabella II.

POPES

Pius VIII, Gregory XVI, and Pius IX.

Descent
LOUIS XIII

LOUIS XIV — PHIL.., DUC D'ORLÉANS

LOUIS LE GRAND DAUPHIN — PHIL., DUC D'ORLÉANS, Regent

DUC DE BOURGOGNE — PHIL.-LOUIS

LOUIS XV — LOUIS-PHIL.

LOUIS (Dauphin) — LOUIS-PHILIPPE, " Égalité "

LOUIS XVI, and XVIII and CHARLES X — LOUIS-PHILIPPE, K. OF THE FRENCH

CONSORT
Descent

Ferdinand IV, K. of the Two Sicilies m. Maria Carolina of Austria.

MARIE-AMÉLIE

Born at Caserta	.	April 26, 1782
Married	. .	Nov. 29, 1809
Died at Claremont	. .	Mar. 24, 1866

Issue :

Ferdinand, Duc de Chartres [1] and d'Orléans . .	1810–42
Louise-Marie (m. Leopold of Belgium) . .	1812–50
Marie-Christine .	1813–39
Duc de Nemours .	1814–96
Françoise . .	1816–18
Clémentine . .	1817–1907
Duc de Joinville .	1818–1900
Duc de Penthièvre	1820–8
Duc d'Aumale .	1822–97
Duc de Montpensier	1824–90

[1] Ferdinand, m. Hélène of Mecklenburg-Schwerin.

LOUIS-PHILIPPE, COMTE DE PARIS — ROBERT-PHILIPPE, DUC DE CHARTRES

MARIE-AMÉLIE DE BOURBON.

LOUIS-PHILIPPE.

CHAPTER FOURTEEN

LOUIS-PHILIPPE, KING OF THE FRENCH
(1830–1848)

MARIE-AMÉLIE was eleven years old when Marie-Antoinette went to the guillotine, and the tragic death of her mother's favourite sister made an indelible impression upon the mind of the child who was to link monarchical France across a span of thirty-seven years during which the nation knew no Queen.

The Bourbon Princess was one of an enormous family of eighteen children, and in babyhood was taught to regard herself as the future Queen of France, for the sisters Marie-Antoinette and Maria Carolina dreamed of marrying their infants. But the first little Dauphin died, the revolution which engulfed France had its repercussion in Naples, and with a French army within sight, the Neapolitan royal family fled to Nelson's flagship, the *Vanguard*, which carried the refugees through a terrible storm to the haven of Palermo. Here Marie-Amélie and her sisters spent their days embroidering banners for the troops who took up arms against the invaders.

Two years later Queen Maria-Carolina took four of her children to visit their elder sisters in Vienna.[1] The journey was dangerous, for French troops seemed everywhere, but Nelson provided an escort, and Russia convoyed the little party across the Adriatic, so two months after leaving Palermo the travellers reached the Austrian capital, where Marie-Amélie met her

[1] One was the consort of Emperor Francis II, the other of his brother, the Duke of Tuscany.

niece Marie Louise, and had an abortive love affair with one of the many archdukes.

She consoled herself with serious reading and many prayers. The family named her " La Santa," and foresaw a convent as her ultimate destiny when the Prince of the Asturias, having been proposed as a possible husband, preferred a younger sister.

When Cardinal Ruffo and the Neapolitans drove the French out of Naples, a family reunion was made possible, and once again beautiful Caserta became a royal residence.

But Napoleon was still all-conquering, and within four years a second flight was necessary.

Others of Marie-Amélie's sisters married, her brothers joined the army, and the remainder of the family lived on the bounty of the English Government in a court composed of refugees as needy as themselves. But a suggestion from Napoleon that Marie-Amélie should marry his stepson Eugène Beauharnais (now Viceroy of Italy) was spurned.

She was twenty-six years old when Louis-Philippe, Duc d'Orléans, came to visit the straitened court.

" I ought to detest you—and yet I feel a liking for you ! " said the Queen, and summoned her daughter.

Louis-Philippe was the son of Philippe Égalité, who had voted for the death of Louis XVI, and had himself gone to the guillotine in a green frock-coat, yellow buckskins, and white piqué waistcoat.

As Duc d'Orléans, Louis-Philippe had offended both parties in France. The Royalists upbraided him with the sins of his father, and remembered that at sixteen he had been an active member of the Jacobin Club ; the Revolutionaries accused him of a treacherous attempt to overthrow the Republic. He had escaped from France, to find himself an Ishmael ; now he had wandered through Switzerland on foot with a single companion until, almost penniless, he contrived to secure a post in a school (under an assumed name) at a salary of seventy-five pounds per annum ; now he had travelled economically in the Scandinavian countries. But wherever the Duke went, France found him dangerous. Wishing him farther from her shores, she bribed him to go to America by the freeing of his mother and brothers, all of whom had been prisoners since the " Terror."

When Louis-Philippe ventured back to Europe, policy dictated a reconciliation with the elder branch of the family, for the Comte de Provence, brother of Louis XVI, had proclaimed himself Louis XVIII when the death of the pathetic child, King Louis XVII,[1] was announced (June 8, 1795). Like Louis-Philippe, the Comte de Provence had been a wanderer, but the Tsar of Russia now permitted him to hold a phantom court at Mittau, where he had been joined by his wife, from whom he had been separated for many years.

During the First Republic, Louis-Philippe had been known by the name which had been adopted by his father, but he went to Mittau incognito.

" Monsieur," said Louis XVIII, " clearly you have much to do to atone ! " and went on to explain that for the future the Duke must renounce ambition, shun Jacobins and revolutionaries, and give to his King that submission and sincerity which was a sovereign's due. The name " Égalité " was to be forgotten.

So re-established, Louis-Philippe was free to mend his broken career ; hence his visit to Sicily and a significant entry in the Journal kept by Marie-Amélie, who saw the hand of Fate in the advent of the thirty-five-year-old Duke.

" Dec. 30, 1808. I have made an acquaintance which will probably influence my whole life ! " She saw Louis-Philippe as " somewhat stout, neither handsome nor ugly, and very polite." As for herself :

---

[1] Son of Louis XVI and Marie-Antoinette, known as " the child of the Temple," who had been given into the charge of a cobbler and his wife. This woman made a death-bed confession, and swore that she had exchanged the King for another child. Forty pseudo-Dauphins appeared in Europe and America after the Restoration.

" My face is long, I have blue eyes . . . a large forehead and not much hair, though what I have is of a
golden hue.   My nose is long and aquiline, and I have
an agreeable mouth, also a round chin with a pretty
little dimple.   My hands are ugly, but I have pretty
feet."

Marriage between Louis-Philippe and Marie-Amélie
presented difficulties, for the Duke was penniless, but
the " King and Queen de l'Émigration," Louis XVIII
and Marie-Joséphine (who were now living in Hartwell,
Buckinghamshire, having been driven out of Mittau
by Napoleon's orders), sent official permission and a
blessing, and Marie-Amélie's parents yielded.   Better
to support their daughter in the world than see her
take the veil, as she threatened to do if thwarted.

The wedding lacked ceremony, since it took place in
Ferdinand's bedroom, he having broken a leg, but
Marie-Amélie found it stirring.

" Knowing the sacredness of the tie . . . I was
filled with emotion, and my limbs tottered under me,
but the Duc d'Orléans pronounced his ' Yes ' in such a
resolute voice that it gave me courage ! "

The bridegroom was content, if less thrilled.
" What an advantage to marry a Bourbon," he wrote
to a friend. . . .   " If I were all that I am not, and if
the times were what they are not, it would be difficult
for me to make a marriage more advantageous. . . ."

(Four months later Napoleon Buonaparte, having
divorced Joséphine, married Marie-Amélie's niece
Marie-Louise, and she was proclaimed Empress of
France.)

The Duc and Duchesse d'Orléans took up their
abode in a corner of the palace until something more
convenient could be arranged.   Their mainstay was a
compassionate pension paid irregularly by England.

Marie-Amélie's first three children were born amid
family dissensions and a Sicilian insurrection which

MARIE-JOSÉPHINE OF SARDINIA (COMTESSE DE PROVENCE).

LOUIS XVIII.

254]

drove her father from the throne and her mother into
exile.   But at last an English man-of-war brought the
news Louis-Philippe had begun to despair of receiving.

"Buonaparte est fini ! Louis XVIII est rétabli et
je pars sur ce vaisseau qui vient me chercher ! " he
cried, too excited to be strictly accurate.

The Duke departed without waiting for his wife.
He had been an exile for twenty-one years, and so
great was his joy on reaching Paris that he kissed the
steps of the Palais-Royal.   The capital was still be-
decked in the white bunting which had been hung out
to welcome Louis XVIII upon his arrival in a British
battleship ;   he and his brother the Comte d'Artois
had made their entries dressed like Wellington (but
no one seems to have noticed the amazing lack of tact),
and beside the King sat Marie-Antoinette's daughter,
now the Duchesse d'Angoulême, erstwhile Madame
Royale, the " orphan of the Temple."

" Which man is our King ? " asked a citizen as the
long procession passed.

"Voilà—c'est le gros goutteux," came the reply.
It was an apt description.

But if France had a King once more, she still knew
no Queen, for Marie-Joséphine had died in exile :
" She was endowed with estimable qualities, and I
never had occasion to find fault with her."   So wrote
Louis XVIII in his Memoirs.   England had given her
a royal funeral and (if no other privilege of the great)
temporary resting-place in Westminster Abbey (1810).

It was to Talleyrand, erstwhile an excommunicated
priest, once an exile in the United States, that Louis
XVIII owed his crown, and France the Restoration.
He had convinced the Emperor Alexander of Russia
that the sanctioned return of the Bourbons was the
only possible solution of the French problem ; he had
convened the French Senate, when only sixty-four
members out of a hundred and forty dared to attend,
and had brought that body to pronounce the deposi-

tion of Napoleon and the election of Louis as a constitutional King :

" The people of France . . . of their own free will, call to the throne Louis Stanislas Xavier, brother of the late King, and after him the other members of the House of Bourbon in the old order."

On the day that Napoleon reached Elba, Louis XVIII passed into the Tuileries wearing a white cockade, which had been pinned upon the breast of his tight, gilt-buttoned coat by the Prince Regent of England.

Alas ! the Bourbons had learnt nothing and forgotten nothing. The King's first act was to refuse to sign the Constitution presented by representatives of the Provisional Government, of which Talleyrand was President, though of his royal graciousness he hinted at granting such a measure in the future.

Louis-Philippe, Duc d'Orléans, was received even more cordially than he had hoped : " I hope I shall see you often, my cousin," said the King. The vast Orléans estates were restored and the past slipped into oblivion. Gone were the days of penury and life among uncongenial relatives-by-marriage. Marie-Amélie and her children were fetched to Paris. Hardly were they installed at the Palais-Royal before she gave birth to her second son, the Duc de Nemours, which enabled her to send a graceful message to the King : " Pray tell his Majesty that he has one more faithful subject ! "

While a humbled Paris did penance on the site of the guillotine and Louis (hoping for a coronation) endeavoured to overcome the scruples of Pope Pius VIII, who declined to accept the fiction that the King had reigned since 1795, the Allies sat in Congress at Vienna. Then on a day in March a frightened messenger brought word that Napoleon had landed in the Golfe de Juan and was approaching Paris.

Anonymous leaflets warned Louis XVIII that his

fate would be that of Louis XVI, but, heavy with his
sixty years, he made a bold stand.

"You see me suffering; it is from gout, not anxiety,"
he told the Diplomatic Corps gravely, but Fouché sent
warning that not a regiment would stand by the King
—and now Napoleon was at Fontainebleau!

Discretion was necessary, and at midnight on
March 19 (1815) a procession of royal carriages left
the Tuileries for Ghent, and at 9 p.m. on the 20th
Napoleon entered the palace.

There followed the Hundred Days, Waterloo, and
the abdication of the Emperor.

The Duc d'Orléans had carried his family to England, where, after a sojourn at Grillon's Hotel in
Albemarle St., he established himself at Twickenham ;
he heard the story of Napoleon's disaster from a
gesticulating compatriot on the pavement at Hammer-
smith when driving to town one day.

But if Louis XVIII returned to Paris " in the
baggage-train of the allies " to show himself in a blaze
of candlelight at the Tuileries, the Duke remained in
England till he had added an English-born daughter
to his international group of children, and when
Marie-Amélie left Twickenham it was with fore-
boding : " Je n'ai pu quitter sans un serrement du
cœur ce paisible séjour où nous avons passé deux ans
tranquilles, loin du monde et ses intrigues ! "—but
the succeeding years spent between Neuilly and the
Palais-Royal were to be the happiest of her life.

She reigned over a salon frequented by the most
brilliant men in France—Talleyrand saw her as " the
greatest of great ladies "—yet she had time to devote
to the still-enlarging circle of children, two of whom
were now attending the Collège Henri-Quatre and
being educated *en bourgeois* according to the King,
who saw in this undignified proceeding further
evidence of the Duke's attempt to ingratiate himself
with the masses.

But whatever ambitions Louis-Philippe was nursing received a check when, seven months after the assassination of the Duc de Berry (heir-presumptive to the throne after his father, the Comte d'Artois), a son was born to the Duchess, and Paris took the baby Duc de Bordeaux to its heart. That Henri IV might live again in Henri Dieudonné, the infant's gums were rubbed with garlic according to the old Gascon custom.

The Pope spoke of the child as Europe's guarantee of peace, the nation gave him the Château de Chambord as a christening gift, and Victor Hugo composed a birthday ode in his honour.

Four years later Louis XVIII died (1824) and was succeeded by his brother as Charles X. Marie-Amélie saw the throne looming near, for the Duc de Bordeaux [1] was a fragile boy.

If Louis XVIII had perforce foregone his coronation, Charles X was of a different mind, and orders were given for a magnificent ceremony despite an almost empty treasury. Talleyrand watched, as he had watched the crowning of Louis XVI and of the Emperor Napoleon.

Marie-Amélie too was present. She saw Charles X anointed with oil from the Holy Ampulla, which, though it had been wilfully destroyed in the Revolution, was now discovered miraculously intact once more, and heard the shouts of "Vive le Roi!" which resounded for a quarter of an hour. After the ceremony Charles touched two hundred scrofulous people, making the sign of the cross on each man's brow and saying: "The King touches thee; may God heal thee!"

There was no Queen to share the King's glory, for the Comtesse d'Artois, that "princesse estimable, mais peu propre par les agréments de sa personne et de son esprit à fixer l'inconstance de ses goûts," had escaped from her husband by dying eighteen years before (1806).

¹ Later to be known as Duc de Chambord.

CHARLES X.

MARIE-THÉRÈSE OF SARDINIA (COMTESSE D'ARTOIS).

258]

The new reign opened reasonably well, for the King promulgated a Charter of Rights—the only liberal act in the six years of his rule—but signs of unrest and a growing majority against the Government were noticeable.

When Charles proved himself a true Bourbon by issuing ordinances (published in *Le Moniteur*, July 26, 1830) which dissolved the newly elected, but antagonistic Chamber, disenfranchised the majority of the electors, and abrogated the freedom of the Press— " that Pandora's box from which emerges all the calamities which desolate the earth "[1]—Louis-Philippe saw that the end was in sight. " The King has violated the Charter ! " announced the Duke.

" Hélas ! mon bonheur est fini ! " cried Marie-Amélie, quick to grasp the implications.

Visitors from Paris brought word of street fighting, the fraternisation of troops and people, and the withdrawal of Charles X to St. Cloud. Fearing that a summons from the King would oblige him to take action with the Royalists, and so antagonise the opposing force, the Duc d'Orléans left Neuilly, and Marie-Amélie remained to face yet another revolution.

The tricolour flew once more above the Tuileries, Paris barricaded its streets, and a group of deputies followed the King to St. Cloud, to find him adamant. In the Chamber men clamoured for the proclamation of a republic, only to be silenced by Thiers,[2] who argued that such a course would embroil France with all Europe ; safety lay rather in offering the crown to the Duc d'Orléans, a prince who was " devoted to the principles of the Revolution."

An inspired article in *Le Globe* attempted to focus public opinion : " La victoire de Paris a proclamé la vacance du trône. . . . Le trône vacant, une grande

---

[1] Robespierre.
[2] Louis-Adolphe Thiers (1797–1877), statesman and historian (son of a locksmith).

question se présente. Quel sera le gouvernement de
la France ? . . ."

Events moved swiftly, and when the King would
have yielded ground, Lafayette cried, " Too late ! "
Already handbills were appearing in the streets.

PROCLAMATION !

" *Charles X* ne peut plus rentrer à Paris. Il a fait
couler le sang du Peuple !

La République nous exposerait à d'affreuses divisions. Elle nous brouillerait avec l'Europe.

Le Duc d'Orléans est un prince dévoué à la cause de
la Révolution.

Le Duc d'Orléans ne s'est jamais battu contre nous.

Le Duc d'Orléans était à Jemappes.

Le Duc d'Orléans est un roi citoyen.

Le Duc d'Orléans a porté au feu les couleurs
tricolores.

Le Duc d'Orléans peut seul les porter encore ; nous
n'en voulons pas d'autre !

Le Duc d'Orléans s'est prononcé. Il accepte la
Charte comme nous l'avons toujours entendue et
voulue.

C'est du peuple français qu'il tient la couronne. . . ."

What stand would the Powers take—those
arbiters of Fate who had effected the restoration of the
Bourbons fifteen years before ?

Charles X and Louis-Philippe both turned to
England's representative in Paris, and Lord Stuart of
Rothesay took counsel with the Russian and Prussian
Ambassadors before sending a negative reply to the
uneasy King :

" We cannot take upon ourselves the responsibility
of offering any counsel. . . . We would merely
recommend his Majesty to lose no time in providing
for his safety and that of the royal family." [1]

[1] F.O., 27, 413, No. 382.

In these fleeting July days three thousand soldiers and twice as many civilians had been killed or wounded in Paris; and that other revolution, when his brother and his brother's wife and children had been carried away from Versailles, was still vivid in Charles's mind. He had fled then as a young man; an old man now, he withdrew from St. Cloud to the greater security of Rambouillet, and with him went the Duchesse de Berry, carrying a revolver to defend the life of her son.

Lord Stuart's reply when Louis-Philippe made a secret approach was uncompromising: " I answered that the oath of his royal highness precluded his possible acceptance of such an offer with honour, and that his elevation [to the crown] could not be sanctioned by any among the Powers which are parties to the Treaties placing the Bourbons upon the throne." [1]

Marie-Amélie took almost as firm a stand when a deputation arrived from Paris, headed by Thiers, bringing word that a strong party wished the Duke to assume the supreme authority.

" My husband is an honest man. He will do nothing against the King," protested the Duchess. But Louis-Philippe's sister Madame Adélaïde, who had shared the vagrant wanderings of his youth, knew more of her brother's mind than did his wife.

" My brother loves his country. He will do anything to deliver it from anarchy! " she exclaimed, adding that she was prepared to go to Paris and make whatever promises were necessary in the name of the Duke.

" Madame, you have given a crown to your family," said Thiers.

Marie-Amélie could not keep back her tears: " Hélas! mon bonheur est fini! " she repeated.

Charles X had come to a decision at last, and wrote to Louis-Philippe: " Mon cousin, j'ai pris la résolution d'abdiquer la couronne en faveur de mon

[1] F.O., 27, 411, No. 370.

petit-fils le Duc de Bordeaux. Le Dauphin qui
partage mes sentimens renonce aussi à ses droits en
faveur de son neveu. . . . Vous aurez donc, en votre
qualité de Lieutenant-Général du Royaume, à faire
proclamer l'avènement de Henri V à la couronne."

But Charles was too late. While some had talked
of a republic, and others demanded that Napoleon's
son should be fetched from Vienna, a few had acted.
If Paris, " troublé dans son repos par une déplorable
violation de la Charte," had defended herself " avec
un courage héroïque," Louis-Philippe was willing to
assist. He was now in the capital, and had taken
control. His first act was to send ten thousand men
to guard the King and escort him to whichever port
he might select ; there was no time to lose, for the
faubourgs were stirring. The Deputiés had declared
the crown vacant and left the peers to an academic
debate on the rights of the Duc de Bordeaux.

By public conveyance, and now on foot by reason of
the barricades, Marie-Amélie brought her seven children to Paris in time to stand beside the Duke when
the Deputies offered him the crown.

" Vive le Roi ! Vive la Reine ! Vive la Famille
royale ! " shouted the people.

Lafayette was there. He had heard the same cry
when standing beside Louis XVI and Marie-Antoinette ; now it was Louis-Philippe's hand that he
kissed.

" Nous avons fait là de bonnes choses, vous êtes le
prince qu'il nous faut ; c'est la meilleure des ré-
publiques ! "

" Quelle journée ! Quelle nation ! Comme l'attitude
de la France devient grande aux yeux de l'Europe, et
comme il est beau d'être appelé à gouverner un peuple
si brave, si généreux, si capable d'attachement et si
digne d'être aimé ! " (So ran the leading article in
Le Moniteur Universel, Aug. 8, 1830.)

Amid his ten thousand guards, his artillery, cavalry, and infantry, Charles X made a dignified journey towards Cherbourg, where two American packet-boats were waiting to carry him to safety. With the abdicating monarch went the ten-year-old " King Henri V," who was never to know crown or throne.[1]

Wrapped in a tricoloured scarf, Louis-Philippe walked to the Chambre des Députés escorted by his family, accepted the title of King of the French, and took the oath required of him :

" En présence de Dieu je jure d'observer fidèlement la Charte Constitutionelle, de faire rendre bonne et exacte justice . . . et d'agir en toutes choses dans la seule vue de l'intérêt, du bonheur et de la gloire du peuple français. . . . Messieurs les pairs et Messieurs les Députés, je viens de consommer un grand acte ! . . ." Louis-Philippe was King of the French " not by act of God, but by the will of the people."

" Vive le Roi ! Vive la Reine ! "

Marie-Amélie watched her husband mount the throne and felt that condolences, not congratulations, should be offered : " I have lost my peaceful home, and I tremble for the uncertain future of my family," she wrote in her Journal.

France had a King and Queen once more, but no tranquillity, for her restless people showed an unwillingness to return to their ordinary avocations. Citizens surged into the palace to insist on embracing their sovereign, and howled through the streets demanding the heads of the late King's ministers.

The royal family moved to the Tuileries, thinking it a safer refuge than the Palais-Royal, and Marie-Amélie found half the nation turning to her for alms :

---

[1] Neither of them were to see France again. They first found refuge at Holyrood, but later France asserted that Scotland was dangerously near her shores, so wanderings began once more. Charles X died at Goritzia in 1836, aged seventy-nine.

though she gave away four-fifths of her income, it seemed but a drop in the ocean of poverty.

" Bread is dear, trade is bad ; to give is my only pleasure," she would say as she sat among her daughters sewing for the poor.

A Queen's children belong to the nation. Two of Marie-Amélie's sons joined the army and one the navy. One daughter married Leopold of Belgium ; another became Duchess of Würtemburg. Ferdinand Louis-Philippe, her eldest born, brought home the Princesse Hélène of Mecklenburg-Schwerin, and in the following year (1838) France celebrated the birth of the Comte de Paris.

Marie-Amélie spent many anxious hours, for in the first decade of Louis-Philippe's reign six attempts were made upon his life, and two upon the throne, one by the Duchesse de Berry, who endeavoured to raise the country on behalf of her son the Duc de Bordeaux, in whose favour Charles X had abdicated, and another by Louis Napoleon, who landed at Boulogne.

Then a close personal tragedy made Marie-Amélie forget her fears, for her eldest son was injured in a carriage accident, and the Queen rushed from the Tuileries to kneel beside him as he lay dying in a wayside inn. Men shook their heads, for the death of the Duc d'Orléans left the succession to children. The Comte de Paris was only four years old, and his brother the Duc de Chartres two years his junior ; France would never stand another long regency.

No one could be blind to the dangerous spread of republicanism throughout the country, where strikes, insurrections, and disturbances of all kinds were frequent, nor was the foreign outlook entirely satis- factory, for two of the Princes made marriages that antagonised the powers,[1] and the National Guard

---

[1] The Duc de Joinville to a Princess of Brazil in 1843, and the Duc de Montpensier to a sister of the Queen of Spain in 1846.

shouted "Vive la réforme" as it marched past the palace.

The signal for revolt was given when, at the eleventh hour, the Government forbade a huge banquet and the Minister of Justice announced that the right of political discussion had never been conferred upon the people.

Once more Paris saw the barricades flung up in her streets, troops were moved, rumours of bloodshed came from Montmartre, and the Guards demanded the dismissal of certain ministers as the price of allegiance. Such a tide could not be stemmed, and presently General de Lamoricière rode through the streets announcing a new Cabinet. The temper of the people changed, and they were demanding illuminations when a chance shot broke the leg of an officer's horse, and he ordered his men to fire into the mob. Revolution came like a thunderclap. It was the sixth through which Marie-Amélie had lived.

Inside the palace the royal family waited, remembering Louis XVI, Marie-Antoinette, and the guillotine.

Outside, the mob made a bonfire of the royal carriages, while the National Guard broke ranks and marched with the people threatening the life of their King.

"Ça ira! Ça ira!" shouted a thousand voices.

A little ahead of the hurrying people rode a man who was a journalist as well as an officer.[1] Possessed of quick wits and the gift of words, he wrote out the abdication of a King, believing that Louis-Philippe could not save both life and crown. He gained entry to the palace and thrust the paper upon the King, who hesitated, but signed :

". . . I abdicate in favour of my grandson, the Comte de Paris. . . ." In much the same phrase Charles X had willed the same crown to his own grandson, the Duc de Bordeaux.

[1] Editor of *La Presse* (F.O. Records).

" You were not worthy of so good a King ! " exclaimed Marie-Amélie to Thiers, as with her arm through Louis-Philippe's, he and she passed out into the gardens, for the end had come.

The Duc de Montpensier followed with the Duchesse de Nemours, Princesse Clémentine, her husband, and six of the King's grandchildren ; two remained behind with their mother, Princesse Hélène, Duchesse d'Orléans.

The party reached St. Cloud, but felt that even here they were not safe, and the journey must be continued, although they were almost penniless.

" Drive them till they drop, Sire, but save yourself ! " said one postmaster, bringing out his best horses, for the news of the sacking of the Tuileries had reached him, and he, like the fugitives, remembered that other revolution and the flight to Varennes. Separation seemed to offer the best chance of escape, so King and Queen drove through the night, taking different roads.   Louis-Philippe had discarded his wig and shaved his whiskers.

In Paris, the Duchesse d'Orléans had carried her children to the Assembly, there to claim the crown for her little son, the Comte de Paris, but the mob invaded the Chambre, driving out the *Députés*, and she too fled for her life.

England was watching the trend of events in France, and presently the British Consul at Havre escorted one " Thomas Smith " on board a packet-boat and bowed to a veiled lady who arrived almost simultaneously.   An hour after the vessel had sailed, gendarmes visited the little cottage where the King and Queen had lain in hiding for nine days.

Once more *Le Moniteur Universel* was to make proclamation (Feb. 25, 1848) : " Un gouvernement rétrograde et oligarchique vient d'être renversé par l'héroïsme du peuple de Paris ! . . .   France a donné au monde l'exemple que Paris a donné à France ! "

The foreign ambassadors were not quite so enthusiastic, although England's representative was inclined to accept the new régime and hinted as much to Lamartine while awaiting instructions : " If France is to be a republic I am sure that the sooner encouragement is given to the virtuous efforts of the men at present in power the better," he wrote to the Secretary of State.

America was the first to take a definite stand through her envoy, Richard Rush, acting on his own initiative.   He remembered that France had been the earliest friend and ally of the United States, and that the recruitment of so great a nation to republicanism could hardly fail to be welcomed across the Atlantic : " Can we be backward when France is looking to us ? " Rush argued, and four days after the *fait accompli* of the Revolution he notified the Marquis of Normanby of his intention and carried his felicitations to the Provisional Government, which received him with surprise.   Rush concluded his formal recognition of the Second Republic by quoting the hope General Washington had expressed to the French Minister at Philadelphia half a century before (that the friendship of the two republics might be commensurate with their existence).

" Vive la République des États-Unis ! " cried the delighted people as the American drove away.

Three weeks later the fugitive King and Queen of the French reached the haven of Claremont, which was put at their disposal by Queen Victoria.   Here Louis-Philippe was to die.

" Not long ago his life was the most important in the world, and his death would have produced a profound sensation," wrote Charles Greville in his Memoirs (Aug. 27, 1850).   " Now it is hardly of more importance than would be that of one of the old bathing women opposite my window. He has long been politically defunct."

Here Marie-Amélie was to live for eighteen years, building up a new life for herself among the children and grandchildren who made a little court around her while across the Channel France still struggled.

The exiled Queen saw the Second Republic merge into the Second Empire, but her interests were in the births, the first communions, the marrying, and giving in marriage of her children's children. She saw the marriage of the Comte de Paris to Isabella, daughter of the Duc de Montpensier, and of his brother to yet another cousin, and she saw the coming of a new generation; she made peace with the Duc de Chambord, from whom her husband had wrested the now lost crown of France.

Marie-Amélie died only four years before Louis Napoleon fell and the Third Republic came to birth. Three of her descendants wore crowns as thorny as her own—Charlotte, daughter of Louise of Belgium, who became Empress of Mexico, Ferdinand of Bulgaria, and that other Marie-Amélie, Queen of Portugal, her namesake and granddaughter.

When dying, the Queen asked that the name inscribed upon her coffin should be Marie-Amélie de Bourbon, Duchesse de Bourbon.

"History cannot be effaced!" they reminded her, and Marie-Amélie yielded: "Alas, to my sorrow, 'Queen of the French'!"

GENEALOGICAL TABLE

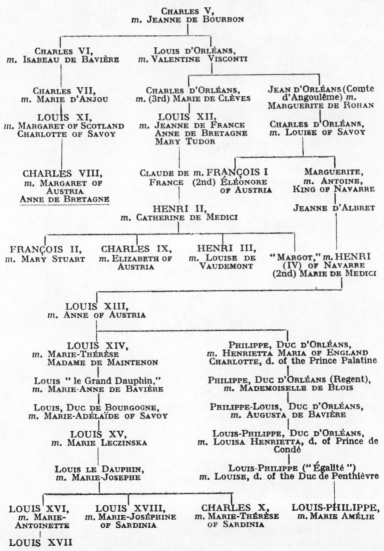

CHARLES V,
m. JEANNE DE BOURBON

CHARLES VI,
m. ISABEAU DE BAVIÈRE

LOUIS D'ORLÉANS,
m. VALENTINE VISCONTI

CHARLES VII,
m. MARIE D'ANJOU

CHARLES D'ORLÉANS,
m. (3rd) MARIE DE CLÈVES

JEAN D'ORLÉANS (Comte
d'Angoulême) m.
MARGUERITE DE ROHAN

LOUIS XI,
m. MARGARET OF SCOTLAND
CHARLOTTE OF SAVOY

LOUIS XII,
m. JEANNE DE FRANCE
ANNE DE BRETAGNE
MARY TUDOR

CHARLES D'ORLÉANS,
m. LOUISE OF SAVOY

CHARLES VIII,
m. MARGARET OF
AUSTRIA
ANNE DE BRETAGNE

CLAUDE DE m. FRANÇOIS I
FRANCE (2nd) ÉLÉONORE
OF AUSTRIA

MARGUERITE,
m. ANTOINE,
KING OF NAVARRE

HENRI II,
m. CATHERINE DE MEDICI

JEANNE D'ALBRET

FRANÇOIS II,
m. MARY STUART

CHARLES IX,
m. ELIZABETH OF
AUSTRIA

HENRI III,
m. LOUISE DE
VAUDEMONT

"MARGOT," m. HENRI
(IV) OF NAVARRE
(2nd) MARIE DE MEDICI

LOUIS XIII,
m. ANNE OF AUSTRIA

LOUIS XIV,
m. MARIE-THÉRÈSE
MADAME DE MAINTENON

PHILIPPE, DUC D'ORLÉANS,
m. HENRIETTA MARIA OF ENGLAND
CHARLOTTE, d. of the Prince Palatine

Louis "le Grand Dauphin,"
m. MARIE-ANNE DE BAVIÈRE

PHILIPPE, DUC D'ORLÉANS (Regent),
m. MADEMOISELLE DE BLOIS

Louis, DUC DE BOURGOGNE,
m. MARIE-ADÉLAÏDE OF SAVOY

PHILIPPE-LOUIS, DUC D'ORLÉANS,
m. AUGUSTA DE BAVIÈRE

LOUIS XV,
m. MARIE LECZINSKA

Louis-PHILIPPE, DUC D'ORLÉANS,
m. LOUISA HENRIETTA, d. of Prince de
Condé

Louis LE DAUPHIN,
m. MARIE-JOSEPHE

Louis-PHILIPPE ("Égalité")
m. LOUISE, d. of the Duc de Penthièvre

LOUIS XVI,
m. MARIE-
ANTOINETTE

LOUIS XVIII,
m. MARIE-JOSÉPHINE
OF SARDINIA

CHARLES X,
m. MARIE-THÉRÈSE
OF SARDINIA

LOUIS-PHILIPPE,
m. MARIE AMÉLIE

LOUIS XVII

CHRONOLOGICAL TABLE

The Capets

	Died
Hugh Capet " the Great "	996
Robert " the Pious "	1031
Henri I	1060
Philippe I	1108
Louis VI	1137
Louis VII	1180
Philippe II	1223
Louis VIII	1226
Louis IX, " St. Louis " . . .	1270
Philippe III " le Hardi " . . .	1285
Philippe IV	1314
Louis X	1316
Philippe V	1322
Charles IV	1328

House of Valois

Philippe VI " the Fortunate " . .	1350
Jean II	1364
Charles V	1380
Charles VI	1422
Charles VII	1461
Louis XI	1483
Charles VIII	1498
Louis XII	1515

House of Angoulême

François I	1547
Henri II	1559
François II	1560
Charles IX	1574
Henri III	1589

House of Bourbon

Henri (IV) of Navarre . . .	1610
Louis XIII	1643
Louis XIV	1715
Louis XV	1774
Louis XVI (guillotined) . . .	1793
Louis XVII (titular King) . . .	1795
Louis XVIII	1824
Charles X (abdicated 1830) . . .	1836

House of Bourbon-Orléans

Louis-Philippe (deposed 1848) . . .	1850

BIBLIOGRAPHY

" L'ouvrage que j'ai entrepris m'a obligé de lire bien des livres ! "
(Aublet de Maubuy.)

La Grande Encyclopédie.
Dictionnaire de Biographie Universelle.
Allgemeine Deutsche Biographie.
Histoire de France. Michelet.
Histoire de France. Henri Martin.
Histoire de France. Mézeray.
Histoire de France. Mignet.
Histoire de France. Lavisse.
Abrégé de l'histoire de France. Mézeray.
Histoire généalogique de la Maison de France. 1647. Les frères
    Sainte-Marthe.
Monuments de l'histoire française. Montfaucon.
Archives Nationales.
Archives du Ministère des Affaires Étrangères.
Archives curieuses de l'histoire de France. Cimber et Danjou.
Curiosités de l'histoire de France. La Croix.
Documents inédits sur l'histoire de France.
Publications de la Société de l'histoire de France. Ed. Dupont.
Intermédiaire des chercheurs. Tomes divers.
L'Art de vérifier les dates depuis la naissance de notre Seigr ----
    jusqu'à nos jours.
Le Grand Larousse.
Mémoires et anecdotes des reines de France. Dreux de Radi
Les reines de France. Celliez.
Bibliographie des femmes célèbres. Anon.
Influence des femmes sur les destinées de la France. Jules de B
Vies des femmes illustres de la France. Aublet de Maubuy.
Les reines de la main droite. Anon.
Les reines de la main gauche. Anon.
Dames illustres et dames galantes. Brantôme.
Éloges et vies des reines. H. de la Coste. 1630.
Femmes de France. Le Roux de Lincy.
Les femmes célèbres de l'ancien régime. Imbert de St. Am
Reines légitimes et reines d'aventure. E. de Lerne.
Essais historiques. Balzac.
Six rois de France. Balzac.

Les rois de France. Lélius.
Questions historiques. J. Loiseleur.
Le Moniteur Universel.

Louis XI

Histoire de Charles VII. Baudot de Juilly.
Pathologie mentale des rois. A. Brachet.
Mémoires. Philippe de Comines. 1464–98.
Calendrier royal pour l'an 1471. Champion.
Règne de Louis XI. Théodore Bénézet.
Louis XI. Jules Zeller.
Histoire de Louis XI (autrement dicte la Chronique scandaleuse).
    Jean de Troyes.

Charles VIII

Histoire de Charles VIII. Godefroy.
Histoire de Bretagne. Daru.
Histoire de Bretagne. Lobineau.
Anne de Bretagne. Le Roux de Lincy.

Louis XII

Vie merveilleuse de Jeanne de Valois. R. de Maulde.
Vie de Ste. Jeanne. Guast.
Louis XII et Anne de Bretagne. La Croix.
Marie d'Angleterre, Reine-Duchesse. C. J. de Boismorand.
Choses mémorables. Seigneur de la Marck.

Francois I

François I. Clarisse Coignet.
François I. Jules Zeller.
Les Amours de François I. Jules Zeller.
Journal de Louise de Savoie.
Journal d'un bourgeois de Paris sous François I. 1515–34.
    Ludovic Lalanne.
Louise de Savoie et François I : trente ans de jeunesse. R. de
    Maulde de la Clavière.
Mémoires du Chevalier Bayard.

Henri II

Famiglie Fiorentini. Conte Pompeo Litta.
Discours merveilleux de la vie de la reyne Catherine de Médicis.
    Estienne.
Vita di Caterina de' Medici. Eugenio Alberi.
Lettres de Catherine de Médicis.

La Diplomatie vénitienne. Armand Baschet.
Relazioni degli Ambasciatori Veneti.
Cour de Catherine de Médicis. Dufour.
Diane de Poitiers. Capefigue.
Mémoires. Tavannes.
Mémoires. Montluc.
Catherine de Médicis, mère des rois François II, Charles IX et
    Henri III. Capefigue.
Catherine de Médicis, par l'auteur de la Vérité sur Marie Stuart.
Lettres d'Antoine de Bourbon et Jeanne d'Albret, par La Croix de
    Vimieux. Marquis de Rochambeau.

FRANÇOIS II

La première jeunesse de Marie Stuart. Ruble.
Œuvres choisies de Brantôme.
" Journal " de l'Hôpital.

CHARLES IX

Dépêches de M. de la Mothe-Fénelon.
Lettres inédites de Charles IX et de Catherine de Médicis et du
    Duc d'Anjou. Roger de Quirielle.
Elisabeth d'Autriche et ses temps. Louis de Beauriez.
Vie de Charles IX. Père de Sorbin.
Les femmes des Valois. Imbert de St. Amand.

HENRI III

Histoire de France sous Henri III. Eudes de Mézeray.
Journal des choses mémorables advenues durant tout le règne de
    Henri III. Anon.
Histoire de France. De Thou.
Louise de Lorraine. Comte de Baillon.
Les femmes de la Cour des derniers Valois. Imbert de St. Amand.

HENRI IV

Le Divorce satyrique. Anon.
Journal du règne de Henri IV. Pierre de l'Estoile.
Les femmes de Brantôme. Henri Bouchot.
L'Alcandre, ou les amours du roy Henri le Grand. Anon.
Les Amours d'Henri IV. Lescure.
Mémoires et lettres de Marguerite de Valois. Guessard.
Confessions catholiques du Sieur de Sancy.
Henri IV et Marie de Médicis. Zeller (d'après des documents
    nouveaux).
Récit de la naissance des enfants de France. Louise Bourgeois.
Mémoires de Sully.
Marie de Médicis. Capefigue.
Gabrielle d'Estrées. Capefigue.

Louis XIII

Histoire de France sous Louis XIII. M. A. Bazin.
Mémoires. Du Bellay.
Mémoires. La Marck.
Histoire de la mère et le fils. Eudes de Mézeray.
Journal. Cardinal de Richelieu.
Le roi chez la reine. Histoire du mariage de Louis XIII et Anne d'Autriche. A. Baschet.
La minorité de Louis XIII. Zeller.

Louis XIV

Louis XIV. Voltaire.
Histoire de France pendant la minorité de Louis XIV. Chéruel.
Entretien familier du roy et de la reyne régente. Anon. 1649.
Anne d'Autriche, Reine-Régente. Capefigue.
Mémoires pour servir à l'histoire d'Anne d'Autriche. Madame de Motteville.
Les reines de France nées Espagnoles. Auguste Noël.
Les amoureuses et les femmes vertueuses du Grand Siècle. Madame de Sévigné. Ed. Babou.
Madame de la Vallière et Marie-Thérèse. G. Gaudy.
Madame de la Vallière et Marie-Thérèse. Duclos.
Anne d'Autriche et Mazarin. V. Molinier.
Lettres. Madame de Sévigné.
Breve historia de la vida y virtudes di Doña Maria Teresa. Buenaventura di Soria.
Madame de Maintenon. Noailles.
Madame de Maintenon. Lavallée.
Madame de Maintenon. Madame de Sévigné.
Mémoires de Mademoiselle de Montpensier.
Mémoires du Cardinal de Retz.

Louis XV

Les filles de Louis XV. Barthélemy.
Journal Anecdotique. Barbier.
Louis XV et Marie Leczinska. Pierre de Nolhac.
Lettres inédites du roi Stanislas à Marie Leczinska. Pierre Boyé.
Vie de la Reine de France Marie Leczinska. L'Abbé Proyart.
Vie de Madame Louise de France. L'Abbé Proyart.
Le Mariage de Louis XV, d'après des documents inédits. Gauthier Villars.
Marie Leczinska. Aublet de Maubuy.
Correspondance et Mémoires. d'Argenson.
La Dauphine. Émile Regnault.
Le fils de Louis XV. Broglie.
Mémoires de Saint-Simon.

Mémoires de Villars.
Mémoires Secrètes. Duclos.
Histoire de l'éducation des princes. H. Druon.

Louis XVI, XVII, XVIII, and Charles X

Louis XVI. Abbé Proyart.
Récit de la Duchesse d'Angoulême (" Madame Royale ").
Mémoires, Tour du Temple, Duchesse d'Angoulême (" Madame Royale ").
Mémoires de Madame Campan.
Marie Antoinette. Marquis de Ségur.
Captivité de la famille royale au Temple. Beauchesne.
Mémoires. Madame de Genlis.
Journal. Madame de Staël.
Histoire de Louis XVIII. A. de St. Gervais.
Le Retour des Bourbons. Gilbert Stenger.
Les renonciations des Bourbons. Closeburn.
Femmes de Versailles. Imbert de St. Amand.
Femmes des Tuileries. Imbert de St. Amand.
Louis XVII. Dubois et Beauchesne.
Le Dauphin fils de Louis XV, ou Vie privée des Bourbons. Ch. de Rozoir.
Mémoires et souvenirs sur la Révolution. G. Lenôtre.
Le drame de Varennes. G. Lenôtre.
La fille de Louis XVI. G. Lenôtre.

Louis-Philippe

Annuaire de la noblesse de France.
Vie de Marie-Amélie Trognon.
Mémoires de la Comtesse de Boigne.

ENGLISH BOOKS CONSULTED

Encyclopædia Britannica.
International Encyclopedia.
The New Encyclopedia.
The Cambridge Modern History.
The National History of France. Funck-Brentano.
History of France. J. R. M. MacDonald.
History of France. Kitchin.
History of France. N. W. Wraxall.
Calendars of State Papers, 1514–15, 1535, 1564–5, 1572–7.
Diplomatic Correspondence (Record Office), 1778–9, 1791–3.
Foreign Office Records, 1830, 1848.
Domestic Intelligence (Record Office), 1793.

History of Scotland. Tytler. (Vol. VI.)
Church and State of Scotland. Rt. Reverend Robert Keith.
Courts of England and France. Richard Rush.
Pictures of the Old French Court. C. Bearne.
Illustrious Women of France. Mrs. Challice.
North British Review, 1869–70.
Genealogical Tables Illustrative of Modern History. Hereford B.
    George.

Louis XI

Margaret of Scotland and the Dauphin Louis. L. Barbé.

Louis XII

A Twice-crowned Queen (Anne of Brittany). Countess de la
    Warr.

François I

François I and Other Historical Studies. Cochran.

Henri II, François II, Henri III, and Charles IX

The Medici. Colonel C. R. Young.
Girlhood of Catherine de Medici. Adolphus Trollope.
Catherine de Medici. Paul van Dyke.
Catherine de Medici and the French Reformation. Edith Sichel.
Later Years of Catherine de Medici. Edith Sichel.
Coligny. Whitehead.
The Last of the Valois. C. C. Jackson.
Elisabeth de Valois. M. W. Freer.

Henri IV

Reign of Henri IV. M. W. Freer.
Henry of Navarre. George Slocombe.
The First of the Bourbons. C. C. Jackson.
Nursery Life 300 Years Ago. Lucy Crump.
Life of Marie de Medici. J. Pardoe.
Richelieu. Sir Richard Lodge.

Louis XIV

Louis XIV. Sisley Huddleston.
Louis XIV. A. Hassall.
Mazarin. A. Hassall. (Foreign Statesmen Series.)
Louis XIV and His Court. Taillandier.
Louis XIV and the Court of France. J. Pardoe.
Marie-Thérèse of Austria. R. J. F. Bright.
Madame de Maintenon. C. C. Dyson.
Madame de Maintenon. Maud Cruttwell.

Louis XV

The Private Life of Louis XV. Mouffle d'Angerville (tr. H. S. Mingard).
Madame du Barry. Karl von Schumacher (tr. D. Richardson).

Louis XVI, Louis XVIII, and Charles X

The French Revolution. Carlyle.
The French Revolution. Gaxotte (tr. W. D. A. Phillips).
The Holland Dispatches.
Travels in France. A. Young.
The Court of the Tuileries. Lady Jackson.
A Friend of Marie-Antoinette. Lady Atkyns.
Lectures on the French Revolution. Lord Acton.
Select Documents of the French Revolution. L. C. W. Legge.
Despatches from Paris. O. Browning.
Letters on France. Walpole.
Last Days of the French Revolution. H. Belloc.
Marie-Antoinette. H. Belloc.
The Private Life of Marie-Antoinette. Madame Campan.
Louis XVI and Marie-Antoinette. A. C. P. Haggard.
Prison Life of Marie-Antoinette. M. C. Bishop.
Louis XVI. C. Stryienski.
Secret Correspondence on the Court of Louis XVI. Anon.
Marie-Antoinette. Clara Tschudi (tr. E. M. Cope).
Marie-Antoinette, Last Days of. Lord R. Gower.
Paris in 1789–94.
Memoirs of Louis XVII. Ed. Lamotte Houdancourt.
Louis XVIII. M. F. Sandars.
Court of Louis XVIII. K. A. Patmore.
The Royal Quartette. Mrs. M. A. Bearne.
Return of Louis XVIII. G. Stenger.
Letters on Events in France since 1815. H. M. Williams.
The Greville Papers.
Life and Times of Louis Philippe. A. E. Douglas.
Journal of Miss Cornelia Knight.
Louis Philippe at the Court of France. R. Rush.
Life of Marie-Amélie. C. C. Dyson.
Letters of Queen Victoria. Vol. I (ed. 1907).

INDEX